Diverse Paths to Modernity in Southeastern Europe

Recent Titles in
Contributions to the Study of World History

The Dragon and the Wild Goose: China and India
Jay Taylor

Land and Freedom: The Origins of Russian Terrorism, 1876–1879
Deborah Hardy

Young Guard! The Communist Youth League, Petrograd 1917–1920
Isabel A. Tirado

Engine of Mischief: An Analytical Biography of Karl Radek
Jim Tuck

Central America: Historical Perspectives on the Contemporary Crises
Ralph Lee Woodward, Jr., editor

The Free Germany Movement: A Case of Patriotism or Treason?
Kai P. Schoenhals

Victims and Survivors: Displaced Persons and Other War Victims
in Viet-Nam, 1954
Louis A. Wiesner

Tsar Paul and the Question of Madness: An Essay in History and Psychology
Hugh Ragsdale

The Orphan Stone: The Minnesinger Dream of Reich
Richard J. Berleth

American Constitutionalism Abroad: Selected Essays in Comparative
Constitutional History
George Athan Billias, editor

Appeasement in Europe: A Reassessment of U.S. Policies
David F. Schmitz and Richard D. Challener, editors

Ritual and Record: Sports Records and Quantification in Pre-Modern Societies
John Marshall Carter and Arnd Krüger, editors

Diverse Paths to Modernity in Southeastern Europe

ESSAYS IN NATIONAL DEVELOPMENT

Edited by **Gerasimos Augustinos**

Contributions to the Study of World History, Number 20

GREENWOOD PRESS

New York • Westport, Connecticut • London

Library of Congress Cataloging-in-Publication Data

Diverse paths to modernity in southeastern Europe : essays in national
  development / edited by Gerasimos Augustinos.
    p. cm.—(Contributions to the study of world history, ISSN
  0885-9159 ; no. 20)
    Includes bibliographical references and index.
    ISBN 0-313-26670-0 (alk. paper)
    1. Balkan Peninsula—Politics and government—20th century.
  2. Balkan Peninsula—Economic conditions. 3. Balkan Peninsula—
  Social conditions. I. Augustinos, Gerasimos. II. Series.
  DR45.D48 1991
  320.9496—dc20   90-38424

British Library Cataloguing in Publication Data is available.

Library of Congress Catalog Card Number: 90-38424
ISBN: 0-313-26670-0
ISSN: 0885-9159

First published in 1991

Greenwood Press, 88 Post Road West, Westport, CT 06881
An imprint of Greenwood Publishing Group, Inc.

Printed in the United States of America

∞™

The paper used in this book complies with the
Permanent Paper Standard issued by the National
Information Standards Organization (Z39.48–1984).

10 9 8 7 6 5 4 3 2 1

Contents

1. Introduction
   Gerasimos Augustinos   1

2. Modernization Through Secularization in Bulgaria
   John Bell   15

3. Belated Modernization in Comparison: Development in
   Yugoslavia and Bulgaria to 1948
   John Lampe   33

4. Self-Management and Development Strategies in Socialist
   Yugoslavia
   Robin Alison Remington   57

5. Development Through the Market in Greece: The State,
   Entrepreneurs, and Society
   Gerasimos Augustinos   89

6. Politics, Nationalism, and Development in Romania
   Mary Ellen Fischer   135

Bibliography   169

Index   173

About the Contributors   177

1

Introduction

Gerasimos Augustinos

Today all of the developed world must confront the changes that are sweeping across Eastern Europe. As for the nations in that area, they face enormous tasks, including creating democratic political systems, restructuring to move from planned to market economies, coping with increased social inequality as a result of opening up to the world market, and dealing with festering nationality and minority problems and disputes with neighbors arising from them. Despite talk about the need to break with the past, the future development of these countries will be influenced to a large extent by their particular historical experiences.

Southeastern Europe is a striking setting in which to consider the problems and prospects of development in the era of *glasnost* from a historical perspective. During the nineteenth century the Balkans were an early example of societies going through the process of nation formation while burdened with economic backwardness. In the twentieth century the area has witnessed dramatic developmental change, while having to cope with the social and cultural dilemmas of modernity.

The two most dynamic political ideologies to emerge in the modern age—nationalism and socialism—have confronted and interacted with one another vigorously in this region. Furthermore, Southeastern Europe remains an area of geostrategic importance where in the recent past the forces of the two most powerful military blocs in the world have confronted one another. In this region of Europe three major religions, Roman Catholicism, Eastern Orthodoxy, and Islam, which are deeply embedded in the popular cultures of the region, have interacted and challenged the process of modernization. Finally, while the Southeast European nations have experienced more growth than the less developed countries of the Third World, they must nonetheless deal with the economically developed states of the world. Therefore, the countries of this region are an excellent example of societies that have managed to create significant economic growth, but yet have developed unevenly because of external and domestic factors.

Few studies have treated the region, with all its ethnic and geographic diversity, as a whole and through a sufficiently long temporal framework. Works dealing with the area in the twentieth century often either begin or end at 1945. Studies that start with this date tend to assume that the upheavals of the 1940s eliminated the previous social and political culture. Those that end with World War II often assume that the national societies that emerged in the late nineteenth century continued essentially in the same form into the twentieth. In addition, the area has been treated selectively by using cultural or ideological criteria. Thus, in some cases the Balkan states have been divided into Central European and Mediterranean societies. In other instances, political criteria have been applied, and the states have been treated according to the bloc to which they belonged. This study seeks to provide an integrated overview of the region. This work is particularly relevant because the effort to aid the states that were part of the Soviet bloc will certainly affect the development of noncommunist nations like Greece as well nonaligned countries like Yugoslavia.

For the general framework of this study, development is taken to be the process by which economic and technological change leads to the transformation of the institutions and values of a society so that the people satisfy their civic, material, social, and individual needs. It is multidimensional change which is shaped and defined by the particular political system, the values associated with it, and the culture of the society.

With regard to the Balkan states, development has meant the emergence of distinct political and social systems shaped by nationalism and the desire for modernization. The changes that have taken place (industrialization, urbanization, a growing public sector providing essential services such as education, communications, and social welfare) have for the most part been rationally motivated and oriented toward providing for people's material wants, though not necessarily their civic interests. The path, the pace, and the outcome of these changes have not been the same in each society. Historic events and personalities—the unique element—as well as the cumulative effect of time have influenced the particular mix of social and political relations. Developmental goals and policies have varied with the particular interest groups in a society and the specific historical conditions of an era. The goals may be self-sufficiency, security, stability, equality, or a higher standard of living. Whatever the aims, the nation-states have had to respond to the constraining limits imposed by the natural environment and the historically determined conditions of interstate relations, both political and economic.

The rationale of this work is to delineate and assess empirically the evolution of distinctive national developmental paths among the states of the region in the twentieth century and at the same time to provide a basis for comparative historical inquiry. The chapters presented here consider how development has been affected by the historically specific and problematic social and economic context. They are intended to help identify the developmental strategies that have arisen in the particular states over the last century as well as to discern developmental variations that have occurred between the various states. This assumes, however, that the Balkan nations have been shaped by a shared inheritance regarding society and the nature of political power that stems from the common factors that have influenced their history, which sets them apart even from other East European societies. At the same time, the peoples of the Balkans have come to see their development as based on values drawn from the common fund of European culture, including the belief in progress and the rational basis of national development.

In analyzing the development of the Southeast European states in the twentieth century, two primary historical verities about the region must be recognized. First, in the Balkans, the overriding determinant was the small power status, politically and economically, of the states that were created there. Second, as the national societies emerged during the nineteenth century, there were already clear indications of the existence of significant trade and agricultural production in the region. This potential did not carry through in steady economic growth and developmental progress. The reason lay both in the structure of the economies (overwhelmingly agrarian, little capital, and inadequate technical and communications infrastructures) and in the policies of the governments of the states in the region. This was the mixed inheritance of the Balkan states in the twentieth century.

This study takes into account three factors that have fundamentally shaped the nation formation of the states of Southeastern Europe. First, the peoples in the region inherited a common legacy out of the imperial world from which they emerged: political authority was distant and indirect, and the socioeconomic world rested on an agrarian foundation. Second, the development of the individual countries have been markedly affected by the pervasive administrative system that was created in each nation-state and used by the various elites and political personalities to promote their interests. Third, the peoples of Southeastern Europe embraced their past and made it the irreducible form of their identity and the validating source of their nationhood.

The peoples of the Balkans have had to face stark choices in the past, which have led them to see themselves as struggling and competing in order to survive. Nations have pitted themselves against imperial rule; nation-states have confronted great powers as well as their neighbors; contrasting ideologies have clashed with one another; and minority ethnic groups have challenged the nation-state. Social integration or cohesion, therefore, has been a surface phenomenon even in the era of nation-states.

Time is another factor to consider in the process of development. Almost a century lies between the emergence of the first state in the region, Greece, and the formation of the last countries, Albania and Yugoslavia. The element of time did not mean a great deal in terms of giving any state the edge in economic growth during the nineteenth century. However, as John Bell demonstrates in the case of Bulgaria, it did make a difference when it came to the creation of the needed administrative, technical, educational, and cultural institutions, which have served development in the twentieth century.

The nineteenth century was a volatile period in the history of the Balkan peninsula. Independent states emerged through the intervention of the European powers. The new countries endeavored to fashion unified societies internally while asserting their right to expand territorially in the name of national liberation to include those of the nations that were outside the state frontiers. Nationalist ideology served a purpose in both dimensions, often through aggression and at the cost of political stability and economic advancement.

As the states of Southeastern Europe were created, their leaders proceeded to establish constitutional/parliamentary political systems, and administrative and educational institutions modeled on those of the developed states in Western Europe. This was done with the expectation that their countries' recognition, legitimacy, and validity as sovereign political units would be enhanced. These institutional structures were also the instruments for the sought-after development into modern societies. Yet, although the state institutions and political life of the Balkan nations resembled those of the developed countries of Europe, the social and economic realities were quite different (what Mary Ellen Fischer in her chapter on Romania denotes as Michael Shafir's contrast between the *pays légal* and the *pays réel*).

From the nineteenth century until the end of World War I the states in the region had to cope with new lands and new peoples. In the aftermath of the Great War the states were forced to look inward. Greece and Bulgaria were flooded with refugees, whereas Romania and Yugoslavia were significantly affected by the new peoples that made them nationality-states rather nation-states. The emphasis was placed on the political integration of the nation. This came after a century in which territorial expansion was in the ascendant and precedence was given to military action rather than to social amelioration and economic development. Efforts to create unified, "national" societies in the twentieth century, however, only place in greater relief the fact that the Balkan states are not homogeneous nations after all.

Development among the Balkan states in the twentieth century must be considered in light of several important issues that relate to the key sectors of political culture, economic structure, and social culture. To begin with, for much of their history the states in the region have been politically dependent vis-à-vis the great powers of Europe. Their development as national societies has been affected by their need for economic ties with the more powerful states while having to confront unwanted political intervention. Perhaps the most significant aspect of development in Southeastern Europe has been the transition from an agrarian to an urban/industrial economy. How this transition was effected, whether through evolution or revolution, has been reflected in the sociopolitical culture. Finally, whatever form the political systems of the states in the region have taken, national integrity has remained the underlying consideration in domestic and foreign affairs. In view of this constant factor, we must consider how government policies and popular responses based on this ethos have helped or hindered the modernization of the Balkan societies.

Bulgaria is a prime example of the possibilities and limits of political and economic development in the Balkans as effected through the secularization of society. In Chapter 2 John Bell examines this problem in his treatment of Bulgarian modernization. Bulgarian nation formation itself began with the effort by intellectuals to assert their cultural and ecclesiastical independence from Hellenic culture, which dominated religion and education among the Bulgarians until the nineteenth century. This effort led to political demands and organized revolutionary ferment against Ottoman rule, which in the wake of Russian intervention resulted in the recognition of a Bulgarian autonomous state in 1878.

Once the principality was created, state institutions and a comprehensive educational system were formed. Educational progress did not, however, translate into economic and social change of the kind to transform the agrarian society. Bulgaria did not have the capital, labor, or markets to make a break with the past and turn to industrialization. Employment in Bulgarian towns became heavily dependent on the state, and politics reflected this demand in the scramble for power and the spoils it offered. The constitutional system of the country allowed urban elites to ignore the need for economic transformation as long as the peasants were politically quiescent by being provided with land for small farms, while the urban world focused its attention on national affairs and the rewards of office.

The populist agrarian movement of Aleksandŭr Stamboliiski, emphasizing the role of the state, the primacy of the peasant and agriculture, and the supportive but subordinate role of industry, attempted to promote modernization by turning away from the outward-looking, nationalistically motivated territorial ambitions of previous parties. Stamboliiski sought to mobilize both labor and education in post–World War I Bulgaria, but traditional political interests prevailed.

The upheaval of the Second World War and the great power realities that issued from it gave the communists an exceptional opportunity. Once in power they struck at the artisan class and small manufacturers who had been the backbone of Bulgaria's pre–World War II commercial economy. Committed to the secular goal of modernization, the communists pushed for an industrial breakthrough by major structural changes in the economy. Their effort, modeled on the Soviet example, emphasized state investment, heavy industry, and central planning. The shift to an industrial, urban economy was accomplished with close trade ties and material assistance from the Soviet Union.

In the process of creating a communist society, the country was mobilized for the development of scientific and technological strength. Yet the need to better manage a more complex society and meet the challenge of a global market had only limited success. Attempts at reform embodied in the New Economic Mechanism in the late 1970s were only partly successful. By the mid-1980s, the economy of the country had become stagnant. These difficulties, combined with a growing resistance to political conformity, gave impetus to a rising demand for political as well as personal freedom. Under the communists Bulgaria made a breakthrough to industrialization through the secularization of society by a committed and authoritarian elite, but without a concomitant commitment to civic education for participatory political life.

In Chapter 3, John Lampe considers the problems of "differentiated modernization" in the Balkans in the first half of the twentieth century by comparing two seemingly dissimilar states. Though markedly different in their national makeup and experience in the Great War, Yugoslavia and Bulgaria shared a strong state administration, a weak oppositional society, and an economy based on a large agricultural sector. The two countries are comparable in that both made economic progress but failed to achieve the needed structural changes in their economies that would permit an industrial breakthrough.

Both Yugoslavia and Bulgaria were limited in their ability to increase their agricultural exports after the Great War in a changing and competitive international market. The turn to foreign banks for needed funding was not effective in helping to transform their economies in the interwar years inasmuch as the loans were needed to cope with existing debt.

During the interwar period the economies of both countries were characterized by small-scale enterprise and a powerful state apparatus that could not be turned to advantage by entrepreneurs who would have wanted to promote private industry. Although the state administrative apparatus increased significantly in the two states, it did not produce a concomitant gain in effective public policy.

Yugoslavia suffered such destruction in the Second World War that it had to find new ways to organize the state. During those years the Partisans' resistance movement mobilized the peasants to a degree unknown before and disciplined them to service and authority. By way of contrast, Bulgaria's role in the war allowed it to retain its economic institutions intact, and the pressures of war promoted the expansion of state agencies. The Bulgarian peasantry survived by attempting to diversify their crops while entrepreneurs turned to small businesses to be free of state controls.

The weakness of the private sector in both states made it that much easier for the communists to consolidate their power after the war. The prospect for private enterprise was indeed dim in these two countries in terms of the competitive market and international trade with its demand for currency convertibility. In Bulgaria the communists were aided by the existing state institutions, which enabled them to put a centralized plan into effect quickly and to rationalize the allocation of human and natural resources. Thus, they were able to move more easily into a Soviet-type model of development. In Yugoslavia the strength of the party, built up during the war, was the key factor because the government ministries had suffered from the dividing up of the country during that time.

As a reaction to the failure of the market system in the 1920s, there was little support for American-style free market economy in Eastern Europe. Postwar recovery was deemed to depend on internal state initiative, especially in developing the communications and education infrastructure and in remaking the backward agricultural sector. The communists, following the Soviet model, established collectivization as a means to provide food for the growing industrial labor sector.

As a consequence, agriculture was left behind in the drive to promote heavy industry in the economy, and "differentiated modernization" occurred.

With Western aid coming in, Yugoslavia began the difficult process of recovery. Tito, desiring to lead the way to a new society as rapidly as possible and backed by a confident party cadre, inaugurated a Five-Year Plan in 1946. But the economy performed badly under such shock tactics. Soviet-style centralized development did not make sense for Yugoslavia with its regional identities and experience in the war. In the wake of the split with Stalin, the Yugoslavs were further impelled to find an alternative development model.

As Robert Remington shows in Chapter 4, the alternative model that the Yugoslavs adopted, socialist self-management, was a strategy for much needed developmental progress and regime legitimacy at home and abroad. After the break with the Soviet bloc, the Yugoslav leadership sought a way to deal with the domestic economic situation, ideological requirements in international affairs, as well as the uniqueness of Yugoslavia's political development, based as it was on nations and regions.

Yugoslav leaders charted a developmental path that included decentralizing the government and the management of the economic system, allowing participation in the economy by various groups—workers, planners, and managers—and turning to the local level for implementation of economic plans. It was a path that was intended to lead to the breakthrough to a socialist society by mobilizing the people.

The alternative model required that the party withdraw from direct day-to-day running of the economy and the government. Thus, the relationship between the party and the state bureaucracy was to be remade, and the hierarchical nature of the party would be altered to allow more "democratic" interaction and input. Inaugurated in 1952, socialist self-management ended the party's monopoly over political life, while the monopoly over party organization remained. Although the initial results were not very promising as party members and workers did not readily take up their assigned roles, an opening was made as the system turned from administration through command to the use of incentives.

By the early 1960s Yugoslav planners believed that it was time to push ahead to promote even more progress. This was to be done by shifting goals from broadly conceived development plans with intensive labor to targeted planning geared to capital investment. Such selective development implied that differentiation would occur, which would create imbalances in economic growth between the country's regions.

The reforms of the 1960s brought unemployment and inequality among the regions of Yugoslavia as the economy failed to hold its own in the booming international market. At the heart of the problem were both economic and ideological contradictions in market socialism. Furthermore, self-management had meant derogating political and economic power to the republic level. The result was that economic development became bound up with ethnically defined politics. Self-management as a way to overcome nationalist politics through local pluralism

had resulted in the opposite taking place. In the early 1970s Tito reacted to the
most vociferous discontent coming from the Croatians by purging local leaders
and rejecting such politics.

The government attempted to create another stratum of self-managing institutions in the mid-1970s by establishing the Basic Organizations of Associated Labor.
But this move only added to the fragmentation of economic development and increased the difficulties of creating a larger market in the country. Tito's political
scheme for Yugoslavia's development after his passing was to parcel out power
among the component units of the federal state. Thus, the center could only mediate
among the republics in dealing with problems of development. By the 1980s,
the country was suffering from a systemic crisis in economic and political life.

The political and economic decentralization that self-management ushered in
was a strategy to mobilize society and provide backing for the government. While
decentralizing politics and economics had its positive side in popular participation in decision making; the other side of the coin was ineffectual central authority to carry out needed reforms and investment decisions to right the ailing
economy. Politically, self-management failed to integrate Yugoslav society. In
the process it raised political demands on the local level.

In Chapter 5, Greece's development since the nineteenth century is seen to contrast with that of the other Balkan states in two important respects. Its agricultural
sector did not provide sufficient foodstuffs for the populace, while the country
was able to draw on the significant commercial wealth of Greeks living outside
the frontiers of the state. In other respects the country may be compared with
its neighbors. During the nineteenth century development was marked by the
significant growth of the state apparatus, a weak industrial sector geared to processing local agricultural products, the pursuit of territorial expansion legitimized
by nationalist ideology, the continuation and enlargement of foreign political intervention, a weak financial position in terms of foreign investment in the country, and a political culture that revolved around the urban world of the court and
party politics based on personalities and clientelism.

With the entry of Eleftherios Venizelos into national politics in 1910, the country
seemed headed for a new era. Moderate reforms and territorial gains in the Balkan
Wars led to the expectation of more territorial and economic growth. But although
Greece was on the victors' side in the Great War, political strife rent the nation.
The destruction of Hellenism in Asia Minor had far-reaching consequences that
burdened the country's development until World War II.

To think of developmental progress in terms of an efficient and productive
agricultural sector, commercial robustness, and vigorous growth in industry after
World War I was simply not realistic. The country faced a staggering problem
in the settlement of the refugees, while development was hampered by a considerable foreign debt and thus a poor financial standing, and a weak communications, banking, transportation, and energy system.

Settling the refugees necessitated land redistribution. The result was a system
of small farms accompanied by rural indebtedness which was not adequately

balanced by greater production, especially with the onset of the Great Depression. The state sought to provide incentives for the investment of capital in manufacturing, undertook the arrangement of major public works projects, and negotiated foreign loans to help with reconstruction and resettlement. Yet, by the end of the 1930s the country still was a net importer of foodstuffs and thus had a negative trade balance that could not be made up by revenue from shipping and emigrant remittances. A large rural population and small enterprises remained the basic elements of the country's economy. In the meantime political life had come full circle to authoritarian, nonparliamentary rule watched over by a returned monarch.

During the Second World War the country suffered unparalleled social dislocation and economic destruction. Under Axis occupation casualties of war, famine, and inflation took a heavy toll on the nation. The social and economic misery produced by the war was compounded by the political struggle that tore the country apart and led to civil war for another four years.

The defeat of the communists in 1949 ended debate about any radical restructuring of the economy and society as Greece was firmly fixed in the Western camp. Rather than experiencing a communist regime committed to revolutionary breakthroughs, Greece turned to economic recovery and political stability under rightist governments.

American aid and administrative oversight helped the country deal with the large number of displaced persons and to build up the wrecked communications and transportation infrastructure. Greece was thus committed to the international market for capital, machinery, technology, and fuel. Internally, the influential role of the state continued—at first, controlling and rationing to bring about recovery and then to promote financial stability, support domestic manufacturers, and stimulate agricultural production.

By the end of the 1950s Greece had not only recovered, but had also made gains in shifting the distribution of the domestic product by lowering the sectoral share of agriculture while raising that of industry. However, industrial investment was directed primarily to housing, transportation, and communications enterprises where there were quick profits as Greece's urban sector swelled with migrants from the countryside.

In the 1960s, while neighboring governments concentrated on breakthroughs by rapid industrialization and mobilizing their societies in a bid for loyalty and legitimacy, Greece was committed to the international market and attempting to create political pluralism. Its development was hampered by reliance on a few specialized agricultural exports, noncompetitive manufactured goods, and ineffective state management of the economy. A new generation of Western-educated specialists sought to effect a developmental breakthrough by rationalizing the management of the economy through planning and state-directed allocation of resources. Politically, it seemed an opportune time as the right gave way to a center–left government under George Papandreou. Raised expectations went awry when political confrontation between parliament and the monarchy triggered military intervention and the anticipated increase in foreign industrial investment and consequent structural change in manufacturing did not materialize.

Economic growth continued for a time under military rule aided by the "peculiarities" in the Greek socioeconomic world. Thousands left the countryside and found employment by either emigrating or starting up small businesses in the cities. As a result, Greece experienced a dramatic demographic and social transformation. Its population became overwhelmingly urban and middle class in social outlook. The country came to rely on the triad of invisible revenues—emigrant remittances, shipping, and tourism—to deal with the balance of payments.

The years of military rule had a profound impact on the nation. Politically, it resulted in the demand for popular participation and pluralist politics. Economically, there was the perceived need to move forward with modernization as part of the growing common economic market in Europe. This also fit in with a foreign policy agenda that called for less dependence on the United States and improved relations with neighboring communist governments.

Membership in the European Community brought significant economic dividends that helped Greece deal with its trade and public deficit, aggravated inflation, and the problem of rural income. Greece has achieved modernity in many respects through the market. Nonetheless, weaknesses in technical training and facilities, market competitive manufacturing, and a large public sector have continued to trouble development.

In Chapter 6, Mary Ellen Fischer focuses on a verity in Romanian history: the economic and political development of the country during the nineteenth century was bound up with the land—those who owned it and the peasant masses who worked it. At the beginning of the twentieth century, Romania's agricultural sector held both the promise of market-oriented production and the peril of rural economic misery and discontent.

The conclusion of the Great War brought Romania both new territories and peoples. With those gains, however, came problems of minorities and hostile neighbors. Building the unity and maintaining the territorial integrity of the nation was a paramount political goal. The country's development between the two world wars was grounded on the great chasm between rural society and the urban, cosmopolitan sector that directed and dominated economic growth. Romania's political elite recognized the need for rapid industrialization but quarreled over the policies to implement it. A small and weak native bourgeoisie, limited and circumscribed foreign investment, and a deteriorating rural sector in terms of production and consumption—all hampered efforts at economic growth.

By World War II, however, a variety of political regimes had failed to establish the national unity of the enlarged state. Economic development failed to take off, burdened as it was by the agrarian problem and then the Great Depression. The internationally recognized integrity of the state was shattered in the war, with territorial dismemberment and control by first one great power and then another. This only heightened the gap in perception and participation in political development between the elites and the people.

The communists tackled the triad of problems facing the country: national unity, sovereignty, and economic growth. Under Gheorghe Gheorghiu-Dej and then Nicolae Ceauşescu, the transformation of Romania from an agrarian to an industrial society was undertaken. This change must be seen against the initial weakness of the party in the country. With little popular support, the communists, with Soviet backing, gained a monopoly of power against their opponents. They ended whatever remained of the large landowning class, ruined the entrepreneurial element, and nationalized industry. In the countryside collectivization was begun, although it was not completed until the early 1960s.

Like the other states in Eastern Europe that followed the Soviet model of development, Romania plunged into rapid industrialization at the cost to the agricultural and housing sector, producing economic dislocation. Stalin's death and the charting of the New Course challenged the Romanian communist leadership. With different signals emanating from Moscow afterward, the lesson seemed to be that Romania's interests would best be served by the country becoming less liable to external pressures even from a fraternal neighbor.

Khrushchev's effort to institutionalize relations between the socialist states in Eastern Europe and to rationalize their development through specialization brought opposition from the Romanians. By the early 1960s, they were opposing this strategy, while continuing to build an extensive heavy industrial base. The regime's stand against the Soviets found resonance among the general population. When Ceauşescu took over as first secretary upon the death of Gheorghiu-Dej, he built his authority and increased his legitimacy by following a moderate line domestically. Promises were made to key social groups to preempt any extraparty opposition that might emerge. His tactics did not increase popular participation or enhance legality in the country. Rather, they helped mobilize the populace while helping to promote a leadership cult.

During the 1970s Ceauşescu turned to greater coercion in society and the Stalinist model of economic development that had been favored in the 1950s. His preoccupation with raising levels of industrial production brought a decline in living standards. Reliance on petroleum and the products derived from it demanded a dependence on imported technology and eventually oil. When profits from exports could not cover the cost of obtaining the needed resources from abroad, the economy turned down. Concurrently, agricultural production fell, further diminishing export revenue and deepening the country's economic crisis.

Ceauşescu chose to deal with the foreign debt problem by instituting draconian measures that allowed the country to reduce its external financial burdens but at a tremendous cost to the nation's living standard. Conditions worsened still more with Ceauşescu's megalomaniac schemes to further increase production by rationalizing industrial and social development throughout the country. This resulted in social upheaval in the rural areas as villagers were forced to concentrate in urban compounds thrown up around the countryside.

Nationalism and socialism had served the communist regime well since World War II. With the fall of Ceauşescu in 1989, communism was discredited. However, relying on nationalism cannot solve the country's major economic and social problems. The communists had achieved national sovereignty, economic growth through industrial development, and the building of a communications and transport infrastructure, increased educational, health, and cultural facilities, and had rationalized the agricultural sector. Unfortunately, all this was done at the cost of exacerbating economic and ethnic divisions and through dominance and coercion rather than accommodation in politics.

Although the states in Southeastern Europe have followed diverse paths to modernity, some similarities in their development may be discerned. The governments in the region worked to mobilize their people in the drive for development, but this only masked deep social and ethnic cleavages. Until the Second World War the social and economic elites, whether landowners or an emerging urban middle class, politicized their social interests by efforts to gain control of the government. In some instances these groups were coopted and neutralized through state power controlled by dominant rulers as occurred in Romania, Bulgaria, and Yugoslavia. During this time the state administrative institutions and the military cradled and shaped the political culture of the Balkan states, with party politics functioning through clientage and favoritism and the playing off of one party against another. This resulted not in a multiparty system that served plural interests in society, but in dominance by one socioeconomic group or political elite. Development needs were subordinated to the drive to gain and keep political power.

A continuing characteristic of the state administrative apparatus into the twentieth century was its growth in size and pervasiveness without necessarily achieving a concomitant efficiency in management. (See the figures for the interwar bureaucracy in Bulgaria and Yugoslavia cited in Chapter 3.)

By the time of the Second World War, however, the primacy of the nation-state was not in question. Rather, the issue was who (group or personality) would dominate. In institutional terms it at first had been a struggle between parliament and monarch. Although it was thrust aside in the other states, this confrontation continued in post–World War II Greece. At critical moments political groups have been willing to resort to swift and extralegal tactics against their opponents, who have been accused of harming the nation. This occurred in Greece in 1922 and 1967, in Bulgaria under Stamboliiski, and under the communists after World War II.

In the years immediately following the Second World War (1945–1948), a key issue in the struggles between rival political groups was the appropriateness of domestically oriented and guided development. Political striving was concentrated on creating unity in state power as opposed to forging political pluralism. The dramatic mid-twentieth-century political upheavals brought "newcomers," in both the social and political sense, to power in four of the states. But politics continued to be a function of elites, albeit new, and of strong personalities in all the countries. Increasingly, however, the governments had to face the political tensions produced by popular aspirations and expectations.

In the interwar era the states of Southeastern Europe, as part of economic development, undertook land reform. However, it was as much a political as an economic issue as the examples of Romania, Greece, and Bulgaria make clear. The governments also sought to finance industrialization from wealth derived by an improved agricultural sector. But it was difficult to compete in the international market of the 1920s; development then turned in the 1930s to the basic question of economic survival. The programs and policies promoted, therefore, resulted in very limited successes. At the same time, the concern with social stability, which was so evident in Romania, for example, pitted various groups against one another. There were the established, indigenous groups versus the newcomers, urban versus agrarian interests, the state administrative sector and its relations with large and small entrepreneurs, and national minorities coping with and confronting majorities. As this book makes clear, whereas all the Balkan governments generally agreed on the need to promote industrialization, the institutional and technical infrastructures were inadequate.

In the aftermath of World War II the Balkans reflected the settlement in Europe as a whole. The region was divided politically, ideologically, and militarily. In the process, however, interstate stability was achieved, and domestic development proceeded apace. In the following decades, with the international system fixed around a bipolar world, the states in the area underwent a dramatic social and economic transformation. It was marked by high rates of economic growth, the consolidation of political control, the movement of labor from the countryside, and the shift to an urban and industrial society. Greece and Yugoslavia took care of some of their economic and social problems by exporting workers, relying on their remittances, and turning to tourism on a large scale. By the 1980s Bulgaria was also encouraging foreign visitors, especially from the West. In the communist states the agricultural sector changed dramatically with the onset of collectivization and the growth of state farms. This process was eventually reversed in Yugoslavia. There were some similarities in all the states with regard to agriculture, however. As the peasants left the countryside in the 1960s, rural labor became scarce. None of the governments, with the exception of Bulgaria later on, allocated adequate investment to promote agricultural growth to the fullest possible extent. The communist states in the Balkans, for ideological as much as economic reasons, did not come to grips with the rural problems that required special effort. Greece's agricultural sector has benefited significantly from membership in the European Community.

Political pragmatism emerged in most of the states (domestic affairs in Romania under Ceauşescu excepted), and ideology became a less intrusive factor in formulating development policies as the need to promote economic growth meant increased reliance on the integrated global economy. All the Balkan states have turned to the developed world to seek out capital and technology in an effort to stimulate their economies and to meet popular expectations for a better material life. Thus, similarities in social expectations have grown among the peoples in Southeastern Europe, which will hopefully promote a better appreciation of each other's place in the region.

This is a critical time for the course of development among the Balkan states as affairs in Europe turn from a world of superpower politics based on the military confrontation of blocs to the recognition of common economic interests and the opportunity for greater initiative by the smaller nations. In Southeastern Europe the nation-states will no doubt continue to act on historically conditioned interests. Yet there is little choice but to become part of the larger European market that is gradually emerging, as well as to work with the other economically developed states in the world. All the countries in Southeastern Europe to some degree face the difficult problem of reconciling the opening up of their economies to the forces of the competitive, developed market with the large domestic role of the state in the public service sector.

As the states in Southeastern Europe seek their way in the new historical era that opened in the late 1980s, the continuing ethnic, religious, and political diversity of their societies ensures that each country will follow a distinct developmental path. This also relates to the long-held goal of the individual nations to assert their legitimacy and equality vis-à-vis the European world culture and political power. Therefore, contradictions inherent between common economic interests and historically specific national cultures, which have existed in Southeastern Europe throughout the twentieth century, mean that developmental imbalances will continue within and between the states of the region.

2

Modernization Through Secularization in Bulgaria

John Bell

In its broadest sense, modernization is understood as adaptation to the new kind of knowledge that began to transform some societies of Western Europe at the end of the Middle Ages and has since involved most of the world in a process of change that is still developing. Among its most obvious manifestations have been the shift from agricultural to industrial-based economies, the movement of the population from the countryside to urban centers, and the development of effective national governments exerting far more control over the human and material resources at their disposal than was possible in the premodern era. Change in the consciousness of individuals is no less important, but more difficult to define or to measure in easily quantifiable terms. Greater openness to change and a higher value placed on individualism seem to be characteristics of members of modern societies compared with their counterparts in premodern environments.[1]

The Era of National Revival

Bulgaria was not one of the original modernizing nations. Modern knowledge and its effects were not introduced among the Bulgarians until the eighteenth century, and then they came as byproducts of changes in the larger political and economic life of the Ottoman Empire. Increasing foreign demand for Ottoman products fostered regional specialization in agriculture and the growth of towns based on artisan manufactures. Over time the expansion of production for the marketing of cotton, tobacco, livestock, woolens, and metalwork created concentrations of wealth, oriented a segment of the population to the larger world, and encouraged a more dynamic outlook. In the towns, guild organizations (*esnafi*) became in many respects more influential than the Ottoman authorities, the Greek ecclesiastical hierarchy, or traditional Bulgarian notables. They were particularly influential in supporting the spread of a secular school system and supporting the growth of national self-consciousness.[2]

The Bulgarian diaspora in the Balkans and the Ottoman and Russian empires also facilitated the introduction of modern ideas in Bulgaria, for it served as a significant conduit linking the Bulgarian lands with the outside world. Bulgarian merchants and craftsmen settled in many Ottoman cities, most of all in Constantinople itself where they formed a community of 30–40,000 by the mid-nineteenth century. Disorders and war had also led thousand of Bulgarians to seek refuge across the Danube, and significant Bulgarian colonies grew up in Bucharest, Giurgiu, Craiova, and Braila. Beyond the Romanian principalities, Bulgarians settled widely in Bessarabia and the southern Ukraine and formed a large merchant colony in Odessa. In the 1820s, the Slavist Iuri Venelin studied the language and customs of the Bulgarian communities and wrote a series of books that called the attention of Russian scholars to Bulgaria and introduced many Bulgarians to their own culture. Smaller Bulgarian communities were founded in other Russian cities, Serbia, and the Habsburg lands.[3]

Some Bulgarians were introduced to the spirit of romantic nationalism by the works of the Serbs Jovan Rajić, Dositej Obradović, and Vuk Karadžić or from Russian sources. In the early nineteenth century, however, outside ideas penetrated Bulgaria mainly through the medium of Hellenism. Greek was the language both of commerce in the Ottoman world and of the Orthodox Church. Bulgarian merchants and ecclesiastics frequently assimilated to the Greek cultural world which was more open to Western and modern influences. Of particular importance was the emphasis modern Hellenism placed on the creation of secular schools. Bulgarian education had been confined to the ''cell-schools'' organized by monasteries or village clergy. While they kept Bulgarian religious culture alive during the centuries of Ottoman domination, they aimed at preparing students for the priesthood, and they consequently stressed the memorization of prayers and liturgy. They also taught the alphabet, but students and clergy who fully mastered reading and writing were exceptional.[4] Possessed of only primitive literacy in their own language, many Bulgarian merchants and guildsmen sent their sons to Greek institutions, and nearly the entire activist generation of the 1820s and 1830s was Greek trained.[5]

Bulgarians learned much from the Greek national awakening, including the methods of building a nationlist movement, but for most people assimilation to Hellenism was not satisfactory. Bulgarians were inspired to assert their own national identity, and many in fact came to dedicate themselves to overcoming the ''Greek cultural yoke'' in school and ecclesiastical affairs. Vasil Aprilov, for example, was born in 1789 to a wealthy merchant family in Gabrovo and was raised in the spirit of Hellenism. He studied in Moscow, Braşov, and Vienna before settling in Odessa, where he read the works of Venelin, discovered his own Bulgarian identity, and dedicated himself to the national cause. Convinced that education was the key to Bulgaria's revival, he persuaded some of his Odessa associates to join him in financing a Bulgarian school in his native Gabrovo. This school, which taught modern subjects in the Bulgarian language, quickly became a model for other Bulgarian communities.[6]

Dr. Petŭr Beron, another son of a wealthy merchant family, studied medicine in Munich and the natural sciences in Paris. He wrote widely on a number of scientific subjects and contributed the famous *Primer with Various Instructions* to the Bulgarian national revival. This text, generally known as the *Fish Primer* (so-called after the illustration on its cover), contained lessons drawn from geography, the physical sciences, and history. After its first publication in 1824 in Braşov, it became extremely popular and was reprinted five times, serving as an alternative to the traditional prayerbooks. In the introduction to his primer Beron argued that secular education in practical subjects was necessary for Bulgarians to prosper in the contemporary world.[7] He advocated the spread of schools with the Bell–Lancaster system as a model. According to this system, which had already been employed in some Greek schools, the most advanced students, having been taught a lesson, in turn teach it to their fellow students or to those on a lower level.[8] This method was employed in the Gabrovo school and was used extensively in the years before the liberation.

Private individuals, guilds, and community organizations, which had greater latitude for action during the period of nineteenth-century Ottoman reforms, sponsored the spread of education, and by 1878 some 2,000 schools were opened. Although not all of them were of high quality or emphasized the dissemination of *modern* knowledge, they provided an important base for further development, helped to create a market for Bulgarian books and a periodical press, and helped create a corps of educated men who would assume positions in the future Bulgarian state.

The work of the schools was supplemented by the *chitalishte*, or "reading-room." This institution was probably brought to the Bulgarian lands by Polish and Hungarian refugees, many of whom settled in northern Bulgarian towns after the defeat of the 1848 uprising against the Habsburg monarchy. *Chitalishta* spread quickly across Bulgaria after the opening of the first one in Svishtov in 1856. Their growth was probably stimulated by an increasing appetite for news that developed during the Crimean War when British and French troops were stationed in some areas of the country. More than just a small library, the *chitalishta* staged lectures, meetings, plays, concerts, debates, and social events. They were centers of adult education and discussion and a focus of community organization.[9]

In the early stage of the Bulgarian national revival, its leaders did not raise the cry of political independence. They aimed first for cultural and ecclesiastical independence from the Greeks, and they believed that it could be achieved within the framework of the Ottoman Empire. In 1870, the Porte—the executive office of the Ottoman government—did indeed recognize an autocephalous Bulgarian Church, headed by an exarch, with jurisdiction over the fifteen dioceses of Bulgaria and Macedonia. Although the Greek patriarch excommunicated its adherents, the exarchate became a leading force in Bulgarian life, representing Bulgarian interests at the Porte and sponsoring the further expansion of Bulgarian churches and schools. It provided some Bulgarians with experience in managing institutions on a national scale.[10]

Inevitably, the growth of national feeling, the inability of the Porte to maintain order or to carry through consistently the reforms of *Tanzimat*, and the examples of Greek and Serbian independence engendered an explicitly revolutionary movement among the Bulgarians. The belief grew that the welfare and progress of the people depended on achieving national independence. Georgi Rakovski formed a Bulgarian legion on Serbian territory in 1862 to send armed bands to harass the Turkish authorities. In Bucharest Liuben Karavelov and Vasil Levski created a Bulgarian Secret Central Committee to prepare for a national uprising. Revolutionary ferment led to the April uprising in 1876 which, though brutally put down, helped to provoke the Russo-Turkish War from which an independent Bulgarian principality emerged.

From Liberation to World War II

Following the liberation, Bulgarian society experienced a number of modernizing changes. National bureaucratic and military institutions were created. Towns expanded, and the traditional pattern of small, crooked, winding streets, cramped dwellings, and isolated neighborhoods gradually gave way to the urban grid system. Western-style housing graced the wealthier areas, and even in the poorer quarters Western furniture and beds supplanted carpets and cushions. Public buildings and monuments gave a new character to town centers. In the countryside, too, signs of new life were apparent. The rural poet, teacher, and political activist Tsanko Tserkovski observed: "Lamps, tables, chairs, shoes for children, combs and so on—we take many new things into our homes casually, for amusement, and by the next day we have grown accustomed to them, they become necessities."[11]

To develop the country's human resources, Bulgarians aimed to continue the tradition of the national revival period by building a comprehensive educational system. Even during the course of the Russo-Turkish War, the scholar Marin Drinov, appointed by the Russians as provisional commissioner of Bulgarian education, laid the basis for the systematization of the educational system, and it was owing to Drinov's urging that a provision was included in the Tŭrnovo Constitution calling for universal, compulsory, free education in the principality. To be sure, this ideal could not be realized with the resources then at the government's disposal, but under Drinov's inspiration and with the direction of the Czech scholar Konstantin Jiriček who served successive education ministers as executive secretary, a system of public instruction was expanded and made to include a growing number of secular subjects.[12] The latter development was not, at least in the early years, opposed by the Bulgarian Orthodox Church, whose leaders professed to see no conflict between secular and religious learning. Metropolitan Klement of Tŭrnovo, himself briefly minister of public instruction in 1879–1880, wrote that "Faith gives us the higher truths of morality, and science illuminates these truths and instills them in us more clearly," to explain his belief that Bulgarians must deepen their commitment to "enlightenment."[13]

The landmark educational reform of 1891 substantially increased the authority of the Ministry of Education over the nation's schools, and for that reason some historians have regarded it as a retreat from the tradition of local initiative and control that characterized the national revival period. But this was outweighed by the substantial increase in resources provided to the schools and by the reaffirmation of the ideals of universal, free, compulsory education. During the 1898–1899 academic year, the first for which comprehensive statistics were collected, 55 percent of the Bulgarian population between the ages of five and fifteen were enrolled in school. This compared to 29 percent in Greece and 15 percent in Serbia.[14]

If there were undoubted signs of progress, they were overshadowed by the fact that in the years after liberation Bulgaria failed to achieve the economic and social transformations associated with modernity. Nor did its democratic political institutions function well or, ultimately, survive. The expectation that national liberation would automatically be followed by Bulgaria's entry into the mainstream of Western development was disappointed. Less than two decades after the creation of the new Bulgarian state, the writer and political activist Mikhalaki Georgiev expressed a growing pessimism: "We strained like eagles high above the clouds, and now we roll in the dust, in the swamp . . . ! If this is the life a free people leads, then such freedom is in vain. We sowed roses, but only thorns have come forth."[15]

Bulgaria's failure to achieve significant progress toward industrialization after 1878 was in part due to purely economic factors. Although the liberation did bring such "prerequisites of capitalist development" as the abolition of "feudal" relations in the countryside, the decline of artisanal production, protection of private property, and control over tariff policy, these were offset by the loss of Ottoman markets and the lack of available capital.[16] Although a native banking system was established, it was too small to support the mechanization of agriculture or the growth of large-scale industry, and the Bulgarian affiliates of major Western banks were reluctant to risk their profits by making long-term investments in the development of Bulgaria's infrastructure.[17] What industrial growth there was concentrated in "premodern" industries, such as textiles, brewing, distilling, and tobacco processing, and not the new metallurgical or chemical industries. According to the director of the Statistical Institute of the University of Sofia, as late as 1936 Bulgaria possessed only about 40,000 industrial workers "in the true West European sense" as opposed to 134,392 artisans.[18] Between 1880 and 1910 the proportion of the population in towns of over 2,000 inhabitants actually declined slightly.[19]

Economic stagnation undermined the state's educational program, as there were not enough productive jobs available for those who were being trained. Since the government was the only major source of employment, Bulgarian students prepared themselves for bureaucratic careers. By 1896–1897, the first school year for which data were collected, the university reported that there were 180 students in the faculty of history, only 81 in the faculties of science and mathematics, and 354 in the faculty of law.[20] Even in institutes set up to provide specialized training in agronomy or commerce, it was found that few graduates actually pursued these careers, the majority ending up as government clerks. One consequence of this development was the growth of political corruption as politics came to be seen as a struggle for the spoils of office, and political parties became "corporations for the exploitation of power."[21] On the other hand, educated Bulgarians who retained a measure of idealism frequently experienced alienation and turned to radical programs of the left or right.

Bulgaria's failure to make significant economic progress after the liberation also had political and social causes. Bulgaria's framework of political institutions was established at the Tŭrnovo constitutional convention. It is traditional to point to the democratic character of the Tŭrnovo Constitution which provided for a unicameral legislature, a cabinet responsible to the National Assembly, universal male suffrage, and an array of civil rights.[22] The economic historian Alexander Gerschenkron even identified the constitution as a major cause of Bulgaria's failure to modernize. By allowing the antimodern impulses of the peasant majority to be expressed through the ballot box, the constitution did not permit any government to adopt the severe economic policies needed to promote industrialization.[23] Gerschenkron failed to note, however, that few of Bulgaria's elections were genuinely democratic; the party in control of the election machinery almost always rolled up a large majority. Moreover, it was precisely when elections were genuine, in the years immediately after the First World War, that a Bulgarian government launched the most serious attempt to modernize the country of any that was made before the communist period. Contrary to Gerschenkron's analysis, the political obstacles to Bulgaria's modernization lay in the undemocratic aspects of the Tŭrnovo Constitution.

In his *The Persistence of the Old Regime*[24] Arno Mayer argued that well into the twentieth century the political and cultural life of Europe continued to be dominated by premodern, "nobilitarian" forces whose roots were in the *ancien régime*. Their hegemony over the middle and lower classes, even through the era of expanded suffrage, was due to a variety of political mechanisms combined with their control of landed wealth and their ability and willingness to coopt the most able members of the class below. Their values and style of life acted as a model for a middle class that aspired to "rise" but lacked self-confidence about its own position in society.

Because independent Bulgaria lacked a landed nobility and aristocratic tradition, Mayer's analysis would seem to fit it poorly. Nonetheless, it offers important clues toward understanding the shape of independent Bulgaria's development. In drafting the Treaty of Berlin, the Great Powers determined that Bulgaria should have a monarchical form of government. This decision injected an alien element, both figuratively and literally, into Bulgarian civil society. Alexander Battenberg, Bulgaria's first prince, was "A favorite nephew of the Tsar, related to the English ruling house, a German prince, the son of an Austrian general.''[25] Mayer characterized the ''nobilitarian'' views of prewar Europe's ruling class as ''undemocratic, hierarchical, and militaristic.'' This was an outlook that Prince Alexander clearly shared.

Battenberg's outlook on life had been molded by his environment. He incorporated in his person both the virtues and the weaknesses of the aristocratic military training which he had received. He was honest and honorable, eager to please his superiors and considerate of his inferiors. He also had a pleasing personality, made friends easily, and was popular with his colleagues. At the same time, however, his knowledge of politics was slight and he was unable to cooperate with people whom he did not consider his equals. He paid great attention to military and court formalities, and it often seemed to the outsider that he was more interested in the forms than in the functions of the military and civil institutions. In spite of his youth and inexperience, he was ambitious to make Bulgaria into a strong military and aristocratic state on the model of the only ones with which he was intimately familiar.[26]

Alexander failed in his attempt to abrogate the Tŭrnovo Constitution with the help of his Russian advisers. His successors achieved more by subverting it through more subtle maneuvers and the cultivation of domestic support. Prince, later Tsar, Ferdinand of Saxe-Coburg-Gotha lacked Alexander's qualities of personal attractiveness, but he was more skillful at mastering the intricacies of Bulgarian politics. Like his predecessor, he was committed to military and aristocratic values and was an enthusiastic player in the ''Great Game'' of diplomacy. Tsar Boris III, though temporarily placed in the background by the circumstances of Bulgaria's defeat in World War I and his father's abdication, cultivated close relations with the high military and was able to rely on them to supplant the constitution with a royal-military dictatorship.

Social position in Bulgaria was determined by wealth, education, and political office rather than by bloodlines or the ownership of a landed estate. Nevertheless, a sort of ersatz aristocracy developed among prominent Bulgarians who absorbed its spirit and values from the monarch and his entourage or from experience in other countries.[27] The growth of this psychology, which centered around the monarch, was visible in the elaborate ceremonial that surrounded Ferdinand's assumption of the title Tsar. It was also apparent in the key political events of the pre–World War II era, the coups d'état of 1923 and 1934, and in the deference shown to the diplomacy of Boris III during the Second World War.

The impact of Bulgaria's monarchy was most strongly felt in policies of resource allocation. Encouraged by the country's unsatisfied territorial aspirations as exemplified by the San Stefano Treaty in 1878, which would have given Bulgaria most of Macedonia and an opening to the Aegean, and the interplay of great power rivalries in the Balkans, the nobilitarian outlook of the court and the political leaders coopted by it fostered the growth of militarism and the tendency to define national goals exclusively in terms of territorial expansion. By the turn of the century, military expenditure and interest payments on the national debt, which was

contracted largely for military purposes, accounted for 44 percent of the state
budget, a proportion that remained approximately constant up to the eve of the
First Balkan War, when military preparations caused it to increase still further.[28]
On a per capita basis, Bulgaria was one of the most thoroughly militarized countries in the world, a fact reflected in the frequently made observation that it was
"the Prussia of the Balkans." Although the Treaty of Neuilly reduced and then
limited the size of Bulgaria's army, after the coup of 1934 military buildup resumed
with spending doubled by 1939.[29]

It is frequently argued that military spending will stimulate the domestic economy
and lead to technological breakthroughs of importance outside the military sphere.
Whatever the validity of this argument for advanced societies, it has no relevance
for Bulgaria in the era before World War II. Because the country imported rather
than produced most of its military equipment, domestic industry was not
stimulated, and resources were simply drained away.[30] Moreover, the militaristic
outlook of Bulgaria's leadership was a vital factor that drew the country into wars
that squandered its economic and human resources without achieving the "national goals."[31]

Bulgaria's failure to achieve significant economic progress in the years after
the liberation provoked broad discontent among ordinary Bulgarians that was given
form in part by Bulgaria's socialists, whose analysis was borrowed from their
Western counterparts, and to a much greater degree by the home-grown Agrarian
movement led by Aleksandŭr Stamboliiski.[32]

From its beginnings at the end of the nineteenth century, the Agrarian movement was explicitly and consciously concerned with the problem of modernization. The village teachers and other members of the rural intelligentsia who provided the core of its leadership wondered why, after twenty years of independence,
Bulgaria had acquired "neither the factories of England and Germany nor the
culture of France."[33]

The answer that Stamboliiski provided was that modernization did not occur
by itself; rather, it had to be nurtured by the state. The monarch and political
parties, composed of diverse economic interests, could not agree on a common
policy, however, and so clung to power by misleading the people through policies
of chauvinism and militarism. The signal fact of modern politics, Stamboliiski
wrote, was the "shameful compromise" between the institution of monarchy and
the political parties to exploit the country for their own interest while ignoring
the plight of the masses. To break away from this system, Stamboliiski advocated
the organization of the population into economic interest groups that could take
consistent positions on issues of economic development. This was, he believed,
beginning to occur in the first decades of the twentieth century as the socialist
parties organized the small proletariat and Stamboliiski's Bulgarian Agrarian National Union (BANU) became the largest political force in the country.[34]

Bulgaria's participation in the Balkan Wars and the First World War represented
a severe setback to the country's development. In human terms alone Bulgaria
suffered more than 460,000 casualties, including 158,000 killed.[35] The diversion

of manpower to the front cut grain production nearly in half and, combined with the loss of imported materials, crippled industrial and artisan production.[36] Suffering and defeat radicalized the population. Tsar Ferdinand fled the country, and the hold of his political followers on the government was broken. The Allies, however, fearing the spread of "Bolshevism" in the Balkans, sought stability by preserving the Bulgarian monarchy and accepting the succession of Boris III.

In the circumstances that surrounded Bulgaria's defeat, the tsar at that time could be nothing more than a figurehead. Genuine elections put the government in the hands of Stamboliiski and the BANU and made the communists the largest party of the opposition. During their years in power, the Agrarians consciously pursued the goal of modernization at the expense of traditional state priorities. Stamboliiski's government directed resources into a massive expansion of the country's school system. In addition to the traditional four years of compulsory elementary school, Agrarian legislation called for three more years of study in the *progimnaziia* (middle school). Over eight hundred *progimnazii* were built during the Agrarian period, and 311 new elementary schools were opened. To staff them, five new institutes of teacher training were created. Agrarian educational reforms also increased the emphasis on practical and scientific subjects in the curriculum and added faculties of medicine, veterinary medicine, and agronomy to the university and opened two "higher academies" in forestry and commerce. Existing professional schools and institutes were directed to reduce the proportion of their curricula devoted to literature and religion in favor of more extensive training in foreign languages, natural science, bookkeeping, and their special subjects.[37]

Compulsory Labor Service (CLS), the most famous of the Agrarians' reforms, was intended to promote modernization in two ways: by mobilizing labor for work on large-scale projects, such as roadbuilding, and by providing the labor conscripts with training in technical skills, hygiene, and work experience. In its initial form, the law on CLS made all men on reaching the age of twenty subject to conscription for one year of labor service. Prominent Bulgarians, appalled at the thought that their children might be compelled to perform physical labor alongside the common people, appealed to the Inter-Allied Control Commission, which put a maximum size on the labor army and required the government to permit the purchase of exemptions. During its first year in operation, CLS employed approximately 30,000 people who worked on the state's model farms and in various state enterprises and construction projects. Before the Agrarian government was overthrown, it was negotiating with France to send labor battalions to work on French farms in order to gain experience with contemporary Western agricultural techniques.[38]

CLS also applied to women, who were liable to perform six months of service upon reaching age sixteen. Although not implemented as fully as CLS for men, battalions of women were trained in cooking and housekeeping skills, telephone and telegraph operation, fruit and vegetable gardening, and the tending of silkworms, bees, and vineyards. While today's feminists will hardly consider such training liberating, in the context of time it marked a sharp break with Bulgarian custom.

In order to allow the Bulgarian smallholder to take advantage of the technology, knowledge of the market, and economies of scale available to large capitalist farmers, the Agrarian government supported the expansion of the cooperative movement. Believing that the cooperative principle could be applied to other areas of the economy, the government also sponsored the formation of cooperatives in commercial fishing and forestry.[39]

To meet the cost of financing its commitment to development, the Agrarian government sacrificed the country's military establishment and traditional foreign policy goals. To be sure, disarmament was required by the Treaty of Neuilly, but it was also a long-standing Agrarian demand.[40] During its years in power, the Agrarian government did not maintain the army at even the level permitted by the treaty. Stamboliiski also pledged to accept the Treaty of Neuilly and the assignment of most of Macedonia to Yugoslavia and Greece. At the end of 1922, he signed the Treaty of Niš with Belgrade, providing for cooperation against Macedonian terrorists who resisted incorporation into the Serb-Croat-Slovene Kingdom.

Agrarian policies struck at the privileges of Bulgaria's elite and seemed treasonous to those who were accustomed to conceiving of Bulgaria's goals as territorial expansion. On June 9, 1923, disloyal elements in the army, the League of Reserve Officers, and Macedonian terrorists[41] overthrew the government and murdered Stamboliiski. Most of the Agrarians' reforms were undone or drastically modified.

In 1931 a reconstituted opposition, the People's Bloc, a coalition that included the Agrarian Union, overcame the government's manipulation of the ballot box and formed a government. It took power, however, during the economic crisis brought on by the world depression, and its inability to alleviate the situation (Bulgaria's GNP fell by more than one-third between 1929 and 1934) led to further political instability and labor unrest. In May 1934 the military carried out a peaceful coup inspired by *Zveno*, an elitist group that drew its membership from intellectual, commercial, and military circles. It advocated "national restoration" through an authoritarian, technocratic regime. The divisive forces associated with parliamentary politics were eliminated by the suspension of the constitution and the suppression of all political parties.[42]

Zveno's political base was too narrow to allow it to consolidate power, and the real beneficiary of the 1934 coup proved to be Boris III. By the end of 1935 he had relied on his own clique in the army to install a thoroughly subservient government. Bulgaria thus ended the interwar period as a royal-military dictatorship, the form of government that had become nearly universal in Eastern Europe.

Given the traditional policies and priorities of the post–1923 Bulgarian governments and the world economic situation, Bulgaria's development stagnated. A recent American study of Bulgaria's national income for 1938 found that modern industry accounted for only 5.6 percent of the total. This was practically unchanged from the proportion in 1926.[43] Artisan production appeared to be gaining ground during this period.

The Communist Era

Compared to its neighbors, Bulgaria suffered little physical destruction during the Second World War. Boris III's policy of alliance with Germany against Great Britain and the United States, but neutrality toward the USSR, kept Bulgarian forces out of combat and avoided foreign occupation, at least until German resistance was crumbling and the Soviet Union declared war. Allied bombing that began at the end of 1943 did more psychological than physical damage, and the internal resistance movement, though real, did not reach major proportions until Bulgaria was near the point of collapse. The country gained territory, since the postwar treaties accepted Bulgaria's retention of the southern Dobruja.

Soviet occupation and the communist consolidation of power, however, radically altered the country's political structure and its international position. Bulgaria's old regime was quickly destroyed. Former political leaders went on trial before "people's courts" that condemned 2,730 to death, 1,305 to life imprisonment, and 5,119 to lesser prison terms before concluding their work in April 1945.[44] The officer corps was purged, and a new security apparatus was created that proceeded to "unmask" an untold number of "enemies of the people." Tsar Boris had died before the end of the war, leaving the throne to his six-year-old son Simeon II, and in September 1946 a popular referendum abolished the monarchy and sent the royal family into exile.

The Bulgarian communists moved more slowly against their partners in the Fatherland Front, the antifascist coalition with the Agrarians, socialists, and *Zveno* that had been formed during the war, but by the end of 1947 they, too, had been destroyed or absorbed into the new communist regime. A team of Soviet jurists helped in the writing of a new constitution, adopted in December 1947, that emphasized the "unity of state power" and provided the legal framework for the building of a socialist system.[45]

The new political leadership was ideologically committed to a program of modernization, at least in the sense of fostering industrial development and of participating in the modern "scientific-technological revolution." To be sure, this was only one side of its activity. The goal of securing political power and liquidating class enemies brought a degree of economic disruption and struck at artisan and manufacturing groups whose knowledge and skills had been the backbone of the prewar nonagricultural economy.[46] Still, despite great human and material cost, Bulgaria's new regime undertook the process of building the foundations of a modern industrial economy, the achievement of which would become the Communist party's proudest achievement and its chief claim to legitimacy.

The American economist George Feiwel estimated that Bulgaria's growth in national income between 1951 and 1967 averaged 9.6 percent annually, and between 1967 and 1974 it was about 7.5 percent.[47] This was accompanied by substantial structural change; the share of industry in national income rose from 37 percent in 1950 to 51 percent in 1972. By 1979 it had reached 58 percent.[48] The late 1970s saw worldwide economic retrenchment, but the Bulgarian economy continued to grow, though at at slower rate of between 4 and 5 percent.[49]

More than any other East European country, Bulgaria replicated the Soviet economic model. It called for the construction of a central planning apparatus that would promote rapid growth of heavy industry through concentrated investment from the state budget. Industrialization would be furthered by the movement of labor from the countryside, made possible by the transition to mechanized collective farms, and by the more extensive use of women in the labor force. Bulgaria's heavy reliance on Soviet experience led to the adoption of a number of organizational forms and investment priorities that were less than ideally suited to Bulgarian conditions. On the other hand, Soviet material assistance also played a significant role in Bulgaria's economic development. Although the exact level of Soviet economic support remains secret, extensive material and technological assistance are visible in such large-scale projects as the Maritsa-iztok energy-industrial complex, the Kremikovtsi metallurgical combine, the Burgas petrochemical complex, and in the nuclear power industry. Bulgarian economic growth is coordinated by treaty with the USSR through the end of the century, although the exact terms of the treaty have never been published.[50]

The international situation that emerged after World War II and Bulgaria's membership in the Soviet bloc created an unusually stable political environment. Whether credit is given to Bulgaria's leaders or to larger forces, the fact remains that since the end of World War II Bulgaria has enjoyed forty-five years of peace. This is already nineteen years more than the longest period of peace (1886–1912) that occurred between the country's liberation and entry into the Second World War, and should not be underestimated as a factor contributing to modernization in the postwar era.

Since 1944 the Bulgarian school system has focused on adapting to the "scientific-technological revolution," concentrating on raising the level of Bulgarian expertise in scientific and engineering fields. To be sure, many skilled teachers and professionals were purged during the communist consolidation of power, and their talents lost to the regime. To this day, appointments to prestigious positions and programs are significantly affected by political considerations and "connections." Nonetheless, in the long run, these factors have been more than offset by the sheer physical expansion of the educational system. Moreover, the curricula of schools and universities were thoroughly secularized and religious education was banned. However deplorable this may have been from the point of view of religious liberty, Bulgarian schools are not required to give equal time to such pseudosciences as "creationism."[51]

At the end of the 1970s, with 86 percent of the eligible population enrolled in secondary education, Bulgaria ranked in seventh place among the world's nations in this category. This was just behind France and ahead of the United States. Of Bulgaria's Balkan neighbors, Greece ranked sixteenth with 77 percent and

Yugoslavia fifty-first with 51 percent. With regard to the percentage of the population between the ages of twenty and twenty-four enrolled in institutions of higher education, Bulgaria ranked ninth in the world, just ahead of Sweden, with 21.7 percent enrolled. Yugoslavia ranked twenty-fourth with 16 percent and Greece thirty-sixth with 11 percent. The emphasis placed on scientific and technological training led to Bulgaria's ranking eleventh in terms of scientific and engineering personnel on a per capita basis (230.3 per 10,000). With 35.5 percent of its scientists involved in basic research, Bulgaria ranked third in the world, behind only the USSR and Japan.[52]

No small country can hope to stand at or near the forefront of scientific and technological progress by itself. Since 1944 Bulgaria has dealt with this problem primarily by availing itself of the opportunity to make use of Soviet institutions. In 1980 it was reported that more than 8,500 Bulgarian citizens had received higher education in the USSR and that more than 1,250 had defended doctoral and candidate's dissertations.[53]

One aspect of postwar Bulgaria's economic and educational policies was the mobilization of women for industrial and white-collar occupations. In this instance Marxist ideology regarding the equality of women and economic necessity combined to oppose traditional values inherited from the centuries of Ottoman domination. The principle of legal equality for women was included in the 1947 Dimitrov Constitution. In subsequent years the government introduced a network of measures (including the legalization of abortion, institutional child care, legislation protecting the employment rights of pregnant women and new mothers) to adapt to and to encourage the changing position of women in Bulgarian society.

The impact of the evolving role of Bulgarian women has so far been small at the highest political levels. Only two women, Tsola Dragoicheva and Liudmila Zhivkova, have sat on the politburo,[54] and only 12 of the 195 full members of the central committee elected in 1986 were female. In other areas of life, however, particularly in the professions, change has been much more visible. At the end of the 1970s, 53 percent of Bulgaria's university students were women. This was the third highest percentage in the world (behind only Kuwait and the Philippines) and compares with 40 percent in neighboring Yugoslavia and 35 percent in Greece.[55]

The pace of Bulgaria's economic development slowed in the late 1970s owing to the worldwide rise in the cost of energy, diminishing Soviet subsidies, and an emerging labor shortage brought on by a prolonged low birthrate. Moreover, despite a number of innovative reforms, Bulgarian experience reflected the general difficulties that Soviet-type systems face in managing more complex and advanced economies. At the end of the 1970s Bulgaria introduced the NEM, or New Economic Mechanism, modeled after the Hungarian experiments in market socialism. NEM was supposed to force Bulgarian industry to meet the quality standards of the world market, but the regime lacked the will to allow noncompetitive enterprises to fail.[56]

The example of *perestroika* provided by the Soviet Union under Gorbachev was initially welcomed and led to the announcement of a grandiose series of reforms. The cornerstone of the reforms was said to be "workers' self-manage-ment" involving the transfer of state enterprises to workers "ownership" and the legalization of a small-scale private sector.[57] The regime failed, however, to clarify the meaning of "workers' self-management" and eventually admitted that little had actually changed in practice.[58.]

More influential have been the long-term social effects of the Bulgarian govern-ment's efforts to modernize. The new generation that grew to maturity under the socialist regime included important elements possessing an outlook that was incompatible with the demands for political and ideological conformity character-istic of the past. Particularly among the specialists, professionals, and intellec-tuals, who constitute the leading edge of Bulgaria's "scientific-technological revolution," there is skepticism toward Marxist dogmas and an aching desire for greater autonomy in personal life. It was precisely this element that provided the core of a revived "civil society" during the 1980s. Organized independent groups, of which the most important were *Ecoglasnost*, the Club for the Support of *Glasnost* and *Perestroika*, and the independent union *Podkrepa* (Support), did not wither under government repression and were clearly catalysts in bringing down the Zhivkov regime.[59]

Modernization rarely occurs smoothly and evenly across all sectors of society. In Bulgaria Todor Zhivkov's long tenure in power—he led the party since 1954 and combined state and party leadership from 1962 to 1989—created an environ-ment of political immobility while considerable change was taking place in the economy and society. Zhivkov's fall opened prospects for extensive and rapid political change. As of March 1990, the Bulgarian Communist party has deleted from the constitution the provision guaranteeing it political hegemony, promised to shift power from the party itself to a government responsible to the National Assembly, accepted the legitimacy of competing political parties, and pledged to abide by the results of free elections. Numerous parties have appeared on the scene, some of them revivals of past political formations, and others, like the Greens, quite new in the Bulgarian context. Some have already split into factions.

Just as the idea of modernization has provided insight into the development of Bulgaria, so the recent turn toward political democracy, should it prove real and lasting, in Bulgaria and the other countries of Eastern Europe ought to lead to a deeper understanding of modernization itself. The concept was formulated at least in part as an alternative to the view that world history should be inter-preted in terms of Westernization, that is, the spread of the ideas, institutions, and values developed in Western Europe and its offshoots to other societies around the world. In the 1960s and 1970s modernization theory suggested that in-dustrialization, urbanization, mass literacy, and effective national government could be achieved through a variety of institutional frameworks. With the addi-tional perspective of another decade it now appears clear that some frameworks work better than others, particularly at sustaining a dynamic engagement with change. Although it is always dangerous to generalize from short-term developments, we should be willing to entertain the idea that democratic political institutions and market economies are more closely intertwined with the process of modernization than we have believed.

Notes

1. The author's understanding of modernization derives primarily from the studies of Cyril E. Black, whose *The Dynamics of Modernization: A Study in Comparative History* (New York, 1966) was a classic in the development of modernization theory. Black also specifically discussed Bulgaria within the framework of comparative modernization in "Process of Modernization: The Bulgarian Case," in Thomas Butler, ed., *Bulgaria, Past and Present* (Columbus, Ohio, 1976), pp. 111–31. Several other chapters in this volume deal with such aspects of modernization as urbanization, demographic and social change, and economic development. For a more detailed account of Bulgarian economic development, see Nikolai Todorov et al., *Stopanska istoriia na Bŭlgariia*, 681–1981 (Sofia, 1981); and John R. Lampe, *The Bulgarian Economy in the Twentieth Century* (New York, 1986).

2. The Bulgarians have produced an immense literature on their national revival. There is a general survey in English by Assen Nicoloff, *The Bulgarian Resurgence* (Cleveland, Ohio, 1987). Of particular importance is Thomas A. Meininger, *The Formation of a Nationalist Bulgarian Intelligentsia. 1835–1878* (New York and London, 1987), which examines the problem in the light of Western social science. An interesting Bulgarian attempt to examine the sociology of the national revival is Rumiana Radkova, *Bŭlgarskata inteligentsiia prez vŭzrazh-daneto* (Sofia, 1986).

3. The penetration of modern ideas into the Bulgarian diaspora is discussed in Cyril E. Black, "Russia and the Modernization of the Balkans," and by Lefton Stavrianos, "The Influence of the West on the Balkans," in Charles and Barbara Jelavich, eds., *The Balkans in Transition* (Berkeley and Los Angeles, 1963), pp. 143–83, 119–42. See also Dimitŭr Kosev, Vladimir Dikulesku, and Virzhiniia Paskaleva, "Za polozhenieto i stopanskata deinost na bŭlgarskata emigratsiia vŭv Vlashko prez XIX v.: (Do rusko-turskata voina 1877–78 g.)," in *Bŭegaro-rumŭnski vrŭzki i otnosheniia prez vekovete: Izsledvaniia* (Sofia, 1965) and V. Diakovich, *Bŭlgarite v Besarabiia: kratŭk istoricheski ocherk* (Sofia, 1930); Krumka Sharova, "Kŭm kharakteristikata na ideinite kontakti mezhdv vŭzrozhdenskite bŭlgari i sŭvremenniia im sviat," in Mito Isusov et al., eds., *Iubileen sbornik v chest na Akademik Dimitŭr Kosev* (Sofia, 1985), pp. 92–100.

4. In his autobiography, Bishop Sofroni Vrachanski (1739–1818), one of the "awakeners" of Bulgaria, wrote of the envy shown to him by his fellow priests because of his ability to read and write.

5. Meininger, *The Formation of a Nationalist Bulgarian Intelligentsia*, p. 70.

6. Nikolai Genchev, *Bŭlgarsko vuzrazhdane* (Sofia, 1988), pp. 149–57.

7. Petŭr Beron, *Bukvar s razlichni poucheniia* (Braşov, Romania, 1824), pp. 2–11.

8. Developed in Scotland and England to save money by reducing the need for teachers to provide basic literacy to "the industrious classes," the Bell–Lancaster system was well suited to Balkan schools where it maximized the impact of trained teachers.

9. Stiliian Chilingirov, *Bŭlgarski chitalishta predi osvobozhdenieto: Prinos kŭm istoriiata na bŭlgarskoto vŭzrazhdane* (Sofia, 1930).

10. The organization of the exarchate and its role in Bulgarian life are examined in great detail in Zina Markova, *Bŭlgarskata ekzarkhiia 1870–1879* (Sofia, 1989).

11. *Zemledelska zashtita* 1, 5 (October 10, 1899), 1. Richard Crampton, *Bulgaria 1878–1918* (Boulder, Colo., 1983) provides an excellent survey of the social and political development of independent Bulgaria in the era through World War I.

12. The establishment of independent Bulgaria's public school system is the subject of Roy E. Heath, *The Establishment of the Bulgarian Ministry of Public Instruction and Its Role in the Development of Modern Bulgaria, 1878–1885* (New York and London, 1987).

13. Heath, *The Establishment of the Bulgarian Ministry of Public Instruction*, p. 307.

14. Iordan Parushev, "Pŭrvata prosvetna reforma v Bŭlgariia prez 1891 g.," *Istoricheski pregled* 43, 6 (1987), 39–49.

15. Quoted in V. de S. Pinto, "The Narodnik Movement in Bulgarian Literature," unpublished dissertation, University of London (1952), pp. 101–02.

16. S. Sh. Grinberg, "Iz istorii razvitiia bolgarskoi promyshlennosti v kontse XIX v. (perekhod k politike proteksionizma i pooshchreniia krupnoi promyshlennosti)," *Uchenye zapiski Instituta slavianovedeniia* 30 (1966), 136–52; I. N. Chastukhin, "Razvitie kapitalizma v Bolgarii v kontse XIX veka," *Vestnik Moskovskogo universiteta: seriia obshchestvennykh nauk*, No. 7 (1953), 55–70; Alexander Gerschenkron, *Economic Backwardness in Historical Perspective* (New York, 1962), pp. 223, 232–33.

17. Lampe, *The Bulgarian Economy*, pp. 29–35.

18. O. N. Anderson, *Struktur und Konjunktur der bulgarischen Volkswirtschaft* (Jena, 1938), p. 13.

19. Kiril Popoff, *La Bulgarie économique, 1879–1911* (Sofia, 1920), p. 11.

20. Kniazhestvo Bŭlgariia–Direktsiia na statistikata, *Statistika za srednite, spetsialnite, profesionalnite i vissheto uchilishta v kniazhestvo Bŭlgariia prez uchebnata 1896–1897 godina* (Sofia, 1905), pp. 166–67.

21. Dimo Kazasov, *Ulitsi, khora, sŭbitiia* (Sofia, 1959), p. 200.

22. Cyril E. Black, *The Establishment of Constitutional Government in Bulgaria* (Princeton, N.J., 1943), pp. 101–10.

23. Gerschenkron, *Economic Backwardness*, p. 226.

24. Arno Mayer, *The Persistence of the Old Regime* (New York, 1981).

25. Egon C. Corti, *Alexander von Battenberg: Sein Kampf mit den Zaren und Bismarck* (Vienna, 1920), p. 57.

26. Black, *The Establishment of Constitutional Government*, p. 137.

27. For a case study of the development of aristocratic consciousness among some Bulgarians, see Nadezhda Muir, *Dimitri Stancioff: Patriot and Cosmopolitan, 1864–1940*. See also the descriptions of life in court circles in Stephane Groueff's biography of Boris III, *Crown of Thorns* (Lanham, Md., New York, London, 1987).

28. Popoff, *La Bulgarie économique*, pp. 483–84.

29. Baiko Baikov, "Politicheska sistema na burzhoaznoto obshtestvo v Bŭlgariia v protsesa na neinata fashizatsiia (1934–1939 g.)," *Istoricheski pregled* 43, 6 (1987), 16.

30. Lampe, *The Bulgarian Economy*, p. 100.

31. An exception should be made for the brief war with Serbia that confirmed the unification of northern and southern Bulgaria. On the other hand, calculated on a per capita basis, Bulgaria suffered the most severe losses of any country involved in the First World War. A. Ts. Tsankov, "Bŭlgariia prez voinata i sled neia," *Spisanie na Bŭlgarskoto*

ikonomichesko druzhestvo," 20, 1–2–3 (1921), 38; G. T. Danaillow, *Les effets de la guerre en Bulgarie* (Fontenay-aux Roses, 1932), p. 603.

32. On the origins of Bulgarian socialism and its analysis of Bulgarian society, see Dimitŭr Blagoev, *Prinos kŭm istoriiata na sotsializma v Bŭlgariia* (Sofia, 1976); Iordan Iotov et al., *Dimitŭr Blagoev: Biografiia* (Sofia, 1979); Joseph Rothschild, *The Communist Party of Bulgaria: Origins and Development. 1883–1936* (New York, 1959); and John Bell, *The Bulgarian Communist Party from Blagoev to Zhivkov* (Stanford, Calif., 1986), pp. 1–20.

33. *Zemledelska zashtita* 2, 14 (January 17, 1901), 1.

34. Stamboliiski's principal ideological statement was *Politicheski partii ili sŭslovni organizatsii?*, first published in 1909. See also John D. Bell, *Peasants in Power: Alexander Stamboliski and the Bulgarian Agrarian National Union. 1899–1923.* (Princeton, N.J., 1977), pp. 57–73.

35. Danaillow, *Les effets de la guerre*, p. 603.

36. Lampe, *The Bulgarian Economy*, pp. 42–45; Leo Pazvolsky, *Bulgaria's Economic Position After the War* (Washington, D.C., 1930), pp. 53–60.

37. Bell, *Peasants in Power*, pp. 176–79; Alexander Velev, *Prosvetna i kulturna politika na pravitelstvoto na Aleksandŭr Stamboliiski* (Sofia, 1980), pp. 9–67; B. Ivanov, "Problemata za trudovoto i politikhnicheskoto obuchenie u nas," *Godishnik na Sofiskiia universitet* 52 (1958), 253–351.

38. Ivan Dermendzhiev, "Organizatsiia na trudovata povinnost v Bŭlgariia 1920–1934," *Godishnik na Sofiskiia universitet: iuridicheski fakultet* 52, part one (1961), 359–451; M. Lazard, *Compulsory Labor Service in Bulgaria* (Geneva, 1922); Bell, *Peasants in Power*, pp. 171–76.

39. Zhak Nata et al., *Istoriia na ikonomicheskata misŭl v Bŭlgariia*, II (Sofia, 1973), pp. 278–86; B. Mateev, *Dvizhenieto za kooperativno zemedelie v Bŭlgariia pre usloviiata na kapitalizma* (Sofia, 1967), pp. 32–34.

40. Stamboliski had opposed Bulgaria's participation in the Balkan Wars and had spent World War I under a sentence of life imprisonment for calling on the population to resist mobilization.

41. The direct complicity of the court has never been conclusively demonstrated. Contemporary observers, however, assumed that military officers would not have undertaken the coup without some indication that they were acting in accordance with the royal will. See Dimo Kazasov, *Bez pŭt i bez idei* (Sofia, 1962), pp. 9–11.

42. A survey of Zveno's program is found in Nissan Oren, *Bulgarian Communism: The Road to Power. 1934–1944* (New York and London, 1971), pp. 11–15.

43. Lampe, *The Bulgarian Economy*, p. 94.

44. These were the government's statistics. Members of the opposition put the toll much higher. Bell, *The Bulgarian Communist Party*, pp. 84–85; Ivan Peikov, "Podgotovka, provezhdane i znachenie na narodniia sŭd prez 1944–1945 g.," *Istoricheski pregled*, 2–3 (1964), 151–70.

45. The consolidation of communist control in Bulgaria is surveyed in Bell, *The Bulgarian Communist Party*, pp. 77–101. See also Mito Isusov, *Politicheskite partii v Bŭlgariia. 1944–1948 g.* (Sofia, 1978); Nikolai Genchev, "Razgromŭt na burzhoaznata opozitsiia v Bŭlgariia prez 1947–1948 godina," *Godishnik na Sofiskiia universitet (ideologichni katedri)* 56 (1962), 181–273.

46. In this respect the recent work of Dimitur Ludzhev, *Drebnata burzhoaziia v Bŭlgariia. 1944–1958* (Sofia, 1985) is exceptionally frank and interesting. See also Ivan Peikov, *Razgrom na svalenata ot vlast monarkho-fashistka burzhoaziia v Bŭlgariia* (Sofia, 1982).

47. *Growth and Reform in Centrally Planned Economies: The Lessons of the Bulgarian Experience* (New York, 1977), p. 270; see also Lampe, *The Bulgarian Economy* pp. 161–63 for informative comments on evaluating statistical measures of Bulgarian economic growth.

48. *Rabotnichesko delo*, April 28, 1979; Feiwel, *Growth and Reform* p. 276.

49. For more recent statistics, see the annual reports published in the *Yearbook for International Communist Affairs* (Stanford, Calif.).

50. George W. Hoffman, *Regional Development Strategy in Southeast Europe* (New York, 1972), pp. 97–99; Lampe, *The Bulgarian Economy*, pp. 139–54.

51. The structure of a system may have a considerable impact on its functioning. For example, in American education, with its emphasis on local authority, effective control over what is taught may rest in the hands of the least modernized segment of the population. This frequently has a broad impact since textbook publishers, in their desire for a mass market, adapt their products to the lowest common denominator. This phenomenon is discussed in Stephen Jay Gould, *Hen's Teeth and Horse's Toes: Further Reflections in Natural History* (New York, 1983), pp. 280–90. In the Bulgarian case, of course, the pseudoscience of Marxism-Leninism exercises a pernicious influence over education in the humanities and social sciences.

52. These figures and comparisons are drawn from George T. Kurian, *The Book of World Rankings* (New York, 1979). It is, of course, dangerous to rely on a few selected indicators, but in Kurian's book Bulgaria consistently ranks in the top fifth on scales associated with modernity. Kurian ranked it twenty-ninth of 190 nations surveyed. His rankings are generally confirmed in Charles L. Taylor and David A. Jodice, *World Handbook of Political and Social Indicators*, 3 ed., vol. 1 (New Haven, Conn., London, 1983).

53. E. Shevchenko, "Sovetsko-bolgarskoe sotrudnichestvo v oblasti vysshego obrazovaniia 1966–1980 gg.," in Pantelei Zarev et al., eds., *Razvitie na naukata i obrazovanieto v Bŭlgariia* (Sofia, 1982), p. 608.

54. Drazha Vŭlcheva held candidate member status from 1974 to 1981.

55. Kurian, *The Book of World Rankings*, pp. 324–25.

56. Lampe, *The Bulgarian Economy*, pp. 199–219, contains a survey of Bulgaria's economic reform efforts. A negative evaluation of their results may be found in *Rabotnichesko delo* (December 23, 1986).

57. Richard F. Staar, ed., *Yearbook on International Communist Affairs—1988* (Stanford, Calif., 1989), p. 249.

58. See, for example, Zhivkov's address to the Politburo in *Rabotnichesko delo* (July 27, 1989).

59. See the entry on Bulgaria in the *Yearbook for International Communist Affairs—1989* (Stanford, Calif., 1989), pp. 299–301.

3

Belated Modernization in Comparison: Development in Yugoslavia and Bulgaria to 1948

John Lampe

Yugoslav development is usually viewed in isolation, largely because of the Tito-Stalin split that launched the country on a separate path after World War II. Its foreign policy of nonalignment was followed by political decentralization and self-management, all in a federal framework that was equally alien to any of its Balkan neighbors. Yet in order to understand the considerable relevance of the thirty years from the formation of the first Yugoslavia to the split itself and to the country's successes and failures since then, some systematic comparison to one of those Balkan neighbors seems instructive. Bulgaria's large Communist party, ethnically homogeneous membership, and long history are as imposing a set of credentials for coming to power as those provided by Yugoslavia's huge wartime resistance and its party's independence from direct Soviet influence.

In comparing Yugoslavia with Bulgaria since the First World War, we must acknowledge some important contrasts. Despite the easily comparable experiences of Serbia and Bulgaria as nation-states until 1914,[1] the first Yugoslavia that emerged from the war was a state greatly enlarged, ethnically divided, and yet victorious. Defeated Bulgaria survived behind slightly shortened borders, its elite embittered and its population swollen by an influx of 220,000 refugees from Macedonia and Thrace. These differences do not, however, vitiate the usefulness of the comparative method. Marc Bloch reminded us long ago that analyses of such differences are potentially more meaningful for near neighbors, "close together in time and space" and sharing "at least in part, a common origin."[2]

Yugoslav and Bulgarian fortunes from 1918 to 1948 clearly differ but still seem to fit into a broader framework based on the uneven course of their modernization. That much-maligned concept still seems useful if we can combine two essential ingredients: the imprecise notion of political culture, that is, the behavioral legacy of the state apparatus and popular consciousness, with the statistical record and social dynamics of economic development, that is, aggregate growth plus structural change. Modern Balkan *political* culture already included the two major phenomena that Western political scientists have fastened on to explain behavior in present-day communist systems: intolerance or weakness of opposition, not yet institutionalized into a totalitarian model à la Karl Friedrich and Zbigniew Brzezinski, and the "bureaucratic politics" of intertwined party and ministerial administrations à la Jerry Hough. Both tendencies helped to generate a powerful state apparatus, stronger than any domestic center of private influence and largely immune to public opinion, though not to internal conflict.[3] For the interwar as well as the postwar period, the political weakness of private economic interests needs to be stressed. The economic pattern during the consolidation of communist power, 1945–1948, not only draws on the earlier predominance of the state apparatus, but also reflects the emergence of a new form of "differential modernization," albeit one that has fulfilled many of the statistical criteria for economic development. According to Robert Tucker's original notion for precommunist societies, the growth of industry, communications, and a modern urban center during the twentieth century transforms the capital city and nationally achieves some aggregate economic growth. However, as he states, it fails to accomplish the structural transformation of the great majority of peasant labor and landed capital into urban workers and factories that is needed for modern industrial development.[4] Tucker has stressed the role of this internal economic dichotomy in attracting educated, urban youth to the communist cause.

My own analysis concentrates on how the international economic context and domestic political culture before 1945 helped to perpetuate the dichotomy of unbalanced modernization into the communist period, now favoring heavy industry as well as state power at the expense of the peasantry, political consciousness, and also a market mentality. The Soviet pattern of totalitarian control and strategy for centrally planned development still bears its share of responsibility. But internal modernization, if viewed as a less benign or less balanced process than its original American advocates assumed, survives as an instructive concept for identifying what difference communist power actually made in the industrialization of postwar Yugoslavia and Bulgaria.[5] More precisely, we may begin to discern why, beyond the obvious Soviet presence in Bulgaria and its eventual absence in Yugoslavia, a different play of political forces led to deceptively similar economic results until 1948 and why similar Communist parties would pursue such different economic policies afterward.

Let us proceed chronologically, examining the international economic setting, the two countries' political cultures, and their internal economic development and policy during the interwar decades, the Second World War, and finally the immediate postwar period. The immediate postwar period will emerge, in larger measure than we used to think, as a consequence of the earlier ones.

The Interwar Era

In neither Yugoslavia nor Bulgaria, as is argued elsewhere,[6] did state administration emerge from the First World War with a clear mandate, let alone any precise plan for modern economic development. The two economies would then find themselves with barely a decade between the end of hostilities and the onset of the Great Depression. Both felt the depression immediately through a drastic decline in international grain prices. Even before, neither the Yugoslav nor the Bulgarian economy had fared well in the international setting of the postwar period. American and Canadian grain had taken over the Balkan share of the Western European market during the war. Afterward, disrupted rail networks to the Black Sea ports made the recapture of these markets doubly difficult. Only the western Yugoslav lands, with less railway damage and initially desperate Central European demand beckoning, were able to approach postwar levels.

This regional advantage boosted Yugoslavia's net export of grain per capita back to 64 percent of the 1901–1913 average by 1926–1930, versus just 33 percent for Bulgaria.[7] The lack of growth in Yugoslav exports of other crops, primarily from the southeast, also contributed to an economic disparity between west and east which may have opened up much more prominently in the 1920s than in the pre–1914 period.[8]

Total exports, in real per capita terms, had risen, however, to less than one-half their prewar level for both Yugoslavia and Bulgaria by 1926–1930. The Bulgarian switch from grain to tobacco exports began with massive sales to Germany during the First World War. It failed to survive the severe drop in world prices in 1925–1926 as a strategy for rebuilding prewar earnings from international trade.

International finance was no kinder to the two economies. Western European capital did make a major new appearance in a number of Sofia banks, as did Central European capital in several Zagreb banks. But the failure of these banks to invest decisively in modern industry or infrastructure is clear. That failure left Bulgaria and Yugoslavia dependent for sizable outside investment on a much reduced Western capital market for loans to their respective governments. Despite Serbia's association with the winning Allied side in the First World War, the Yugoslav government enjoyed little better access to foreign funds. The expensive Blair loan (for construction of a railway line from Zagreb to the Adriatic coast) of $45 million from the United States in 1923 did finance some railway construction, but it was also used to pay interest on a still larger Serbian war debt to the United States ($62 million). Proceeds of a similar French loan the following year went largely for armaments. Two belated loans to Bulgaria in 1926 and 1928 totaled $30 million. The obligation to pay as yet uncollected reparations put the Bulgarian state debt per capita in 1920 at four times the Yugoslav figure, burdened only by war and relief debts, but only one-quarter more by 1930.[9]

More important, the Western financial system encouraged the national banks and central governments of the two countries to restrict their note issuance and budgetary expenditures in order to place their currencies on a stable basis within the reconstituted Gold Exchange Standard. By 1926 both countries had achieved this goal, at least informally, but the cost was high. Deflationary measures raised taxes and reduced budget expenditures just as the postwar recovery was entering its crucial phase. Real note issuance per capita was cut by over one-quarter for Yugoslavia from 1920 to 1926–1930 and by over one-half for Bulgaria.[10] Exchange rates for the Yugoslav dinar and the Bulgarian lev were again overvalued, as they had been before the First World War, discouraging exports still further. In return for these high, stable exchange rates, the two economies awaited improved access to Western capital markets. It had not come by the time the depression ruined their credit ratings, along with those of other agricultural exporters.

Bulgaria's political reaction against the international setting of the 1920s was undoubtedly deepened by the stigma of defeat and the threat of reparations. The notion that Bulgaria had no friends among the Western allies would eventually generate some support on the right for a German connection in the 1930s. But during the first postwar years, the country's political culture was nurtured more by the left than by the right. The Bulgarian Communist Party (BKP) found that its opposition to the lost war and its support for the Russian Revolution quickly swelled its membership, especially among the growing number of industrial and transport workers in Sofia and other towns. For a few years it was the largest of the urban-based parties.[11]

The Agrarian Union (BZNS) of Aleksandŭr Stamboliiski polled twice as many votes as the BKP in the relatively free elections of 1919–1920 and dominated the countryside. His genuinely radical regime (1919–19232) set a number of neglected precedents for one-party rule outside the ministerial and military bureaucracy, which until then had been the principal formative influence in Bulgarian political culture. As the largest occupational group in Sofia before the war, this bureaucracy became an end in itself. Its power and the corrupting effect of *partisanstvo* (placing political allies in civilian positions) had undermined the emergence of a healthy multiparty system from the same direction as had Tsar Ferdinand's personal policy of divide and rule.[12] Stamboliiski's four-year regime undermined it from another direction, viewing state power not as an end in itself but as a vehicle for one party's restructuring of Bulgarian society.

Agrarian precedents for communist measures twenty-five years later began with Stamboliiski's arrest of Bulgaria's wartime leaders in late 1919 for having led the nation into what was commonly called a catastrophe. For a time, moreover, he weighed the possibility of trying the accused before "people's courts" convened outside the existing judicial bureaucracy. He did not do so in the end, and none of the defendants received the death penalty, as would virtually all who were charged after the Second World War. The Agrarians did, however, go ahead with restructuring the educational system to further their party program, opening many new rural schools and attempting to place them under the control of local BANU committees. Stamboliiski's minister of education introduced vocational training, but he also purged some political rivals from Sofia University and wanted to eject more. Stamboliiski took advantage of the new Tsar Boris's initial weakness to place the army under direct control of his government. He himself became minister of war. His party's Orange Guard militia soon exceeded the 10,000 members authorized by the peace treaty, while the regular army was prevented from reaching its maximum of 20,000. Stamboliiski's attraction to what he called "the unity of state power" may be seen in his repeated efforts to bypass the authority of the state bureaucracy in order to secure his party's right to represent the national interest.[13] As internal opposition to his policies grew, he increasingly characterized the other parties as too dangerous to permit any collaboration.

Only one of the Agrarians' major economic policies succeeded in bypassing the ministerial apparatus. This was the prudent land reform of 1920, whose redistribution of properties over 30 hectares was carefully prepared over a six-month period, with the assistance of the BANU network of cooperatives throughout the country. Implementation of the redistribution and the granting of exemptions for larger holdings applying modern methods to export crops were left largely in the hands of the cooperatives and local Agrarian committees.[14]

The party's other economic policies rested on state controls implemented by the ministries in Sofia. The first of them was the abortive Grain Consortium of 1920–1921. Set up to collect and export grain at monopoly prices above the low level of the world market, the Consortium's profits were intended to go mainly toward state construction of badly needed grain elevators. Pressure by private grain traders, mainly Western European representatives, on the Allied Reparations Commission plus the wheat surplus on the world market forced Stamboliiski to abandon the project by late 1921. Yet a precedent had been set for Hranoiznos, a sales monopoly for grain and other foodstuffs founded in 1930. As we will see, the monopoly would grow during the Second World War and greatly facilitate communist control of agricultural trade afterward.

Another precedent for the post–1944 period was the institution of compulsory labor service.[15] From 1920 forward, all young men twenty years of age were drafted into uniformed battalions for one year's service. Stamboliiski saw this service not, as Hitler would later, as a device to circumvent treaty limits on a standing army, but as a way to instill national discipline and to provide agricultural or industrial training. Some 30,000 were drafted in 1920. Numbers fell by one-third after Stamboliiski's demise in 1923, but the service continued to build bridges, roads, railways, and even factories into the 1930s and again after 1944 under the auspices of the Communist Youth organization.

The Agrarians' policy toward industry made no significant change in the role the state would play until after 1945. Contrary to contemporary Western opinion, Stamboliiski did not oppose modern industrial development as long as it made full use of the Bulgarian potential for agricultural processing.[16] Nor did he continue to object, as he had before the war, to the formation of industrial cartels, as long as state controls were sufficient. Here, as in other areas of economic policy outside of land reform, his inclination was to rely on the executive power of the central government rather than on local party committees or private self-interest.

The result of tax and tariff exemptions for even small firms and the spread of cartels did not discourage the emergence of large-scale industrial firms, especially in metallurgy and other producers' goods.[17] The average size of the Bulgarian enterprise qualifying for exemptions rose insignificantly, from thirty-six to forty-one employees, between 1921 and 1929. Horsepower per worker declined, as did the share of incorporated firms in the enterprise total. A small domestic market and a growing need for costly imported inputs also discouraged large-scale production. It was, therefore, essentially smaller enterprises that were responsible for striking rates of growth for aggregate industrial output—13.3 percent for 1921–1931 and 6.9 percent for 1935–1941.

The political consequences of the industrial growth without structural change were twofold. The political leverage of the industrial owners remained very limited, as witnessed by the ease with which the state ended most exemptions and took over the cartel apparatus in the 1930s. The leverage of industrial workers was even smaller nationwide than their size, but their concentration in Sofia and several other towns overcame their scattering among small workplaces to create fertile ground for communist recruitment, especially in the 1930s. By then they had become the largest occupational group in Sofia. In 1932 they succeeded in electing a communist city council, although the result was quickly annulled.

In the post–Stamboliiski years Bulgarian political culture returned to the pattern of internal struggle between party leaders, the ministries, the army and the tsar. The tsar and the army emerged victorious in the 1930s, inaugurating in 1934 a series of "nonparty regimes" that left all party structures save the illegal Communists to atrophy.[18] The Agrarians were increasingly divided between domestic and émigré factions, and ruled again only briefly in a 1931–1932 coalition.

Bulgaria's last powerful prime ministers were the two who succeeded Stamboliiski. Their party affiliations were less important than the contribution each made to the growing Bulgarian tradition of political intolerance. Aleksandŭr Tsankov (1925–1926) was a protofascist professor who was himself implicated in Stamboliiski's murder and who could not come to terms with his own coalition partners. Andrei Liapchev (1926–1931) was more accommodating, but, perhaps because of his Macedonian origins, he permitted the IMRO (Internal Macedonian Revolutionary Organization) irredentist movement to operate freely and to deal violently with opponents. Yet all three men shared more positive traits. They had been trained primarily in economics and were disposed to solve the country's problems through internal economic development rather than through initiatives abroad.

Yugoslavia's political leadership remained in the hands of lawyers turned politicians until 1929. Then King Aleksandar's so-called royal dictatorship started a series of nonparty regimes that would continue past his asassination in 1934. The strong-willed economist Milan Stojadinović would head such a regime in the late 1930s. By then it was too late in the depression and too close to the Second World War for his newfound notions of state-sponsored industrial growth, independent of the international economy, to have any meaning other than projects suited to Nazi Germany's military preparations.

The patterns for the first Yugoslavia's political culture and economic development had already been set during the 1920s. These patterns included political intolerance, a weak private sector, small-scale enterprise, and a powerful state apparatus along the Bulgarian lines just elaborated. They need not be treated in similar detail for Yugoslavia. But major regional divisions within the country, reinforced by varied influences from Western or Central Europe, did constitute crucial differences. Almost from the outset, the ensuing struggle did not result in the widely presumed Serbian hegemony from Belgrade as much as a stalemate that satisfied no one politically and that impeded economic growth, let alone development.

The Vidovdan Constitution of 1921 successfully centralized control of the army and local police in the hands of the Serbian-dominated ministries of War and Interior in Belgrade. Only in Macedonia and Kosovo, however, did these instruments of power provide the leverage needed to control local political parties and private economic activity. Initial Serbian advantages in levels of taxation proved difficult to maintain or manipulate from Belgrade. The new central bank located in Belgrade was indeed the direct successor to the Narodna Banka Kr. Srbije. However, its conversion of Austro-Hungarian crowns in the western Yugoslav lands to dinars in 1919–1920 at a rate of five to one had prompted Croatian and Slovenian financial interests to withhold buying stock in the new central bank. Enough native and Central European funds collected in the large private banks in Zagreb and Ljubljana to make these western lands essentially independent of credit from the new Narodna Banka Kr. Jugoslavije.[19] The rapid recovery and advance of these lands in the early postwar years, facilitated as noted earlier by lack of war damage and the desperate needs of nearby Austria and Hungary, stood in sharp contrast to a Serbian economy that had to replace all its industry and most of its transport.

During this postwar period the Serbian political spectrum fragmented into first three and then four parties (and five if we include the communists). Thus ended the emerging two-party system dominated by the Radicals and their network of rural clubs before the war.[20] Afterward Radical governments could obtain a parliamentary majority only within a coalition drawn in part from other Serbian parties. Nor could the Radical party keep from splitting up during the last years under its legendary leader, Nikola Pašić. (He died in 1926). In the western Yugoslav lands, Croats and Slovenes were represented in large measure by a single party each, the Slovenian clericals of Monsignor Korošec and the Croatian Peasant party of Stjepan Radić. Radić ignored the National Assembly in Belgrade until he accepted the post of minister of education in 1925. An ill-fated trip to the capital city in 1928 resulted in his assassination at what were perceived to be Serbian hands. (Actually, a Montenegrin deputy fired the shots.) King Aleksandar's royal dictatorship never really broke the resulting stalemate. Croat representatives, following the Hungarian tradition in Habsburg politics of boycotting unresponsive bodies, did not return to Belgrade for a decade. The huge peasant majority's suspicion of central government authority reinforced stalemate even in Serbia. Their resistance to ministerial authority had already been well developed in prewar Serbia, Austria-Hungary, and the Ottoman Empire.

In the principal cities of Ljubljana, Zagreb, and especially Belgrade, a more complex political culture was evolving. Central European influences predominated in the first two. In Belgrade, however, French thought and culture were widely admired in the wake of the wartime alliance. Moreover, thousands of Serbian soldiers, had been allowed to continue their education in France while Belgrade was first occupied and then during rebuilding.[21] Native Yugoslav and other European influences, especially Italian, came with migrants from Croatia, Slovenia, and Dalmatia to what was now the capital of their country. Over 20,000 Russian émigrés also collected in Belgrade, as in Sofia, and made more of a cultural contribution than in the Bulgarian capital. Politically, however, they were tied to the past and eschewed any connection with revolutionary Russia.

American-style media of mass communication pushed the Yugoslav capital toward the future. A proliferation of publications, including the European-level daily paper *Politika* and others, along with telephones, radios, and especially Hollywood films, began to break down ties to church and village, if less so to the patriarchal family. Replacing these traditional ties were personal, occupational, or political goals. As occupational opportunities contracted during the 1930s, attraction to new political directions, and to the Communist party in particular, began to spread among the student population, numbering 8,000 at Belgrade University. Even family ties began to fray.

As in Sofia, factory and transport workers had meanwhile become the largest occupational group in Belgrade and Zagreb. They were largely responsible for the Communist party (KPJ) winning 32 and 25 percent of the respective votes in those two cities in the 1920 elections for the Constituent Assembly. In addition to other industrial towns, the KPJ attracted the support that had won it 12.3 percent of the overall vote mainly in Macedonia and Montenegro, and mainly as a protest against Serbian hegemony.[22] Illegal after several party members, acting on their own, assassinated the interior minister in 1921, the KPJ saw its membership decline sharply. The party did not become attractive again to workers until the depression created widespread unemployment in the major cities.

Meanwhile, the rapid rate of economic growth that had marked the early interwar period, primarily because of advances in the western Yugoslav lands, trailed off. Real crop value was still only 90 percent of the prewar figure per capita by 1929. Modern manufacturing grew by just 4 percent a year in constant price value for 1923–1929, after exceeding 6 percent for 1918–1923. For the later period, the Bulgarian rate exceeded 13 percent. Overall Yugoslav growth for these years fell short of a 2 percent average.[23] During the depression decade of 1929–1938, Yugoslav manufacturing could manage only an annual increment of 2.4 percent, exactly half the real Bulgarian rate. Crop production in real per capita terms, and therefore overall national product as well, nearly matched the Bulgarian rate of 2 percent a year.[24]

Several reasons were behind this poorer Yugoslav performance. The expansion of grain cultivation and export in the western and northern lands just after the war lost much of it rationale when the Hungarian and Austrian economies began to recover. Nor should we minimize the problems of putting together a national market for labor and capital as well as for goods from territories whose economic relations with each other had previously ranged from limited to nonexistent. The first Yugoslavia's political stalemate also played an important retarding role.

The considerable size of the state apparatus made the failure of public policy all the more significant. Although the Bulgarian state bureaucracy had risen fourfold from its prewar level to 87,000 by 1930, the Yugoslav figure had jumped sevenfold to 280,000 by 1925, nearly double the Bulgarian total in per capita terms. By 1925 expenditures for Yugoslavia's state budget were also double the real per capita level in the prewar component parts, in contrast to Bulgarian expenses which barely matched the prewar level. A high protective tariff was passed in 1926, and new direct taxes were levied. Both failed to collect projected budget revenues. The government increasingly relied on the indirect turnover tax (*trosarina*). It was increased on four occasions between 1924 and 1934, rising in Serbia as much as in the western lands and discouraging production of the foodstuffs to which it applied. The large Yugoslav Army, unrestricted by treaty stipulations, and a bigger defense budget were, of course, partly responsible for the greater Yugoslav expenditure. As Ivo Banac has rightly argued, another reason was surely the desire of the central government in Belgrade to take control of the new country with a ministerial bureaucracy that was overwhelmingly Serbian.[25]

In the economic area especially, this effort was nonetheless a failure. A state Agricultural Bank could not be created until 1929, the start of the depression decade. The separate ethnic cooperative networks hindered rather than facilitated its founding. The strong Croatian and well-funded Slovenian cooperative networks saw little reason to collaborate with their Serbian counterpart in pooling credit facilities, let alone establishing a single bank to coordinate their activities in Belgrade. In the event, the belated bank did extend most of its credit to Serbian borrowers. A grain export monopoly, Prizad, was set up in 1930, but, unlike Bulgaria's Hranoiznos, it did not extend its controls to the internal market nor reduce price differences between surplus and deficit regions. The same kind of regional stalemate prevented the passage of a law for industrial encouragement on the Bulgarian and prewar Serbian pattern until 1934, and then under army auspices as part of a rearmament program. Rearmament went further in Yugoslavia than in Bulgaria, culminating in the new state-owned iron smelting facility in Bosnia in 1938. State enterprises, if we include the railways and the tobacco monopoly, accounted for 15 percent of Yugoslavia's industrial capital by 1938, about the same fraction as in Bulgaria.[26] But the reputation of the Yugoslav central government for effective intervention in the national economy was much poorer and with good reason. Active measures had typically come too late and were undermined even in their eventual execution by regional rivalries. These rivalries precluded any resolution except a federal one.

The Second World War

The Second World War sundered the first Yugoslavia into a series of occupied areas and the native fascist, puppet state of Croatia (NDH), which included most of Bosnia-Hercegovina and Dalmatia. The German area of occupation covered Serbia and the Banat, and the Italian area the Dalmatian and Montenegrin coast. Bulgaria administered Macedonia. In addition, Hungary annexed the Bačka (west of the Banat region of the Vojvodina) and Germany and Italy most of Slovenia. No nationwide economic institution (and there were few of them before the war) could have survived this set of divisions. Their regional successors were discredited both by collaboration with the occupation forces and by lack of positive accomplishment.

The Serbian economy and population bore the heaviest burden, as in the First World War, but none of the other Yugoslav areas could be said to have done well, with the exception of those inhabited by ethnic Germans.[27] Nazi grain requisitioning in Serbia relied precisely on the prewar Prizad organization. Its prewar staff had been replaced with Serbian collaborators and its management with German administrators. Prices were minimal, and interest in improving techniques of cultivation was nonexistent. After the bad harvest of 1942, the Macedonian lands found themselves dependent on grain deliveries from Bulgaria's Hranoiznos. They failed to receive what they needed from its depleted reserves. The huge Croatian state contained a majority of prewar Yugoslavia's areas of grain deficit. This, together with the requisitions of German and Italian troops, made the task of the NDH's Food Economy Division, or Pogod, an impossible one. Charged with constructing an internal grain monopoly through the existing cooperative network of the Croatian Peasant party (HPSS), it could not collect the necessary reserves to feed the smaller towns in particular. Pogod succeeded only in helping to discredit the HPSS.

Financial institutions and industry fared no better. The Yugoslav central bank ceased to exist with the German attack in April 1941. The NDH and the various occupying authorities proceeded to set up their own banking systems and to issue their own currency. Trade and other transactions between the separate areas were quickly reduced to a minimum. By 1943 black market rates for rapidly expanding issues of these assorted currencies had slipped to 5 to 10 percent of face value. German, Italian, or fascist Croatian authorities took over existing industrial or mining facilities to insure that most of their production was exported for the German war effort. In the case of Serbia, the German occupation dismantled modern industrial plants for shipment to the Reich.

Politically, the significance of the Second World War was not just the destructive occupation, and the consequent mandate to find some federal framework within which to reconstitute Yugoslavia, but also the dynamics of the spreading Partisan resistance. The readiness of its communist leadership to confront the occupation forces militarily won the Partisans increasing support as the occupiers committed war crimes and then began to lose the war. Filling the Partisan ranks overwhelmingly were peasant youths, most of whom had a limited education and had never even been to Belgrade or any other large town. Most were Serbs or Montenegrins, accounting for over 90 percent to begin with and still over one-half by 1944.[28] The Serbs were increasingly *prečani*, from eastern Croatia in particular, where the danger of *Ustaši* massacres drove most able-bodied Serbs from their villages into the hills. This location outside the territory of Serbia proper may have helped free most of these peasant recruits from the obsession with defending Serbdom alone which plagued the more geographically compact, if more loosely disciplined Chetnik movement of Draža Mihailović. Partisan service also exposed many of its members to a structure of command which, though strict, depended on the flexibility and initiative of local units for survival against a larger, better equipped opponent.

If this sort of political perspective and experience would eventually serve postwar Yugoslavia well, the military and myth-building nature of the wartime experience was hardly one to prepare the Partisans' huge peasant majority well for postwar economic modernization. Yugoslav communist strategy, unlike that of their Greek counterparts, was to concentrate on the front lines rather than to strive for socialist political consolidation behind them. But military necessity encouraged the exercise of or acquiescence to arbitrary, unquestioned authority.

At the same time, the charter myth of the unfailingly heroic Partisan movement began to take shape. Its romantic vision of the violent, reckless individual in the service of the common good drew deeply on the upland, Dinaric ideal of personal honor and heroism, unspoiled by civilization, whether in the service of the Serbian patriarchal clan or the Croatian local community.[29] There was a darker side to these upland norms. They included brutal, merciless treatment of opponents and a hostility toward the impersonal norms of market behavior that extended to glorifying banditry against strangers. None of these attitudes would help to make market socialism work in the period after 1950, when many of these once teenaged peasant Partisans found themselves in positions of industrial as well as urban authority.

The Bulgarian experience during the Second World War laid important economic groundwork for the postwar practice of central planning which, unlike the brief Yugoslav experiment with this Soviet approach, has endured to the present. The economic institutions of Bulgaria's prewar state remained intact throughout the war. Their management rested completely in Bulgarian hands, despite the close external alliance with Nazi Germany. Only with the start of Anglo-American bombing raids in late 1943 was there any destruction of their Sofia headquarters or any disruption of their daily duties. The expansion of these duties during the war effort would prove invaluable for the communist consolidation of power that followed.[30]

Four existing institutions and two new agencies were primarily responsible for the wartime growth in official leverage over an already weak private sector. The grain export monopsony Hranoiznos, whose authority extended to internal distribution, was quickly recalled to life. Its initial list of five controlled items (wheat, rye, cotton, flax, and hemp) had grown to twenty-three by 1943. Virtually all vegetable products were included. The only major crop excluded was tobacco. Its marketing and export to Germany were in the hands of the state's tobacco monopoly, taken over from French interests in 1940, as well as in the hands of the Bulgarian Agricultural Bank and the cooperative network. By 1943 that network had come to include some fifty producers' cooperatives. They used more modern methods, including tractors, and worked more days than the typical peasant smallholding. Their yields were therefore higher, and their income was two-thirds greater.[31]

Two new agencies were less successful than the four old ones, but the scope of their ambitions paved some of the way for central planning. Both the Directorates for Civilian Mobilization (DGM) and for Foreign Trade had been created in 1940. The DGM sought annual production plans from all manufacturing enterprises, but less than one-half complied. In 1942 the DGM joined the Ministry of Agriculture in drawing up Bulgaria's first Five-Year Plan, for 1942–1946. Mainly agricultural, it proposed consolidated and expanded cultivation, with prices and income under complete state control. But repeated grain requisitions beyond announced quotas discouraged peasant participation. The Foreign Trade Directorate concentrated on providing credit and badly needed fertilizer and other imports to the agricultural sector. The programs of both directorates were undermined in 1943. As during the First World War, the army created its own competing agency to mobilize economic resources.

Meanwhile, Bulgarian peasant smallholders and private owners of manufacturing enterprises were retreating not only from this expanding state apparatus, but also from modern, large-scale production. Peasants turned first to bean cultivation and then to milk production in order to avoid the low sale prices, high quotas, and other regulations of the Hranoiznos regime. As that regime became more comprehensive, smallholders moved into grape and other fruit cultivation. This was diversification, but hardly modernization.

Large-scale industrial firms faced labor and growing input shortages. The mobilization of an 800,000-man army was followed by the dispatch of 20,000 workers to factories in Germany. Promised German deliveries of crucial supplies for manufacturing, as with fertilizers for agriculture, failed to appear on time or in the designated amounts.[32] Metallurgy was especially hard hit. Only the processing of fruit pulp increased significantly, with production rising some sixfold. For 1939–1944, the share of specifically state enterprises in overall industrial production fell from 9 to just 5 percent. Plans for new state enterprises to manufacture caustic soda, calcium, and even synthetic rubber appeared on the DGM's drawing board for 1942 and again in 1943 but never materialized.

As a result, private owners began to set up new, small enterprises, free from the problems of state contracts or DGM controls, and to produce consumer goods for the heavy demand and high prices of the domestic urban market. Almost 1,000 firms were established, increasing the 1939 total by one-third to 4,000 by 1944. Most were single owners or simple partnerships in one enterprise only. Most just met the minimum size of ten workers and 10 horsepower to qualify for tax and import tariff reductions. This influx reduced the average size of all Bulgarian industrial enterprises from twenty-nine to twenty-six workers over the 1939–1944 period.

The few private concentrations of economic power were further weakened by the Anglo-American bombings of 1943–1944. Not only were some larger plants damaged, but so was much of the residential property in the center of Sofia. These apartment buildings, in the fashion of present-day Athens, had attracted more private investment than manufacturing.

Political Revolution and State Planning: The Communist Era

Partly because of the weakness of the private economic sector, postwar consolidation of communist power proceeded more rapidly in Bulgaria and Yugoslavia than elsewhere in Eastern Europe. For Bulgaria, however, the strength of existing state institutions was of comparable importance. For Yugoslavia, the strength of the Communist party and the impetus of its wartime successes and mythology were instead decisive. Not surprisingly, the result was Bulgaria's slower but more successful transition to Soviet-style central planning than Yugoslavia's, with its reliance on the ministerial apparatus.

The Bulgarian Communist party (BKP) saw its membership jump from a modest 14,000 in September 1944 to 422,000 two years later. By 1945 its leader Georgi Dimitrov had returned from two decades of Soviet exile, and by 1946 he was prime minister. Over half of his cabinet were BKP members, and the rest were allies in the wartime Fatherland Front. The army had been purged of 3,000 officers and the state bureaucracy of 30,000 officials. Hastily convened "people's courts," on the pattern pioneered by Stamboliiski in 1919, handed down 100 death sentences to leaders of the wartime government and another 2,700 to lower ranking defendants. From the outset communist control of the ministries of Justice and Interior was decisive in convening these trials, as well as in the wholesale replacement of the existing police force with a "people's militia." In his recent party history, John Bell emphasizes the central role of these ministries in the BKP's assumption of local as well as national power. He rightly downgrades the role of the Fatherland Front's communist-dominated local committees as "highly romanticized."[33]

In the Bulgarian communist consolidation of economic power, the existing state framework was even more important. The apparatus and the authority of Hranoiznos were so preeminent that no decree was needed to nationalize foreign trade. The same organization served nicely to eliminate private wholesale trade in most agricultural goods. The communist militia aided in outright requisitions. Tobacco, fruit, and a few vegetables lay outside their purview, but the Bulgarian Agricultural Bank and the network of credit cooperatives were soon buying virtually all these crops for the state at fixed prices.[34]

The party's Politburo quickly transformed the wartime Directorate for Civilian Mobilization into its own Higher Economic Council (VSS). As early as the spring of 1945, ostensibly in response to a growing fruit shortage in the towns, the Council nationalized the plants for processing fruit pulp which had grown so rapidly during the war. Accelerating urban inflation from the last months of the war forward justified the Council's decision to impose price controls.

These controls, together with the role of the central bank (BNB) restricting note issues and credit, did in fact limit aggregate inflation for the entire period 1944–1947 to 86 percent, a much lower figure than in neighboring Yugoslavia or Romania. The capital and deposits of the Bulgarska Narodna Banka had already far exceeded those of all private banks combined in 1944. The remaining private banks, long since shorn of the German or Italian affiliations that had replaced French or Belgian capital during the war, accounted for only 11 percent of total bank capital when the BNB finally absorbed them all in 1947.[35]

By 1948 the further transformation of the Higher Economic Council into a Soviet-style State Planning Commission, in full control of nationalized industry as well as trade, drew on more than the ideological commitment of the BKP's leadership in general and of Traicho Kostov, who was most responsible for economic policy, in particular. The post–1944 dynamics of private industrial growth made nationalization appear to be a more rational policy than Western observers have previously assumed. The mushrooming of smaller firms which had begun during the interwar period and continued during the war moved ahead even more rapidly after 1944. Some 1,500 were founded by mid-1947, increasing the total number of enterprises by one-third. Skilled labor flocked to these essentially artisan shops, and the average size of an industrial enterprise fell again, from 26 to 24. Thus, the large enterprises already under state control lacked skilled labor as well as raw materials. Unskilled labor demobilized from the army could find few jobs in the towns. Over 20 percent of the industrial workforce was unemployed by 1947. The regime's nationalization of all private manufacturing at year's end absorbed these small firms; so began a painful, hasty, but more understandable process of consolidating them into modern, technologically advanced enterprises.[36]

The coordination of labor supply and other inputs that would be required for such consolidation outside a freely functioning market economy fell to the State Planning Commission (DPK). Created in January 1948, the Commission found its work facilitated not only by the Two-Year Plan already drawn up by its communist predecessor, the VSS, for 1947–1948, but also by the continuing existence, from before the First World War, of the best state statistical service in Southeastern Europe. The Main Directorate for Statistics (GDS) and most of its trained staff had been efficiently merged into the DPK by March 1948. Here was an advantage in the transition to central planning, which was conspicuous by its absence in postwar Yugoslavia. The postwar statistical apparatus derived in part from a broader Bulgarian advantage; more university graduates had been trained in technical or scientific subjects in the interwar period, and more had survived the war.[37]

For both countries, private economic interests were distinguished not only by internal weakness, but also by the dim prospects posed for them by any great reliance on the market mechanism in general and by multilateral trade in convertible currencies with the developed Western economies in particular. Neither had previously conducted significant trade with the United States, the major Western economy to emerge strengthened in the immediate postwar period. Little wonder that we have no record even of noncommunist support, anywhere in Eastern Europe, for the strongly held American vision of free, multilateral trade as the best path to postwar recovery and growth.[38] Contemporary observers throughout Eastern Europe drew the opposite lesson from the interwar experience. They stressed the failures of the market mechanism during the 1920s, rather than the autarkic tendencies of the 1930s which American policymakers from Cordell Hull forward believed had deepened the depression, encouraged Nazi hegemony, and led directly to the Second World War. The last period of advantageous multilateral trade in Eastern European memories was the now distant decade before the First World War.

The necessities of postwar recovery further encouraged reliance on internal state initiative rather than the international market mechanism. So did two longer term imperatives for economic modernization which had emerged from the interwar experience throughout the region. These were the needs to broaden the access to technical education in the major towns and to enlarge the access to electricity and modern agricultural equipment in the countryside.

Although the Bulgarian commitment to these two long-term goals was held as firmly by the Agrarians as by the Communists, the international economic context unequivocally pointed toward bilateral ties with the Soviet Union. This direction could only assist the BKP. Prewar debts owed primarily to France and the specter of postwar reparations to be imposed by the United States and Great Britain, as well as Yugoslavia and Greece, made chances for any Western credits or other assistance virtually nil. Here was a noncommunist rationale for exchanging the heaviest dependence of any of the Eastern European economies on German trade by the late 1930s for a similar Soviet connection, especially if that connection might also protect the Bulgarian economy from any serious burden of reparations. Initial Soviet deliveries of badly needed oil, cotton, fertilizer, and farming and railway equipment in 1945–1946 created an import surplus that pushed the Bulgarian side to export more to the USSR. Off went fruit pulp, wine and particularly tobacco in sufficient quantities to make the Soviet share in total Bulgarian exports 95 percent for 1945 and over 50 percent thereafter.[39] The Soviet practice of paying 1933 prices for Bulgarian tobacco would draw a futile, eventually fatal protest from Traicho Kostov (who was executed in the Stalinist purges in 1949); it served to reduce still further the volume of tobacco, Bulgaria's most saleable product, that was available for export elsewhere.

The domestic political context did not favor Communist ascendancy as much as did the international economy. True, the wartime alliance with Nazi Germany had discredited those elements of the prewar political leadership associated with the war effort or simply with the monarchy. Unlike Yugoslavia or Romania, however, there was also a large, nationwide noncommunist party essentially untainted by wartime collaboration. The Agrarian Union attempted to overcome its debilitating interwar divisions and to unite again briefly after 1944. First, the return of the other Georgi Dimitrov, the émigré Agrarian leader, and then the aggressive, independent leadership of his successor, Nikola Petkov, swelled party membership, primarily among the peasantry, to perhaps 150,000 by 1946. The Agrarians' appeals to the Anglo-American members of the Allied Control Commission, and to the American Minister Maynard Barnes in particular, postponed one election in 1945 and allowed Petkov and his followers to continue publishing an opposition paper until 1946.[40] The strength of the Agrarian resurgence may be judged from the communist decision to split the party and create its own Agrarian Union. We also see testimony to Agrarian strength in the harsh treatment meted out to Petkov and all other members of a largely democratic opposition as soon as the Allied Control Commission disbanded in 1947. The Agrarians would, of course, pay a high price for having sought Anglo-American support and for allowing themselves to become the focus for most domestic opposition to a Communist regime. The Bulgarian tradition of political intolerance for opposition parties was not new, however; it had been building, as we have seen, since before the First World War.

The principal economic result of the Agrarian opposition was probably to delay the start and to moderate the nature of the collectivization process in the countryside. Even though producers' cooperatives had already existed since the 1930s and had grown to some fifty during the Second World War, few others were formed after the one hundred in 1945. Less than 4 percent of arable land had been collectivized by 1947. Growing Agrarian strength in the countryside helped to keep membership in these new Communist collectives voluntary.[41] Land rents and residual ownership for members apparently represented too little compensation for low delivery prices, assorted controls, and some forced requisitions. At the same time, the valuable Agrarian network of credit cooperatives and their links to the once powerful Bulgarian Agricultural Bank (BZB) were left to history. Bulgarian agricultural modernization was thereby dealt a setback from which it would not recover for at least a decade.

Agrarian strength and institutions aside, the Communist blueprint for postwar Bulgarian development was drawn directly from the Soviet experience of the 1930s. Collectivization would eventually be required as the least expensive way of extracting a food surplus for a vastly enlarged industrial labor force. Investment would be channeled overwhelmingly into heavy industry. Already in 1946, when the Higher Economic Council drew up its Two-Year Plan for 1947–1948, agriculture received only 6 percent of state investment even before the full nationalization of industry.[42] The plan for new electric power stations was the one priority project that would also benefit agriculture. This early underinvestment in agriculture and the resulting deficiencies would teach Bulgarian communist planners a lesson they would learn more quickly than their counterparts elsewhere in Eastern Europe, including Yugoslavia. Before they learned that lesson, late in the 1950s, their scanty investment in a forcibly collectivized agricultural sector imposed a new "differential modernization" on the Bulgarian economy, which favored heavy industry as well as the state bureaucracy over the countryside, a policy that was less different from the prewar pattern than they imagined.

The Yugoslav economy also experienced this sort of differential modernization in the immediate postwar period. It occurred, however, in a more hasty and disjointed fashion that would make the weaknesses of central planning unmistakable.

Politically, the Yugoslav Communist party faced significantly less opposition to implementing its own program, including the nationalization of industry, if not the collectivization of agriculture, than did the Bulgarian party. No rival Yugoslav party had won a nationwide following during the interwar period. The war years had further fissured and weakened these other parties, through emigration, persecution by the occupying forces, or collaboration with them. German authorities left little of Belgrade's ministerial bureaucracy intact and restricted its authority to Serbia.

The only other native administration during the Second World War was in Zagreb, capital of the puppet Croatian state. It was collaborationist by definition. What survived of the interwar army spent the war in German prison camps inside the Reich. Tito's Partisan army exceeded half a million men by late 1944. Its control over internal security was never challenged by small numbers of British and American troops stationed with the Allied missions in Yugoslavia. No Allied Control Commission ever existed.

The Communists themselves had no intention of sharing power even with fellow opponents of the prewar regime. Their Communist cadres were bursting with young, confident recruits from the largely peasant Partisan ranks. The party leadership could legitimately claim some right to rule the country after the long military resistance to occupation which it had personally led. At the same time, neither its Bolshevik ideals nor its wartime experience included tolerance for opposition. The leadership's initially proclaimed readiness to share political power within its Popular Front Coalition or to tolerate democratically based opposition outside it evaporated by the end of 1945. First, the most viable party outside the Front, Milan Grol's Democrats, and then the major source of opposition inside it, Jaša Prodanović's Republicans, were stifled. Control of the judicial system facilitated communist attacks and intimidation against these parties.[43]

Economically, the Yugoslav Communist party faced a more daunting task than its Bulgarian counterpart. Physical destruction and human suffering were far worse. Although these desperate circumstances made state initiative and control seem essential simply to supervise the recovery, the institutions and physical apparatus of central government were largely missing. The peasant backgrounds and formative military experience of most party cadres gave such men little technical training but plenty of overconfidence in confronting the longer term task of industrial modernization.

Moreover, the international economic context was more complex, if less threatening, for Yugoslavia than Bulgaria. As a partner in the Allied victory, the Yugoslavs looked forward to the prospect of some Western aid (e.g., a $300 million credit from the United States) even beyond the massive U.N. Relief and Rehabilitation Administration (UNRRA) deliveries that poured in, some 70 percent of which were American supplied, until 1947. No further American aid would in fact appear until after the Tito–Stalin split. Assistance for industrial recovery was anticipated from German and Hungarian reparations. They were slower to come, as was anticipated Soviet aid. Meanwhile, substantial imports from Western Europe, albeit almost entirely UNRRA deliveries, generated a Yugoslav interest in restoring the prewar volume of agricultural exports to pay for future imports. This issue, however, diverted attention away from industrialization only briefly. Party leaders were attracted to Soviet-style development based on heavy industry, while the Western European markets were too accessible to American grain for this interest to endure. Imports from the USSR never went beyond 23 percent of total Yugoslav value; this was in 1946 when exports to the Soviet Union peaked at 43 percent of a tiny total. Much of this export amount came from the several joint Soviet-Yugoslav companies, whose price policies and arbitrary actions formed the economic basis of Yugoslav communist disenchantment with Soviet tutelage.[44]

The Yugoslav economic recovery from 1945 to 1947 was further burdened by serious deficiencies in central coordination but was nonetheless remarkable. The *obnova*, or renewal, succeeded in topping the modest prewar level of industrial production by 1947 and in pushing agricultural production to 93 percent of the 1938 level by 1948.[45] In Serbia alone, some 90 percent prewar productive capacity was operating, if not fully employed again, as early as mid-1945. The similarity of the Yugoslav and Bulgarian recoveries to prewar levels is deceptive, given the far smaller war damage suffered by the Bulgarians.

A Fund for Recovery in Yugoslavia was set up under the control of a communist Ministry of Finance and Planning Commission. Its resources included the $428 million worth of supplies delivered under the UNRRA program of war relief, a larger sum per capita than Bulgaria received from the Soviet Union. Yet the Fund's centralized administration was its weakest point. Detailed research by the Yugoslav historian Branko Petranović reveals that these and other ministerial authorities operated without any sort of comprehensive economic plan for 1945–1946 and suffered serious shortcomings in coordination.[46] Only agriculture and state properties operated under partial plans, which were often overridden by the military priorities of the huge 800,000-man army or divided among several ministries. Where ministerial approval was required for expenditures, usually wherever credit was required, delays and arbitrary decisions were the rule. These practices only made shortages in raw materials inescapable and skilled labor worse.

How then was the rebuilding of the industrial plant and infrastructure, as well as the revival of agricultural production, accomplished in the face of these failings at the supposedly all-powerful center? Perhaps the center, lacking Bulgaria's institutional infrastructure, was not that powerful. The sources of success would in fact appear to lie with the interaction of UNRRA aid with lower levels of administration, with those ministries that were subdivided into republic-level sections, and with local-level competitions that pitted one project's workforce against others. UNRRA aid provided most of the equipment and supplies: tractors for the first collective farms, rolling stock for railways, and electrical equipment, tool, saws, and coal for industry.[47] Even the massive UNRRA supplies for grain-deficit areas stimulated the rebuilding of the infrastructure because of the need for port facilities to unload such shipments and rail lines to transport them inland. Significantly, it was the ministries of Agriculture and Construction that were subdivided into sections for each of the six republics. Local committees of party activists organized competitions for every conceivable project, whether rebuilding a factory or a railway line or transporting grain, timber, or other scarce supplies to deficit areas. These competitions involved no central coordination but became a permanent method for organizing projects.[48] Their widespread success may perhaps be traced in part to the national attraction to group rivalry with an identifiable opponent, as distinct from the much less appealing prospect of impersonal market competition between individuals. A more certain impetus was postwar enthusiasm to rebuild after so much death and destruction. The party's zealous young cadre, fresh from victorious combat themselves, could readily tap this kind of energy. The absence of a surviving ministerial apparatus and an experienced bureaucracy in Belgrade was probably an advantage in helping this local enthusiasm to circumvent a multiplying set of centralized procedures.

When, however, Tito and most of the party's leadership decided in 1946 to rush ahead with an initial Five-Year Plan, two years ahead of Bulgaria and the rest of Eastern Europe, its young cadre and its newly reconstituted ministries performed badly. The targets set for industrial and agricultural production for 1947–1951 were by all accounts wildly exaggerated.[49] They projected an increase in industrial production of 38 percent a year, or nearly 400 percent overall. They expected agricultural output to rise 87 percent over the 1939 level, leaving a substantial surplus for export as well as for feeding a large number of new industrial workers, all on the basis of just 7 percent of planned investment. (Recall the equally low Bulgarian percentage.) The inputs needed for meeting these targets and for opening a variety of modern metallurgical plants were simply not available, even before the Tito–Stalin split of 1948 prompted a sharp reduction in supplies from the Soviet Union and its Eastern European allies. The end of UNRRA supplies in early 1947, was especially damaging to the plan's prospects.

The rapid nationalization of industrial enterprises, which was essentially complete by early 1946, versus late 1947 in Bulgaria, did not offer the expected advantages to the party's management of the economy. The communists' greater political leverage in postwar Yugoslavia combined with the large fraction of industrial property, which had been operated under German or Italian auspices during the war, to permit the permanent nationalization or at least temporary sequestering of most major enterprises with little effective protest, either domestically or from Western representatives.[50] Such communist control did not, however, encourage Western suppliers to deliver machinery and inputs that were required to modernize or expand production in the larger enterprises for metallurgy and oil refining. These enterprises were concentrated in the western half of the country, in central Slovenia and Croatia, but also in Bosnia, near the major iron mines, and along the Dalmatian coast.

In the eastern half of Yugoslavia, in Serbia, Macedonia, and Montenegro, there were some large mines, but most of the manufacturing enterprises were on a small scale similar to the situation in Bulgaria. In these regions of Yugoslavia, wartime destruction and the postwar political atmosphere prevented a similar influx of skilled labor into a large number of new small firms. Yet the same task of combining these small enterprises into large, modern factories confronted Yugoslav party leaders and economic officials earlier. They were well aware of the importance of rational consolidation, but inexperienced communist planners and managers typically could not make the transition from reconstruction to modernization within these few years.

We must add to these industrial difficulties an agricultural sector where collectivization had proceeded only slightly beyond the minimal amount of arable land so organized in Bulgaria, 6 percent versus 3 percent by late 1947.[51] The Yugoslav party's leverage for carrying out a successful Five-Year Plan was clearly too limited. The loss of Soviet and Eastern European supplies following the Tito–Stalin split was therefore not the first but the final step in pointing the Yugoslav economy away from Soviet-style central planning as a viable strategy for economic modernization. A number of large banks did manage to survive the process of nationalization with their separate identities intact.[52] They would serve as the institutional models for a financial network which would tie together the self-managed enterprises emerging in the 1950s, with virtually no central planning apparatus to coordinate their activities.

The system of market socialism which would take final shape in the 1960s was therefore a legitimate heir not only to the special Yugoslav legacy of separate regional identities, but also to the particular experience of the 1940s. The country's political culture and economic institutions had too little experience with the "unity of state power," in the phrase of the Bulgarian Agrarian Aleksandŭr Stamboliiski, as well as the Bulgarian communist constitution of 1947, to carry out a successful Soviet-style strategy for rapid industrialization.

Notes

A longer, earlier version of this chapter appears in Roland Schonfeld, ed., *Industrialisierung und gesellschaftlicher Wandel in Südost Europa* (Munich: Südost Europa Gesellschaft, 1989).

1. John R. Lampe, and Marvin R. Jackson, *Balkan Economic History, 1550–1950: From Imperial Borderlands to Developing Nations* (Bloomington: Indiana University Press, 1982), pp. 159–277.

2. See Bloch's essay on comparative economic history in Frederick J. Lane and J. C. Riemersma, *Enterprise and Secular Change* (Homewood, Ill.: Richard D. Irwin, 1953), p. 498.

3. Stephen White, John Gardner, and George Schöpflin, *Communist Political Systems: An Introduction* (New York: St. Martin's Press, 1982), pp. 14–24, 43–51; Archie Brown and Jack Gray, eds., *Political Culture and Political Change in Communist States* (New York: Holmes and Meier, 1979), pp. 1–25.

4. Robert C. Tucker, *The Marxian Revolutionary Idea* (New York: W. W. Norton, 1969), pp. 12–22.

5. A brief summary and critique of this American approach may be found in Daniel Chirot and Thomas D. Hall, "World System Theory," *Annual Review of Sociology* 8 (1982), 81–106.

6. See John R. Lampe, "Unifying the Yugoslav Economy, 1918–1921: Misery and Early Misunderstandings," in Dimitrije Djordjevic, ed., *The Creation of Yugoslavia, 1914–1918* (Santa Barbara, Calif.: ABC–Clio Press, 1980), pp. 139–42; John R. Lampe, *The Bulgarian Economy in the Twentieth Century* (London: Croom-Helm, Ltd., 1986), pp. 42–45; Lampe and Jackson, *Balkan Economic History, 1550–1950*, pp. 376–82.

7. Tables 10.6 and 10.12 in Lampe and Jackson, *Balkan Economic History* pp. 343 and 365. Also see pp. 358–65.

8. Lampe, "Unifying the Yugoslav Economy, 1918–1921," pp. 139–56.

9. Lampe and Jackson, *Balkan Economic History, 1550–1950*, pp. 382–94.

10. According to Table 11.2 in Lampe and Jackson, *Balkan Economic History*, p. 384, real note emissions per capita for 1926–1930 were 38.5 dinars versus 22.4 in 1911 for the Yugoslav lands and just 24.5 leva for Bulgaria, versus 25.4 in 1911.

11. John D. Bell, *The Bulgarian Communist Party from Blagoev to Zhivkov* (Stanford, Calif.: Hoover Institute Press, 1986), pp. 21–37.

12. Richard J. Crampton, *Bulgaria, 1878–1918: A History* (Boulder, Colo.: East European Monographs, 1983) makes this sad political story the centerpiece of his excellent survey of the period.

13. John D. Bell, *Peasants in Power: Alexander Stamboliiski and the Bulgarian Agrarian National Union, 1899–1923* (Princeton, N.J.: Princeton University Press, 1977), pp. 149–68, 213; Aleksander Velev, *Glavni reformi va zemedelskoto pravitelstvo* (Sofia, 1977).

14. Lampe, *Bulgarian Economy*, pp. 51–60.

15. The standard source remains Max Lazard, *Compulsory Labor Service in Bulgaria* (Geneva, 1922).

16. Nikolai Todorov, et al., *Stopanska istoriia na Bŭlgariia. 681–1981* (Sofia, 1981), p. 328.

17. Lampe, *Bulgarian Economy*, pp. 68–74.

18. See the section on the 1930s in Richard J. Crampton, *A Short History of Modern Bulgaria* (Cambridge University Press, 1987), pp. 107–19.

19. Lampe, "Unifying the Yugoslav Economy," pp. 147–52. For a different view, sharply critical of Serbian policies and procedures, see Ivo Banac, *The National Question in Yugoslavia* (Ithaca, N.Y.: Cornell University Press, 1983), pp. 214–25.

20. For details, see Banac, *National Question*, pp. 141–201; Branislav Gligorijevic, *Parlament i politicke stranke u Jugoslaviji, 1919–1929* (Belgrade, 1979). A brief summary is Joseph Rothschild, *East Central Europe Between the Two Wars* (Seattle: University of Washington Press, 1974), pp. 204–35. The best running account of interwar political life may be found in the confidential Annual Reports of the British Foreign Office, in Great Britain, Public Records Office, FO 371.

21. Dr. Vuksanovic-Anic, "Urbanisticki razvitak Beograda u periodu igmedzu dva svetska rata," *Istorija XX veka* 9 (1968), 459–510.

22. Ivo Banac, "The Communist Party of Yugoslavia During the Period of Legality, 1919–1921," in Banac, ed., *The Effects of World War I: The Rise of the Communist Parties*, War and Society in East Central Europe, Vol. 13 (Atlantic Highlands, N.J.: Atlantic Research and Publ., 1983), pp. 180–230. Ivan Avakumovic, *History of the Communist Party of Yugoslavia*, Vol. 1 (Aberdeen: Aberdeen University Press, 1964).

23. Table 10.5 in Lampe and Jackson, *Balkan Economic History, 1550–1950*, pp. 338–40.

24. Tables 12.2 and 12.14 in Lampe and Jackson, *Balkan Economic History*, pp. 438–39 and 484. Also see Marvin R. Jackson, "National Income and Product in Southeastern Europe Before the Second World War," *ACES Bulletin* 24, 3 (1982), 73–103, and his "Agricultural Output in Southeastern Europe, 1910–1938," *ACES Bulletin* 24, 4 (1982), 49–87.

25. Banac, *National Question*, p. 217, reproduces a table prepared by the Croatian economist Rudolf Bicanic which quantifies the Serbian preponderance in the state bureaucracy. For a contemporary British view stressing the divisions and deficiencies of Yugoslav administration, in Serbia as well, see Great Britain, Public Record Office, FO 371, Confidential Annual Report, Yugoslavia, 1925, pp. 34–38.

26. Marvin R. Jackson and John R. Lampe, "The Evidence of Industrial Growth in Southeastern Europe Before the Second World War," *East European Quarterly* 16, 4 (January 1983), 392–98, 403–409. Lampe and Jackson, *Balkan Economic History, 1550–1950*, pp. 500–503.

27. Lampe and Jackson, *Balkan Economic History*, pp. 544–54, 569–71; Branko Petranović, "O promenama u drustveno-ekonomskoj strukturi Jugoslavije u toku narodnoslobodilacke borbe, 1941–1945," *Prilozi za istoriju socializma* 6 (1969), 57–72.

28. Table 4.1 in Leonard Cohen and Paul Warwick, *Political Cohesion in a Fragile Mosaic: The Case of Yugoslavia* (Boulder, Colo.: Westview Press, 1983), p. 64.

29. David A. Dyker, "Yugoslavia: Unity Out of Diversity," in Brown and Gray, eds., *Political Culture in Communist States*, pp. 70–77.

30. Lampe, *Bulgarian Economy*, pp. 105–20.

31. Lampe and Jackson, *Balkan Economic History, 1550–1950*, pp. 541–44.

32. The imported share of industrial inputs fell by one-half from 1937–1938 to 1941–1943, from 29 to 14 percent. Lampe, *Bulgarian Economy in the Twentieth Century*, p. 117.

33. Bell, *Bulgarian Communist Party*, pp. 79–96. Also see Vladimr Migev, "Politicheskite aspekti v izgrazhdanieto i razvitieto na durzhavnite organi, 1944–1958," in Tsvetana Todorova and Mito Isusov, eds., *Bŭlgarskata durzhava prez vekovete*, vol. 2 (Sofia, 1982).

34. Lamp, *Bulgarian Economy in the Twentieth Century*, pp. 124–27.

35. Ibid., pp. 130–32.

36. Ibid., pp. 132–36, 141–43; Zl. Zlatev, "Socialist Industrialization in Bulgaria," in Mito Isusov, ed., *Problems of the Transition from Capitalism to Socialism* (Sofia, 1975), p. 176.

37. Table 12.21 in Lampe and Jackson, *Balkan Economic History, 1550–1950*, pp. 503–504. See Petŭr Shapkarev, *Statistiko-ikonomicheski etiudi vukhu narodnoto stopdanstvo na NR Bŭlgariia* (Varna, 1982), 189–229, for a first-hand account of this integration.

38. Robert A. Pollard, *Economic Security and the Origins of the Cold War, 1945–1950* (New York: Columbia University Press, 1985), pp. 1–58, provides a prudent summary of American economic policy in this period.

39. Tables 13.2 and 13.3 in Lampe and Jackson, *Balkan Economic History, 1550–1950*, pp. 524–29; Grigor Popisakov, *Ikonomicheska otnosheniia mezhdu NR Bŭlgariia i SSSR* (Sofia, 1968), pp. 27–40; Angel Nikov, *Bŭlgaro-suvetski otnosheniia, 1944–1948* (Sofia, 1978).

40. Bell, *Bulgarian Communist Party*, pp. 87–96. Also see Michael M. Boll, *The Cold War in the Balkans: American Foreign Policy and the Emergence of Communist Bulgaria, 1943–1947* (Lexington: University of Kentucky Press, 1984).

41. Lampe, *Bulgarian Economy in the Twentieth Century*, pp. 124–25; Vl. Migev, "Borbata sreshtu kulachestvo i negovoto likvidirane v Bŭlgariia, 1944–1958," in Kh. Khristov, ed., *Iz istoriia na stopanskiia zhivot v bulgarskite zemi* (Sofia, 1984), pp. 44–49.

42. Lampe, *Bulgarian Economy in the Twentieth Century*, pp. 141–42.

43. A controversial Yugoslav critique of the opposition's suppression is Vojislav Kostunica and Kota Cavoski, *Party Pluralism or Monism, Social Movements and Political System in Yugoslavia, 1944–1949* (Boulder, Colo.: East European Monographs, 1985). Also see *Foreign Relations of the United States* 4 (1947), 820, 838, and A. Ross Johnson, *The Transformation of Communist Ideology, The Yugoslav Case, 1945–1953* (Cambridge, Mass.: MIT Press 1972), pp. 32–33.

44. Joseph Bombelles, *The Economic Development of Communist Yugoslavia, 1947–1964* (Stanford, Calif.: Hoover Institute, 1968), pp. 39–45; Vladimir Dedijer, *The Battle Stalin Lost* (New York: Grosset and Dunlap, 1972), pp. 73–96; *Foreign Relations of the United States* 5 (1945), p. 1266; 4 (1947), 855–56.

45. Tables 13.6 and 13.11 in Lampe and Jackson, *Balkan Economic History, 1550–1950*, pp. 538–39 and 561.

46. Branko Petranović, *Politicka i ekonomska osnova narodne vlasti u Jugoslaviji za vreme obnova* (Belgrade, 1969), pp. 256–304.

47. George Woodbridge, *UNRRA*, vol. 2 (New York: Columbia University Press, 1950), pp. 138–70.

48. Petranović, *Politicka i ekonomska osnova*, pp. 339–49.

49. Bombelles, *Economic Development of Communist Yugoslavia*, pp. 24–39; Rudolf Bicanic, *Economic Policy in Socialist Yugoslavia* (Cambridge: Cambridge University Press, 1973), pp. 22–32; Branko Horvat, *The Yugoslav Economic System* (White Plains, N.Y.: M. E. Sharpe, Inc., 1976), pp. 6–12.

50. Johnson, *Transformation of Communist Ideology*, pp. 35–39; *Foreign Relations of the United States* 5 (1945), 1293; Petranović, *Politicka i ekonomska osnova*, pp. 233–55.

51. Bombelles, *Economic Development of Communist Yugoslavia*, pp. 17–23.

52. Lampe and Jackson, *Balkan Economic History, 1550–1950*, pp. 551–53; M. Golijanin, *Bankarstvo Jugoslavije* (Belgrade, 1977), pp. 39–42.

4

Self-Management and Development Strategies in Socialist Yugoslavia

Robin Alison Remington

Yugoslavia emerged from World War II with a revolutionary political leadership legitimized by a successful indigenous struggle for national liberation. That leadership's political experience was limited to a prewar clandestine organization within a revolutionary subculture and wartime party building. These activities took place on the run amid battles with Germans and Italian forces, complicated by a simultaneous civil war between the communist-led Partisans and the royalist Chetnik resistance movement.[1]

There was a wide gap between the core party leaders—those who had joined before the war and were already deeply committed to social revolution, Marxist-Leninist ideology, and the Soviet model of political and economic development—and the party rank-and-file that flowed in from the Partisan army. These young, often peasant soldiers revered Tito because he led them to victory. They accepted the promise of a brave new world with scant understanding of its ideological foundations or what commitment to Soviet development strategies and Comrade Stalin entailed.

Geographically, Yugoslavia was a dividing line between east and west. Unresolved border disputes that continued to fester after 1945 were a factor in Yugoslav international relations and security considerations. Efforts at political consolidation and economic development had to deal with the legacies of Austrian and Ottoman imperialism under which the South Slavs had acquired distinct, indeed conflicting, political cultures and achieved very different levels of economic development. There was also the fallout from the failed effort at political integration during interwar Yugoslavia. Bitter ethnic hostility was exacerbated by wartime atrocities, while, as John Lampe describes, the war had drastically depleted Yugoslav human and economic resources as well.

Nonetheless, the country came out of war with a sense of self-confidence and self-reliance. Notwithstanding Allied aid and belated Soviet assistance, the

Yugoslav Partisan army had essentially won the national liberation struggle themselves. The party had made the transformation from a small underground revolutionary organization of some 12,000 members to a ruling party of some 140,000.[2]

The party leadership was by far the most consolidated in Eastern Europe, securely allied with Moscow within the mainstream international communist movement. It had what it thought was a sure thing in the Soviet model of socialist development.

This is not the place for a detailed discussion of the Yugoslav break with the Soviet Union in 1948.[3] For purposes of this analysis the consequences are more important than the causes. Yugoslav resistance to the penetration devices of the Stalinist interstate system and doctrinal disagreements concerning the substance of postwar proletarian internationalism that led to the expulsion of the Yugoslav Communist party from the Cominform in June 1948 shattered the ideological prism of the Yugoslav party leadership. As a result, the Yugoslav road to socialism detoured onto, as Robert Frost would say "a road less travelled by that made all the difference."

Once the reality sank in that Soviet hostility was not a mistake, but an inescapable political conflict, the Soviet model of socialism and Moscow's development strategies became patently inappropriate. Stalin miscalculated when he said that he would shake his little finger and Tito would fall. The Soviet leader was right, however, in his assessment that his problems with the Yugoslav party were rooted in "conceptions different from our own."

Yugoslav-Soviet differences arose spontaneously from the habit of autonomous decision making that Yugoslav party leaders had become accustomed to during wartime. This autonomy took in the Yugoslav armed forces' natural military self-confidence after the war that made the role of Soviet military advisers uncomfortable, if not redundant, and Tito's regional revolutionary ambitions. The conceptions that Stalin complained of were latent, almost subconscious.

Stalin's displeasure became a full-scale campaign to replace Tito and his supporters with a more submissive Yugoslav leadership. Soviet military maneuvers, economic blockade, and purges of "Titoists" in other East European parties made clear that reconciliation was not in the cards. Thus, the need for an ideologically acceptable Yugoslav alternative to the Soviet model became a domestic and foreign policy priority. In this sense foreign policy imperatives flowing from Yugoslavia's expulsion from the socialist camp and the Soviet threat to Yugoslav security became the impetus for the elaboration of Yugoslav socialist self-management as a theoretical model of political and economic development.

Yugoslav theorists turned to the young Marx, looked to the experience of the Paris Commune of 1871, and studied Fabian socialism with G.D.H. Cole. The result was a commitment to a participatory, self-managing socialism which was formally accepted at the sixth Party Congress in 1952, symbolized by the party's change of name to League of Communists of Yugoslavia (LCY).

The Yugoslav Alternative

Yugoslav self-management is a process of decentralization, debureaucratization, and de-etatization (i.e., taking the state out of the business of managing enterprises and public services), and democratization. This form of participatory socialism is based on the assumption that within socialist society many interests may legitimately be expressed and, notwithstanding its vanguard role, the Communist party is not a mind reader. It assumes that specific conditions lead to situations that may require different solutions and that those who must live with those situations can contribute positively to their solution. It assumes that domination reduces opportunities for genuine political development. The essential characteristics are the legitimation of socialist pluralism in what Edvard Kardelj came to call the "pluralism of self-management interests,"[4] the prevention of the concentration of power, and regulation based on the equal rights of those concerned.

In the broader sense of political development, self-management in the economy, local government, and public services was seen as a means of political mobilization and socialization that would work toward ending political alienation. There was a utopian agenda, what might be called a search for development as self-realization, that has something in common with contemporary Gandhian development strategies, although it did not involve the religious aspect or the emphasis on pooling local resources.

Political Repercussions

From the narrower institutional perspective, however, the move to self-managing socialism required a substantial overhaul of the Yugoslav Communist party that added up to far more than a decrease of economic power within the enterprise. Self-management mandated a change of function in which the party officially withdrew from day-to-day running of the government and redefined its function as that of political-ideological education. This required restyling tactics for implementing party policy as well. The Leninist command mode of the party exercising its leading role was no longer appropriate. Party members were supposed to persuade both local government bodies and self-managing organizations in the economy of the merits of party policies, to work as individuals in these new self-managing institutions without pulling rank or reverting to institutional leverage. In this sense self-management meant reorganizing institutional relationships between party and state bureaucracies.

It also gave more autonomy to local units, thereby reordering hierarchical relationships within the party itself. As for democratic centralism, the centralist aspect was expected to be an increasingly silent partner. The emphasis was on inner-party democracy and eliminating bureaucratic behavior. Tito himself spoke of the "withering away of the Party" along with the state.[5] Of course, there would still be a general party line, but in the absence of specific orders, local party branches were expected to decide for themselves what to do and how to do it rather than referring back to the center.

Although these changes were underway even before the Sixth Party Congress in 1952, that meeting put the official stamp of approval on the decision to abandon the Stalinist model of political development for a vastly decentralized form of party organization still in the process of becoming. The change of name to the League of Communists of Yugoslavia (LCY) in itself upgraded the regional (republic) party organizations, chipping away at the hierarchical prerogatives of the federal party. At the same time the People's Front was transformed into the Socialist Alliance of Working People, an umbrella organization of officially sanctioned interest groups such as trade unions, veterans associations, professional organizations, and individuals designed for purposes of political mobilization and election organization.

Thus, the LCY gave up its monopoly over political life, while retaining its monopoly of party organization.[6] This was a self-management democratization from above. In terms of political development, it increased the number of legitimate political actors, redefined the function and tactics of the hegemonic party, reorganized the party's relationship to society, and substantially weakened its coherence by introducing ambiguity into the rules of the political game.

Although the results were certainly not what had been desired, they may well have been feared and could have been more or less expected. There was major institutional confusion. Some members went too far in interpreting the new rules, and others not far enough.

Party members were used to behaving in a certain way. Many did not understand how to play an "ideological-educational" role. They were accustomed to giving orders. Often they had no talent for persuading. Nor were those who were suddenly expected to decide local policy for themselves comfortable about doing so. They hesitated, fumbled, and fell prey to anxiety and doubt. Many could not adjust to the change in dominant-subordinate status. What did it mean to "wither away" as a party and at the same time be individually responsible for the work and behavior of society as a whole? Perhaps not surprisingly, party membership declined for the first time from 772,000 in 1952 to 654,000 in 1954.[7]

The meeting of the Central Committee in June 1953 at Brioni attempted to draw the line, to push "withering away" into a vague future, and to reinstate some party discipline. This attempt to take two steps back on the road to decentralization further divided the leadership itself, ultimately leading then Vice President Milovan Djilas to publicly insist that the LCY was not "withering away" fast enough. His call for a new democratic socialist party and his subsequent analysis of Yugoslav Communists as a new class of Red bourgeoisie would echo down to the 1980s. But that is getting ahead of the story.

Economic Consequences

With regard to economic development, the legal basis of self-management in the economy rests on two laws that were on the books before the Sixth Congress: (1) the Basic Law on the Management of State Economic Enterprises and Higher Economic Associations by the Workers Collectives (June 1950) that replaced the economic role of the state with the principles of worker management and social ownership and (2) the Law on Planned Management of the National Economy (December 1951), which began Yugoslavia's transition from a command to a market economy. Deborah Milenkovitch summarizes four basic characteristics that distinguished the emerging Yugoslav market socialism from other command economies, other forms of decentralized socialism, and free enterprise economies: (1) an economic plan; (2) market methods of resource and product allocation; (3) production by independent enterprises; and (4) management by workers whose incomes are a residual.[8]

The principle of increased enterprise autonomy came to life in the form of an infrastructure of workers' council and management boards as concrete expressions of the concept of "factories to the workers." From the perspective of economic development, the expectation was that the shift from party to professional management would raise the level of expertise among enterprise directors, thereby improving management efficiency. It was assumed that the opportunity for worker participation in management would combine an assumed visible correlation between productivity and wages to stimulate enterprise production.

Not surprisingly, as with the political dimension of the Yugoslav experiment, gaps existed between principle and practice. Initially, the new system had little real impact on the system of centralized administrative planning. Workers' councils were elected in a limited number of enterprises and controlled very little of the available funds. Management boards were often under the thumb of enterprise directors, whereas party members continued to have a disproportionate influence in the early self-managing institutions.

Nonetheless, the stage was set for replacing administrative-command relations with a system of economic incentives. The Soviet system of central planning was abandoned for "social plans" which at the enterprise level were indicative rather than compulsory. Step by step during the 1950s, changes took place in the handling of capital goods, enterprise income distribution, liquidation of unprofitable enterprises, agriculture, investment funds, the price system, and the banking system.[9]

This period resulted in a Yugoslav economy characterized by increasing reliance on economic criteria in production and distribution, by growing economic power of the banks, and by increased authority of local communes over local enterprises. Indeed, Dennison Rusinow argues persuasively that, notwithstanding the workers' councils, local government and party were the winners when it came to decision making in the local economy or local enterprises.[10]

In terms of economic performance the move away from the Soviet economic model appeared to be a major success story. By 1953 the economy had recovered from drought and stagnation. An economic boom developed that swept the second Five-Year Plan of 1957–1961 to completion in four years. According to Yugoslav sources, the material product of self-managing enterprises (social product) grew by 12 percent; industrial output was up by 14 percent.[11] Indeed, Yugoslavia's growth in GNP in the 1950s and 1960s outranked that of Austria, West Germany, and Japan as well as most of the country's East European neighbors.[12]

Differing interpretations of that success in the Yugoslav political and economic context became the dividing line between decentralizers and centralizers in the heated debate that surrounded the Five-Year Plan for 1961–1965. Before we move to the divisions among Yugoslav economists and politicians over real or token market socialism, we should consider yet another aspect of the Yugoslav alternative.

Domestic–Foreign Policy Linkages

In terms of foreign policy, the Yugoslav alternative model of socialist development directly challenged Soviet hegemony and the existing dominant-subordinate relationship between the Communist Party of the Soviet Union (CPSU) and other communist and workers' parties. Yugoslavia no longer recognized a "leading role" or center within the international communist movement. The demand for national roads to socialism emphasized the need for socialist pluralism, for ideological self-determination in the socialist camp. It stressed sovereignty, noninterference in internal affairs, and mutual advantage. The logic of self-management thereby paved the way for Yugoslav participation in the nonaligned movement developing among the newly independent countries in Asia, Africa, and the Middle East. That foreign policy option had economic and ideological dimensions that interacted with self-management as a development strategy.

With the break with Moscow in 1948, Yugoslavia became de facto nonaligned. Notwithstanding their differences with the Soviets, Yugoslav party leaders were committed to a socialist revolution and had no desire to switch allies in midstream, even if that option had existed, which is doubtful. As Moše Pijade expressed the Yugoslav position after 1948, there is no law that small and medium-sized states must "jump into the mouth of this or that shark."[13]

This political situation became foreign policy in the 1950s, undoubtedly in part because of Yugoslav-Indian contacts within the United Nations. Nonalignment offered Yugoslavia an alternative to the LCY's isolation from Soviet-East European socialism without political strings. It allowed relations with the West without subordination, while opening the door to new trading partners and markets in the South. It was an acceptable compromise between those Yugoslavs who sought further democratization and those who looked wistfully for a socialist identity.[14]

Moreover, from the perspective of the Yugoslav leadership, it reinforced the domestic turn to socialist self-management as a road to political and economic development. Thus, according to Kardelj, self-management and nonalignment are reciprocally and essentially related:

Self-management . . . and the nonaligned policy of Yugoslavia constitute two basic, essential components of the Yugoslav social being, closely interrelated and mutually conditioned. . . . If it were not for its system of socialist self-management, Yugoslavia's nonaligned position would not be possible . . . and vice-versa, without nonalignment, Yugoslavia could not successfully develop its system of socialist self-management.[15]

Some scholars of Yugoslav politics would argue that, even if Yugoslavia had remained domestically Stalinist, the split with Moscow would have led Tito to a nonaligned foreign policy. Yet, for Yugoslav policymakers domestic and foreign policy imperatives operated in tandem during the early 1950s. Subsequently, Tito may have been tempted to backtrack during Khrushchev's flattering efforts to woo Yugoslavia in 1955–1956. However, Soviet duplicity at the 1957 Moscow meeting of ruling Communist parties shut the door to Soviet-Yugoslav rapprochement.

Under the pressure created by the second Soviet-Yugoslav dispute, the LCY Party Program of 1958 reaffirmed the party's commitment to socialist pluralism, continued democratization, and expanding self-managing institutions in the economy and society. At the same time renewed security concerns vis-à-vis Moscow made the need for a nonaligned foreign policy more compelling.

These domestic-foreign policy linkages reflected the initial economic successes of the move to self-management as well. By the 1960s there was an impetus toward further modernization, designed to make Yugoslav currency convertible and to allow closer integration of the Yugoslav economy with the international economic system. Not only the political imperatives of the second Soviet-Yugoslav split, but also perceived economic targets of opportunity offered by the international political economy added momentum to the drive to expand the arena of market socialism. This process crystallized in the economic reforms of 1965.[16]

Perestroika the Yugoslav Way

Long before Mikhail Gorbachev tackled the problem of restructuring the Soviet economy, Yugoslav economists and party leaders struggled with the question of how to overhaul the country's still largely command economy so as to take advantage of the twentieth-century scientific-technical revolution. These efforts epitomize the dilemmas facing Soviet-East European reformers today. As was the case almost three decades ago, conflict generated by the unequal distribution of benefits, the burdens of change, hopes and fears of political consequences, and the momentum of reform radicalizes and creates factions among its supporters, brings new players into the political game, and increases the opposition of those who stand to lose power, privilege, or economic security under the new rules.

By the early 1960s the economic boom associated with the first decade of self-management convinced economists from the more successful sectors of the Yugoslav economy that the time had come to push ahead. In their view the real problem with self-management was the ratio of principle to practice. They wanted to opt for real instead of token market socialism, to allow enterprises that could not make a profit to go out of business, to truly reward initiative and entrepreneurship. In this scenario the modernization of the economy would be based on organization theory, advanced technology, and exports to an international market.

From a development perspective this was an effort to switch from a broad-gauged, labor-intensive development strategy to capital-intensive selective development.[17] Such selective development implied easing up on efforts to equalize the economic level of the Yugoslav republics and provinces. The strong would grow stronger; the weak would slide further behind. In terms of individual enterprises, the weak would go under.

As expected, the chief opponents of the reform were those who would be left out under the shift to selective development. Yet the politics of economic reform blurred the "north–south" divisions because the projected changes substantially increased republic and provincial economic as well as political autonomy. An alliance was created between economic reformers in the more economically advanced "north," managerial-technical elites in economically strong enterprises, and republic and provincial politicians whose instincts were substantially more political than economic (or who perhaps calculated that the reforms could not be implemented without their collaboration). These supporters of change were joined by advocates of party democratization and liberalization in the cultural sector.[18]

Opponents of the reform argued that "market socialism" pushed to that degree amounted to capitalism, that socialist egalitarianism was being abandoned to create a new privileged class, that the less advanced republics and provinces would be still further disadvantaged, that a socialist society could not walk away from its welfare obligations, and finally, that the economy could not afford to have so many unprofitable enterprises going bankrupt at once.

The reformers convinced federal party leaders. Even Tito spoke out in favor of their platforms. As opponents predicted, however, when the reforms of 1965 were introduced, they quickly became the focus of bitter political struggle during attempted implementation. The reform steamed ahead when the leader of the opposition, Alexander Ranković, head of the security forces and the veteran's union, was removed after a bizarre report of attempts to bug Tito's personal premises in what appears to have been Byzantine maneuvering on the part of the head of army intelligence.

Supporters of reform rejoiced prematurely, however. The Yugoslav economy was not strong enough for this great leap forward into international economic waters. It did not take off as the supporters of market socialism predicted, and unemployment skyrocketed. Admittedly, external economic conditions had become less favorable, but on balance the opponents of the reform had been right about the consequences for the economy.

With Ranković's fall, unemployment was alleviated by allowing Yugoslav workers to join the ranks of the *gastarbeiter* in West Germany, Austria, and Switzerland. But this was not enough to stem the growing discontent over evident

inequalities, economic hardships in depressed sectors, and the ideological ambivalence surrounding such symbols of market socialism as the Dior Department
Store in the center of Belgrade which in 1970–1971 infuriated my prewar partisan landlady into open criticism of party policy. Her visceral anger was articulated
by a challenge from the left that accused the party of having lost its ideological
center. On one level, this involved the Praxis group of Marxist humanists[19]
whose criticism went beyond the level of tolerance for inner party democracy.
On another and still more forceful level, the discontent crystallized during the
massive Belgrade student strike in June 1968.

The students demanded jobs for Yugoslavs at home. They objected to party
privileges and the bottleneck to political access created by the generation of partisans known "as the club of 41." There was no substitute for having taken part
in the national liberation struggle as an initiation into political power. Those who
had fought, while in their twenties, had easily another fifteen to twenty years
before they made room for the university-educated generation of party cadre that
came after them. The students wanted knowledge and technical training to count
more than political connections or military history in hiring at the managerial
level. They wanted a more genuine democratization of party life, less corruption
as they saw it, and a return to socialist morality.

Whatever the inconsistencies of the simultaneous demand for egalitarianism
and liberalization, the Belgrade strike laid bare the ideological and economic contradictions of market socialism. It struck at the heart of the party's weakness when
it came to political socialization. Historically, "socialist morality" has meant com-
pensating for unequal levels of development, assuring employment, and protecting the weak. On the other hand, the market in principle allocates resources according to productivity, liquidates unprofitable firms, and rewards the strong.

Tito brilliantly coopted the students by acknowledging the correctness of their
criticism and appealing to them to help him regenerate the party. Of course, in
the meantime they had to return to classes and examinations. Just what course such
party renewal might have taken remains a mystery. Before the university reopened
in the fall, "allied socialist" soldiers put an end to neighboring Czechoslovakia's
reform agenda, aborting Dubcek's search for socialism with a human face.

Once again, as in 1958, the compulsions of an external threat papered-over
deepening political-economic conflicts and swept aside the tensions that surfaced
with the 1965 reform. Students joined the party in large numbers. There was
a sense of solidarity and at least the illusion of cohesion. Tito himself euphorical-
ly announced that the national question had been solved.[20] Based on that false
optimism, he set out to stage-manage his own succession in a manner that legitimized and dramatically escalated historically conflicting South Slav nationalisms.

Self-Management and the National Question

According to Marx, class struggle is the engine of historical progress. Nationalism functions as one of the means by which the bourgeoisie dominates and

divides the working class. In this sense it is the antithesis of proletarian internationalism, which by definition is retrogressive and is destined to land on the rubbish
heap of history. Thus, communist political systems include national integration
along with modernization and political and economic development among their
primary public policy objectives. In instances of conflict between class and national interests, party and state officially represent the working class against national dissidents.

From the beginning the Yugoslav Communist party struggled against South
Slav nationalisms as an enemy of party unity. On assuming power, party leaders
believed that wartime partisan solidarity reinforced by a formal commitment to
multinational federalism would buy time while the socialist revolution redirected
nationalist passions into class identity.[21] As with the Soviet Union, the goal was
nationalist in form and socialist in content.

Yet political life has a way of spilling over the edges of theory. After the
Bolsheviks captured the Russian revolution, Stalin transformed Lenin's concept
of "permanent revolution" into that of "socialism in one country," which was
equated with russification at home, substituting Russian national communism for
proletarian internationalism within the international communist movement.
Domestic power was based on an historically powerful Russia, which continued
to dominate the much weaker nations within the Soviet Union, socialist ideology
and rhetoric notwithstanding.

In 1918 for the first time the interwar Kingdom of Serbs, Croats, and Slovenes
brought together South Slav peoples whose national identities had been forged
during centuries of occupation and repression. That attempt at integration did
not survive the tensions produced by conflicting political expectations and behavior
patterns, the authoritarian and intolerant aspects of political development, and
the inability to institutionalize some kind of nationwide political parties. Rather,
a proliferation of national and ethnically based parties squabbled until the first
Yugoslav state collapsed into a royal dictatorship in 1929. The rise of the Croatian fascist Ustaši (a puppet government under the Axis powers) in retaliation
and the subsequent mutual wartime atrocities left scars on national psyches that
had to be overcome. Whereas Soviet communists built on Russian nationalism
despite their official class priorities, Yugoslav communism required that Serbian
nationalism be restrained and the Serbian historical vision of a greater Serbia be
replaced by a South Slav federation so that the smaller nations and nationalities
would have an incentive to participate instead of opting out.

These policy implications of Yugoslavia's history and domestic national-ethnic
balance of power were initially submerged in the postwar revolutionary euphoria.
Then the break with Moscow added new and complex dimensions to the Yugoslav
national question.

Undoubtedly, Tito rode out Soviet efforts to get rid of him because the Yugoslav
party and army held firm. He was supported as the liberator of the country, a
popular hero; he was seen as the Yugoslav David holding off the Soviet
Goliath.[22] Nonetheless, the Yugoslav party's insistence on national roads to

socialism internationally created domestic spinoffs for center-republic relations within Yugoslavia. From the beginning self-management was equated with expanding republic and provincial autonomy both economically and within the party itself. The logical consequence of a League of Communists of Yugoslavia was to strengthen the territorial party organizations. Since the republics and provinces were largely synonymous with the nations and nationalities of Yugoslavia, this opened the back door to ethnic politics—the door that the party had tried to nail shut as it set out on the path of socialist construction.

Some scholars argue that Yugoslav political leaders, far from being unaware of the implications of self-management for national and ethnic politics, deliberately tried to achieve socialist pluralism via social fragmentation. In this view, Yugoslav self-management strives to institutionalize local, communal interests in an elaborate system of checks and balances precisely to prevent national and ethnic conflicts from taking over republic and provincial relations.[23] This would make the architects of Yugoslav self-management the predecessors and practitioners of what Arend Lijphart subsequently describes as the conditions necessary for consociational democracy.[24] My own suspicion is that the result was not the intent.

Whatever the intent may have been, with the campaign for market socialism and the selective development strategies in the 1960s, republic and provincial party organizations were clearly divided along territorial, bureaucratic lines reflecting a range of economic and political interests. The emergence of regional political actors motivated by acceptable, in-system economic nationalism dovetailed with government support for Macedonian nationalism as an instrument in handling relations with Bulgaria[25] and the acceptance of the Bosnian Muslim campaign for national status as a component of foreign policy aimed at influence building among Muslim countries in the Middle East and North Africa.[26] In short, foreign policy objectives stemming both from security considerations and Yugoslavia's role in the nonaligned movement combined with the ideological propositions of self-management to obscure the differences between good and bad nationalism in the Yugoslav context.

This increasing ambiguity as to what was permissible was at times tantamount to the federal party's blessing national activity as a counter to the challenge from the left following the illusion of national unity after the long, hot summer of 1968 that transformed the Prague Spring into a winter of discontent. In this environment class and national interests appeared more compatible. Public defense of national interests became acceptable.

Notwithstanding Marx's open condemnation of South Slav nationalism as a negative historical force, the prophet of proletarian internationalism's own statements as revolutionary practitioner (what Peter Zwick has called situational nationalism)[27] blurred the ideological issues. In this situation, perhaps inevitably, a campaign for genuine, participatory federalism attached itself to Tito's effort to spell out the guidelines for his own succession via the constitutional amendments of 1971.

Advocates of national self-determination within Yugoslavia as well as in international politics challenged the submerging of national identities in working-class interests as defined by the federal party. As the head of the Croatian Central Committee's ideological commission put it: "There cannot be a federation of equal, self-managing communities, if there are no possibilities for formation of the League of Communists both on a class and national basis.[28]

This is not the place for a detailed discussion of the fate of the Croatian mass nationalist movement.[29] For our purposes, it is not important whether the popular movement captured the Croatian party leadership or whether that leadership miscalculated in its effort to use broadly based support in its struggle to expand Croatian political autonomy and to exert control over the foreign currency generated by Croatian enterprises and tourism. The point is that spontaneous ethnic politics became a factor in both interrepublic and center-republic relations. Notwithstanding the purge of the Croatian party leadership at Karadjordjevo, symbolically at the hunting lodge of Serbian kings, the handwriting for federal republic relations in post-Tito Yugoslavia was on the wall.

There followed the streamlining of the federal League of Communists and the purge of republic and provincial leaders who were "nationalistically minded." This was not a return to Leninism. It was at worst a flirtation. With the Eleventh LCY Party Congress in 1978, the centralization–decentralization pendulum swung back in the direction of Kardelj's "pluralism of self-managing interests" away from the federal center. Moreover, the officially tough-minded constitution of 1974 retained the essence of the republic-center relationship spelled out in the unacceptable amendments of 1971.

According to the constitution, the federal government retained responsibility for foreign policy, defense, and a united market, although no one was quite sure how such a market would be protected or, more to the point, achieved.[30] Other responsibilities devolved to the republic, provincial, or communal levels, with a strong effort to keep the republic and provincial politicians in check by increasing communal authority. A new layer of self-managing institutions in the form of Basic Organizations of Associated Labor (BOALS) was set up to counter the development of monopolies and to further free the economy from direct political meddling. The new system was codified in the 1976 Law on Associated Labor.

From the perspective of economic development, however, this proliferation of self-managing institutions was a distinctly mixed blessing. Increasing the number of economic actors with localized vested interests made the task of maintaining, or more accurately creating,[31] a united market more difficult. As D'Andrea Tyson put it, "having led the way to these reforms, the party has been unable to contain the fragmentation of interests they have created."[32]

As for political development under the 1974 constitution, Tito was to remain president of the party and the country for life. He would be followed by collective, rotating party, and state presidencies. It was assumed that this territorial-functional (the party organization in the armed forces was also dealt into the game) division of powers would work in the context of a strengthened federal party and provide maximum pressure on republic and provincial politicians for policy implementation. The return of the political pendulum in the direction of decentralization in 1978 cast a shadow over those expectations.

The weak links in the succession machinery set up by the 1974 constitution did not appear during Tito's lifetime, however. Interrepublic-provincial conflicts continued to be brokered by Tito personally rather than negotiated or resolved. The godfather of Yugoslav communism spent his last two years on the political stage in a duel with Fidel Castro over the fundamental principles of nonalignment abroad[33] and continued his domestic campaign to assure his place in history.[34] In post–Tito Yugoslavia there would be no room for flamboyant, charismatic authority on the merry-go-round of collective leadership.

In fairness, Tito was undoubtedly right when he said there was no acceptable successor on the political horizon, that the best that could be hoped for was agreement on a political mechanism. Unfortunately, at the end Tito forgot or ignored the fundamental Marxist principle that politics is a function of economic relations. He spent his energy constructing a political solution for political, national and ethnic, and territorial bureaucratic conflicts unmindful that his own lack of attention to the consequences of domestic investment strategies and the Western debt that skyrocketed during the 1970s risked turning the projected collective leadership into a house of cards.

The Titoist Solution

The post–Tito Yugoslav collective leadership is a complex, cumbersome political machine.[35] There is a separation of power and personnel between the highest party and state bodies; a carefully regulated balance of power between regional party organizations that essentially control who represents them at the center in party and government alike. This may be the most elaborate quota system in the world. There are four key elements.

1. Federalization of the party into nine parts (the regional parties plus the party organization in the Yugoslav armed forces).
2. Interrepublic and provincial consensus as the standard decision-making procedure.
3. Territorial and ethnic keys for political jobs at all levels.
4. Rotation schedules that incorporate the principle of deprofessionalization of politics in theory and prevent any vestige of cadre job security in practice.

The unintended consequence of what the growing ranks of critics call the "parcelization of power"[36] was to strengthen the regional rivals for federal power and expand the number of unofficial political actors in the interrepublic and provincial and center regional political game.

Notwithstanding the lingering affection for Tito and attempts to use him as an integrating symbol, the federal party was rapidly reduced to mediating between powerful republic and provincial competitors for declining resources.

The Thirteenth Party Congress of the League of Communists of Yugoslavia in 1986 recognized and warned against emerging economic and political crises. At that time the crisis was perceived in terms of economic imperatives, the need to address "inadequate mechanisms and methods" of implementing the system, and the search for party unity and cohesion.[37]

By autumn 1988 a pervasive sense of systemic crisis had become the central reality uniting politicians, workers, and housewives. As a foreigner who has visited Yugoslavia first as a student, and then as a scholar, for twenty years I experienced that crisis as a wave of insecurity, anxiety, and alienation eroding the quality of life of my friends and colleagues.

Within Yugoslavia there was general agreement that the economy and political system alike were in crisis. There agreement ended. There were differences on the nature of the political and economic crises facing Yugoslavia, conflicting priorities, and competing agendas.[38]

With regard to what was to be done, there was agreement that to overcome the state of crisis a three-pronged reform of the economy, the political system, and the party was required. Beyond a general and almost desperate faith in "the market," there was no agreement on where to start and how to go about such reforms. In principle the market as the answer was combined with emphasis on the need for "democracy and pluralism." However, politicians advocating such solutions had very different things in mind, while democracy and pluralism created still another range of expectations at the level of mass politics.

These crises are tangled and overlapping, feeding on and exacerbating one another. They are deeply rooted in what many Western observers see as the golden age of Tito's Yugoslavia. There are three crises: (1) an economic crisis complicated by (2) a crisis of political legitimacy and institutionalization that has been made more difficult to resolve by (3) a crisis of party identity. Although it is somewhat artificial to separate them, it is logical to begin with the economy.

The Economic Crisis

During the 1970s Yugoslav politicians, like the leaders in other East European and developing countries, adopted a "buy now, pay later" development strategy. Policymakers and enterprises alike took advantage of the willingness of Western bankers to recycle OPEC dollars in the form of substantial loans. Hard choices of resource allocation were postponed. Then the boom collapsed. The favorable international conditions disappeared. Faced with escalating oil prices, world recession, and Western protectionism, the country could no longer avoid the consequences of uncoordinated borrowing and unwise investments.

As the debt grew, so did the anxiety of Yugoslav economists. Certainly, by the mid-1970s the academic debate on the causes of inflation indicated that the problem was linked to mistakes in development policy and governmental errors in fiscal and monetary policy.[39] Efforts were made to apprise Tito of the situation. Tito, unwilling to accept sound economic advice, did not devalue the currency and left the country with what we think was roughly a $20 billion hard currency debt. (No one seemed to know for sure until a team of consulting economists tallied federal and republic-provincial debts. Indeed, until 1982 the actual amount was treated as a governmental secret.)

Within days of his death in 1980, the post–Tito collective leadership devalued the dinar, and the all too familiar cycle began. The Yugoslav economy reeled under the burden of debt-servicing. The International Monetary Fund (IMF) and Western bankers came to the rescue. After much haggling and lost time, debts were rescheduled at the price of yet another austerity program. With each cycle the downhill slide of living standards continued, inflation accelerated, and the ranks of unemployed increased.

The structure of this economic spiral was put into place with the Krajger Commission's Economic Stabilization Program in 1983 that established official priorities under IMF supervision. Not surprisingly, then Prime Minister Milka Planinc's efforts to turn "market socialism" from a slogan into an instrument of economic reform ran into the buzz saw of opposition from those who were asked to pay the price.

As with the economic reforms of 1965, conflict generated by the unequal distribution of benefits and the burdens of change, by hopes and fears of political consequences, functioned as a break on the drive to overhaul the Yugoslav economy. Indeed, the economic and ideological dividing lines that Dennison Rusinow identified between economic rationalizers and their opponents remain much the same.[40]

The political dynamics of the 1980s operated on a different plane altogether. The constitution of 1974 rewrote the rules of the political game in such a way as to eliminate the cross-cutting cleavages that generated the economic and political alliances in support of reform twenty years earlier. Moreover, in the context of the Titoist solution that gave the republic and provincial leadership virtually everything demanded by the Croatian mass movement of the early 1970s, there was no reason for republican politicians to accept economic disadvantage for political gains vis-à-vis the federal center. In the deepening politics of scarcity, there was actually every reason to defend one's own economic turf.

The new players in the post–Tito Yugoslavia do not have Tito's charismatic authority. They are further handicapped by the role of the IMF as a referee imposing unpopular penalties that restrict economic policy options. In these circumstances it is not surprising that public confidence in the federal party steadily declined. In 1985 the results were somewhat better than might have been expected.[41] There was a small favorable balance of trade, industrial production had inched up, and hard currency from tourism had increased by 12 percent. The foreign debt appeared to have stabilized at $19.7 billion. For the moment the decline in the standard of living was reportedly halted.

When Branko Mikulić took over as prime minister in 1986, the economy had done well enough that IMF supervision was no longer required. But whatever advantages Mikulić inherited soon disappeared under the weight of half-hearted

reforms, skyrocketing inflation, and scandals such as the AGROKOMERC af-
fair.[42] There is no need here to reiterate the scorecard of the Mikulić government's declining credibility.

Whatever his weaknesses, the prime minister had a right to complain that his
government was burdened with blame for a political and an economic crisis it
had not created. Rather, these crises were the product of decades during which
"others made decisions."[43] Previous decisions had led to a decline in labor productivity, inefficient investment, and disturbances in the structure of the Yugoslav
economy.

The implication of economic mismanagement during Tito's lifetime is clear,
and it supports the views of most economists both within and outside of Yugoslavia.
Notwithstanding some differences on detail, they appear to agree that the severi-
ty of the current economic crisis is directly related to the time lost when Tito
refused to take politically distasteful, though needed, measures to preempt emerging economic problems. Those who have come after him may be accused of in-
decisiveness, continued mismanagement, knowing or unknowing complicity in
corruption, political ineptitude, and inability to get the country out of disaster.
In fairness, however, the post–Tito collective leadership has consistently wrestled
with an economic crisis that Tito refused to face, under much less favorable
economic and political conditions than those Tito confronted in the 1970s. This
brings us to the political dimensions of the Yugoslav crisis.

Crises of Political Legitimacy and Institutionalization

Ever since popular sovereignty replaced the divine right of kings, establishing
political legitimacy in any multinational state has been a complex, essential, and
frequently illusive task. The attempt to do so in the first Yugoslav state resulted
in ethnic hatreds, terrorism, and, eventually, genocidal wartime atrocities.

After the war, the legitimacy of the Yugoslav Communist party was rooted
in what Western scholars call a revitalized belief system[44] based on the founding myth of Partisan solidarity and a federal political system established to fulfill
Tito's promise that the Partisan army fought not only against the German and
Italian occupiers, but also for the equality, unity, and brotherhood of the Yugoslav
nations and nationalities.

With Yugoslavia's expulsion from the Cominform in 1948, a security component was added in the form of an external threat. The party, therefore, defended
Yugoslav independence. It stood up to Stalin and created an indigenous alternative to the Soviet model; a home-grown, participatory socialism. These components of legitimacy were reinforced by Tito's charismatic authority, his ability
to broker regional conflict, and his international prestige as a leader of the nonaligned movement.

Tito was the George Washington of postwar Yugoslavia, symbolizing Yugoslavia
in story, song, and political jokes. After a quarter of a century of political dependency, there was much understandable nervousness about "after Tito" what?

Tito died on May 4, 1980. At first he was a living memory, still a forceful voice for Yugoslav unity. The afterglow of the Tito personality cult was summed up in the slogan "After Tito—Tito." But this was wishful thinking. Tito had symbolized Yugoslavia, embodying the myth of Partisan solidarity. He arbitrated student strikes, and ethnic crises, and he whipped regional party leaders into line behind the center. He was the last living statesman of stature from the World War II era and the only living architect of nonalignment. He walked on a world stage, larger than life, and like the Indian banyan tree, he dwarfed other political leaders in his shadow.

Lesser politicians who jumped on and off the merry-go-round of collective leadership once a year (and in the case of the party-state presidencies, every two years in the job of party secretary) could not be a satisfactory substitute for thirty-five years of charismatic authority. Moreover, the Titoist solution had deliberately set out to institutionalize a mechanism, not to find a Tito lookalike.

Post-Tito central politicians had a distinctly unenviable job. On the one hand, they desperately cultivated the afterglow of the Tito cult as the most powerful force for Yugoslav unity. On the other, Tito had left the Yugoslav economy standing on glass legs. His refusal to devaluate, to stop borrowing, and to retrench went against the warnings of his economic advisers. His successors had to pay the bill and somehow cope with the $20 billion Western debt they had inherited. Whatever Tito's political advantages, they did not want to take the blame for the economic mess.

Gradual and delicate efforts to disassociate themselves from Tito's economic mismanagement did little to improve their popular image. The perception of ordinary Yugoslavs was that when Tito died their standard of living began a steady downhill slide, and the price of everything went up. The collective leadership had none of the reassuring psychological aspects of Tito's godfather image. Moreover, with no one and everyone responsible, the people were even deprived of someone to blame.

Today there is not even an external threat to distract attention from their economic woes. In these days of *perestroika* and *glasnost*, Mikhail Gorbachev sounds remarkably like Alexander Dubcek of twenty years ago. The Soviet danger is not a unifying factor. If anything, Soviet reforms resemble rather than reject the Yugoslav alternative. Thus, in post–Tito Yugoslavia foreign policy security concerns no longer function as a unifying force, while economic imperatives associated with market socialism and the challenge of the European Economic Community's enhanced integration in 1992 have thus far worked against federal politicians rather than strengthening them.

Given the seriousness of the economic crisis facing Yugoslavia, the legitimacy of any post–Tito politician should logically be based on economic performance. In the eyes of Yugoslav workers, housewives, students, and pensioners, satisfying IMF restrictions does not equate with economic credibility. They have an understandable visceral objection to the theory of fighting inflation with inflation.

The federal government has taken the brunt of the backlash. Combined with the consequence of increasingly fragmented power, this has strengthened regional politicians who have sought legitimacy as defenders of regional interests and have cultivated national and ethnic constituencies. In their search for support, republic and provincial leaders in turn have rehabilitated ethnic populism which had been declared tantamount to counter-revolution during the "Croatian events" of 1970–1971.

This ongoing crisis of legitimacy in post–Tito Yugoslavia is reflected in the (Belgrade journal) NIN poll taken at the time of the Thirteenth Party Congress in 1986. Of some 4,500 respondents, 73 percent thought the party had been fulfilling its leading role "inadequately, barely, or not at all."[45] Despite some early optimism with respect to the Marković government's commitment to structural economic reform, inflation steadily climbed to an unmanageable and virtually unbearable 2,000 plus percent by the end of 1989. In these circumstances, the results of such a poll before the January 1990 Fourteenth Congress would likely have been even less encouraging.

Many observers both within and outside of Yugoslavia apparently concluded that the Titoist solution had set off a runaway decentralization in which the party and government center had essentially withered away.[46] This problem has been aggravated by the way in which that solution has been institutionalized so as to continually reinforce regional power at the expense of the center.

It is constitutionally impossible to overhaul the post-Tito political machinery without the consent of all the republics and autonomous provinces. Whether or not one goes as far as Vojislav Koštunica's assessment that the Yugoslavs "are prisoners" of a system they cannot change,[47] substantive reform clearly requires establishing mutual advantage and achieving a common denominator of agreement on the nature of systemic change. Yet, from the perspective of political institutionalization as conceived by Samuel Huntington in his classic study of political order in developing societies,[48] the League of Communists of Yugoslavia suffers from too little or at best uneven political institutionalization. If we apply Huntington's indices of adaptability, complexity, autonomy, and coherence to the LCY, we could say that, whereas the party has chronological adaptability, it is in the midst of its first major generational transition from what some call "the club of 1941," the revolutionary generation, to previously unknown leaders who will inevitably be judged by their political and economic performance.

The autonomy of the federal as well as the republic and provincial parties has been weakened by the de facto shift from class to national and ethnic constituencies as the primary reference group. In principle, consensus as a procedural requirement for policymaking was intended to ensure coherence. Increasingly, however, sectarian national and ethnic politics have substituted public passion for consensus building. There are no agreed upon rules of republic and provincial conflict resolution these days. Nor could there be if politicians were actually expected to come to agreement under the glare of television cameras.

The Crisis of Identity

The twin crises of legitimacy and institutionalization are compounded by an ongoing identity crisis within the party itself. This problem is not new, nor is it necessarily bad. Ever since the commitment to socialist self-management at the Sixth Party Congress in 1952, there has been ambivalence about what the shift to an educational and ideological leading role meant. There has been ongoing difficulty in sorting out an appropriate relationship to self-managing institutions; periods of withdrawal alternate with aggressive efforts to impose direction. Confusion has arisen over how the party should relate to the pluralism of self-managing interests. Now there are new challenges to face.

Currently, Yugoslavia is locked in a struggle between those who want to overhaul the Titoist solution and those who want to abandon it. The thrust of the 1989 amendments to the Serbian and Yugoslav constitutions was to reverse the parcelization of power, reestablish Serbian authority over the two autonomous provinces, and integrate the Yugoslav economy. These amendments largely represent Serbian objections to the Titoist solution and support the Serbian version of political reform. They appear to have been reluctantly backed by the Slovene party leadership as the best economic package they could obtain.

In the short run, the Serbian party strongman Slobodan Milošević's resort to street politics and playing the Serbian card succeeded in replacing or intimidating his provincial opponents into giving up their constitutional position under the 1974 constitution. It remains to be seen whether in the long run that is a Pyrrhic victory.[49] Meanwhile, the arena of struggle shifted to the drafting commission for a new Yugoslav constitution and maneuvering surrounding the "extraordinary" Fourteenth LCY Congress which was scheduled for December 1989.[50] In order to allow time for the republic and provincial congresses that had to take place before the Federal Congress could meet, the Fourteenth Congress was postponed until late January 1990 by which time the handwriting was on the wall.

As neighboring Communist parties and governments toppled like so many humpty-dumpties, it is not surprising that the LCY yielded to popular pressure for democracy and pluralism and gave in to Slovenia's and Croatia's demands for a multiparty system. These concessions did not go far enough to prevent the Slovene delegation from walking out. It is important to keep in mind that, although the Slovene League of Communists has walked out of the Congress and split with the federal party, as of this writing (March 1990) Slovenia is still a functioning part of Yugoslavia.

Clearly, Prime Minister Marković's call for a "new socialism" requires "new political thinking" by party members.[51] What is the role of the League of Communists of Yugoslavia in a democratic, pluralist society? What is the relationship of the party to their political forces, including former Slovene comrades? What does the notion of inner party democracy mean? The party congress simultaneously underscored the urgency to find answers and the depth of disagreement.[52]

The Balance Sheet

In considering the legacy for political development flowing from the founding Congress of Yugoslav socialist self-management, it is clear that a number of the problems that threaten the cohesion of Yugoslavia at the end of the twentieth century might be considered birth defects of the Yugoslav alternative.

First, the change of function and reorganization of the institutional relationships within the League of Communists left the party with a deep-seated identity crisis. It has manifested itself in a political decentralization–centralization pendulum that has characterized Yugoslav politics for three decades.

Second, given the national and ethnic basis of the Yugoslav republics and the autonomous provinces, the shift in the balance of power between the center and the regional parties at the Sixth Congress de facto relegitimized ethnic politics. It thereby set the stage for the tug-of-war between "nation" and class priorities that has become the hallmark of post–Tito Yugoslavia.

Third, strengthening the power of the communes in the economy undoubtedly fostered local initiative. However, it also led to powerful local protectionism, which in Yugoslavia's export-driven economy of the 1980s has hindered national investment policy, acted to prevent liquidation of unprofitable enterprises, and thwarted the center's efforts to encourage small private enterprises.

Fourth, political mobilization via the pluralism of self-managing interests tied the notion of democratization firmly to economic decentralization. This linkage between political democracy and enterprise autonomy continues to severely limit the options of post–Tito Yugoslav prime ministers struggling to deal with the need for economic stabilization and the relentless imperatives of debt-servicing in hard currency.

In fairness, the following points concerning the beleaguered Yugoslav federal politicians are in order. In my view, their weaknesses are magnified, and their accomplishments are undervalued. If we look back to the somewhat hysterical media speculation of "after Tito," during the ten years before the giant of Yugoslav communism died, which ranged from collapse into ethnic civil war, a military coup, or Soviet domination, the answer is none of the above.[53]

For all its warts and weaknesses, the Titoist solution survived the transition from charismatic authority to collective leadership and avoided the paralysis of winner-take-all factional struggles at the top. It kept the complex political machinery from grinding to a halt. It grappled with conflicting economic priorities and faced tough choices that Tito himself refused to confront.

The post-Tito leadership put in place an unpopular austerity program and made enough progress so that it came out from under six years of IMF supervision of the Yugoslav economy. That Prime Minister Branko Mikulić dissipated many of the advantages he inherited does not negate that accomplishment. Mikulić did not live up to his reputation. However, it is not a sign of systemic collapse for a prime minister to resign. An underlying rule of democracy, as Harry Truman would have said, is for those who cannot take the heat to get out of the kitchen.

Whereas the collective leadership fell short of its goal of economic stabilization, their economic record is not as bad as it looks to their increasingly alienated constituents, who have to pay up after decades of living beyond their means. Measured against other states caught in the trap of international indebtedness, Yugoslavia has shown some economic progress and perhaps too much self-discipline. In 1989, foreign currency reserves and Western exports increased. The Western debt dropped from around $19 billion to $16 billion, which is light years ahead of the Polish economy with a debt that grew from $26 billion in 1980 to a reported $40 billion over the same period.[54]

The system has mechanisms for establishing temporary economic measures such as the subsequently modified 1985 law centralizing foreign currency, a law enacted despite determined Croat and Slovene opposition. Consensus did not amount to political paralysis. It slowed the government's ability to act, but it did not freeze it. Nor is that always a disadvantage. Centralized power can move faster. However, in the Yugoslav context this has not been a guarantee against a wrong decision or an assurance of the ability to implement unpopular economic reforms. For all his authority, Tito could not or would not push through the campaign for market socialism in the 1960s. As for lack of accountability, Tito himself could not be held responsible for the economic mismanagement of the 1970s that created the problems that now torment his successors.

Self-Management: An Economic and Political Assessment

If we consider self-managing socialism as a participatory economic development strategy, it has an uneven track record.[55] Self-management in the economy undeniably worked better in the Yugoslav "north": where Austrian traditions and a work ethic facilitated participation. By contrast, in the Yugoslav "south" five hundred years under the Turks and low levels of economic development worked against the system. Nonetheless, workers in all parts of Yugoslavia had a channel for participation and a weapon against managerial abuses that had not existed before. Expanding enterprise autonomy was indeed a reality.

At the national level under socialist self-management, the Yugoslav economy advanced sufficiently that the World Bank categorized it as a newly industrialized country. During this period investment patterns did much to eliminate the differences between rural and urban Yugoslav life, if not between republic and provincial levels of economic development. Yugoslavia has made substantially greater economic progress than many medium-sized, developing countries buffeted by the international economic cycles over which they have no control. Even with perfect economic management such countries were not masters of their fate in the international political economy of the 1980s.

This is not to defend poor investment strategies or the corruption so evident in the AGROKOMERC scandal. Whatever the former prime minister's deficiencies, he was right in asserting that the central government's inability to control runaway inflation was as much due to the unwillingness of regional party leaders and powerful enterprises to play by the rules as a lack of decisiveness at the federal center.[56] The center does not have the power to implement unpopular policies without republic and provincial cooperation. In fact, the politics of scarcity and the pressures of an export-driven economy politicized the economic nationalism of the 1970s into dangerously sectarian politics. That was not necessarily the fault of either worker participation in decision making or of socialist self-management as a development strategy.

Commitment to self-managing institutions in government and the economy have undoubtedly exacerbated the problem in two specific arenas. First, although provincial autonomy has probably not been the only reason for the continued lag in economic development in Kosovo and other depressed sectors, it is hard to refute the argument that the inability to monitor the use of the Federal Fund to assist the less developed regions contributed to the problem.[57] To whatever extent future aid is given in the form of direct investment in enterprises, it may come closer to accomplishing its objective.

Second, there appears to be an intrinsic conflict of interest between the drive for profit by Basic Organizations of Associated Labor and the imperative to export to hard currency markets in order to service foreign debts. There is no convincing evidence that those who insist that the answer is "real self-management" have sufficiently refined economic instruments to bring about an environment in which what is good for individual Yugoslav enterprises is also good for the national economy under the compulsion of a $16 billion hard currency debt. On the other hand, with or without self-management weaker enterprises and the communes that depend on them would resist going bankrupt for the general good.

Moreover, the underlying flaw in the almost desperate faith in market socialism these days is that in order to have a market, consumers have to have money to spend. Increasingly, many ordinary Yugoslavs are finding it impossible to live on their salaries until the end of the month, and many of those who do make ends meet can only afford food and their electric bill. The goal of increasing exports is essential. Realistically, however, export markets are hard to break into or expand on. In the meantime, no matter how high the quality, very few of my Yugoslav colleagues could afford to pay $20 to $35 for a pair of women's winter boots when the average salary of PhDs in the social sciences has shrunk to less than $100 a month. What will the workers who produce those boots do when there is no domestic market or when they cannot produce for less and earn enough to survive?

In the search for political accountability, socialist self-management and the League of Communists alike have lost credibility. Yet, for the most part self-management is irrelevant to the clash of economic forces under which the Yugoslav economy staggers. Contrary to the opinion of some critics, self-management did not create the problems, and contrary to the hopes of its supporters, self-management is not the answer to relief that can come only through negotiations with international financial circles.

Politically, socialist self-management did not socialize Yugoslav workers and generations of increasingly educated youth into accepting even the ideological-educational role of the League of Communists as it was intended to do. It did not create autonomous, politically unalienated citizens. It did not work perfectly.

Nonetheless, it did raise the political expectations of a largely apathetic Balkan society. Yugoslavs now believe that their voices should be heard and that their complaints should be taken care of. Self-management cannot be termed a failure because workers marched into parliament and demanded responsible economic policies and accountable politicians. One goal of self-management was to politicize the working class; that the result is uncomfortable for those in power does not diminish the value of that success.

Nor is it a failure of self-management when the Slovenian League of Communists decided that other legal political parties should be allowed, or indeed when mass rallies became instruments in the struggle between the Serbian and Kosovo party leaderships. I have more reservations about Milošević's taking over the Serbian press and creating a climate in which Serbian party members and academics who disagree with his tactics hesitate to say so. Yugoslav socialist self-management created channels for articulating multiple political, economic, and social interests. It fundamentally changed the rules of the political game so that a dogmatic, once centralized Communist party accepted a pluralism of political interests, if not yet parties, long before the rest of East Central Europe. It created an environment in which the LCY came to understand that in Yugoslavia class identities could not replace national passions; that class and national interests must coexist.

For at least seven years the much weakened political center continued to mediate with considerable success among increasingly powerful republic and provincial actors. The federal party had not withered away; rather, it had changed its function. Undoubtedly, party democratization and debureaucratization never reached what many party members would consider satisfactory levels.

Despite the rhetoric of systemic crisis and breast beating, however, the Thirteenth Party Congress in 1986 brought in a central committee with 127 new members out of 165. All but four members of the party presidency were replaced. The average age of the new presidium was roughly fifty and that of central committee members forty-five. Thus, the generational transition from the "club of 1941" proceeded smoothly, almost unnoticed. Notwithstanding the increasingly sectarian tone of interrepublic and provincial politics, for the most part rotation schedules have been routinely observed. This process of generational turnover accelerated in a much more controversial fashion with the leadership changes that took place in Vojvodina, Kosovo, and Montenegro in 1988–1989.

On the national or ethnic front, the federal government did not solve the Kosovo problem. As of 1989 it had not mismanaged it so badly as to create another Northern Ireland or Lebanon, or even Punjab. In this regard, the repercussions of the successful Serbian campaign to reestablish constitutional and security authority over the autonomous provinces remain to be seen. Although the intention was

to protect Kosovar Serbs and Montenegrins, the immediate result was to escalate
protest on the part of Kosovar Albanians, most recently in the form of violent
outbursts that followed an instance of mass hysteria by ethnic Albanian teenagers
and schoolchildren.[58] Whether these children were victims of ethnic-motivated
attack as believed by Albanians, of separatist provocation as believed by Serbs,
or of accidental food poisoning, such incidents underline the deepening climate
of distrust that feeds the cycle of violence.[59]

In these circumstances, the decision of the Yugoslav presidency to appoint a
commission to examine all cases of persons killed or wounded in Kosovo is needed
to contain conflict situations. Its demand that provincial, republic, and federal
politicians work together on a "different development concept" for the Kosovo[60]
is a precondition of any political solution. Without such cooperation, the quality
of life for Kosovar Serbs and Montenegrins as well as the ethnic Albanian majority of the population will steadily decline regardless of where constitutional
authority resides.

The foreign policy of the collective presidency has maintained Yugoslav influence in the nonaligned movement, retained Yugoslav credit in the West without
giving up its independent political judgment, and expanded trade with the East.
Indeed, currently the most sensitive Soviet-Yugoslav issue is the roughly $2 billion
balance of trade in favor of Yugoslavia, which the Yugoslavs consider to be a
debt and want the Soviets to pay.

These accomplishments are unlikely to give much comfort to alienated constituencies, whose negative reaction correlates with their economic sufferings. Much
depends on whether Prime Minister Marković's economic package of reforms
gives Yugoslav workers and housewives (most of whom hold jobs outside the
home as well) some relief.

Finally, although to compare de-Titoization with de-Stalinization is an exag-
geration,[61] the viability of socialist self-management requires a hard look at the
Tito myth. Self-management gave a rationale to his refusal to play by Soviet-
defined rules of interparty politics. It also supported and gave credibility to his
role within the nonaligned movement. Finally, self-management enhanced Tito's
international prestige and met his domestic and foreign policy needs. But Tito
was always uncomfortable with the spontaneous way in which this Yugoslav alternative kept getting out of control. He distrusted spontaneity, disliked having the
League of Communists share power, and feared the consequences of legitimizing national and ethnic politics.

Tito both symbolized and undermined self-management as a development
strategy. It was not the self-managing institutions that weakened the leading
role of the League of Communists of Yugoslavia so much as Tito's insistence
on playing the leading role himself. He was a grand showman, whose political
style was more like holding court than that of a team player. He was unwilling
to step aside, unwilling to accept the fact that "real" self-management is incompatible with dependence on charismatic authority. Tito thereby reduced those
who would come after him to bit players, roles that left them ill prepared to

run the complex political machinery he left them or to manage the economic burdens they inherited.

Tito's historical role has to be reevaluated before a systemic balance can be restored. However, the Tito myth is so deeply intertwined with the ideological foundations of socialist self-management, so integral to its credibility, that the consequences of de-Titoization are unpredictable.

Today many Serbian reformers see Tito's Yugoslavism as a deliberate attempt to destroy legitimate Serbian nationalism and to deny Serbs a national identity encouraged among non-Serb nations and nationalities.[62] They insist that the parcelization of Serbia must be reversed before the country can set out on the path to economic reform. Not surprisingly, Slovenes and Croats put the priorities in the opposite order, whereas Kosovar Albanians carry Tito's picture in protest rallies against Serbian domination. These differing reform agendas require revealing Tito's weaknesses and defending his historical role, respectively. But polemics centered on the search for the bad and good Tito are only another diversion.

Conclusion

Yugoslav policymakers are caught in the cycle of debt-servicing and IMF-imposed austerity programs that increasingly undermine both their credibility and the viability of self-managing socialism. Self-management outlasted Stalin. The Soviet threat increased Yugoslav cohesion. It remains to be seen whether this participatory strategy of political and economic development can survive an export-driven economy, IMF prescriptions, and the pressures generated by the projected 1992 Common Market integration.

A consensus has been reached on the core of the reforms—independence of enterprises without strong state influence, market criteria, equal status of enterprises under all forms of ownership, "profit as the ultimate objective."[63] Yet demands to proceed with market socialism have been combined with the contradictory insistence that the means for getting there, that is, the instruments of economic reform, not be put into place prior to "equalization of all economic sectors; private to social, foreign to domestic, agricultural to everyone else." This is a classic Catch 22. As one Croatian daily summed up the government's dilemma: "The tragedy of Ante Marković's government lies in the fact that its term belongs to a time when there is no economic policy measure which equally hits and benefits everybody."[64] The Sarajevo newspaper *Oslobodenje* went further: it attacked the prime minister's program as a sellout to capitalism and predicted that his government was doomed in any case.[65]

As during the aborted campaign for market socialism in 1965, analysts are in deep disagreement as to who will pay the bill for needed change. Genuine economic reform means closing down some 10 percent of Slovene firms. In Montenegro as many as 80 percent of the enterprises could go bankrupt. It is difficult not to agree with the Belgrade political scientist Kosta Čavoški, who flatly concluded,

"No Montenegrin politician can accept that sacrifice no matter what he believes about market economies."[66]

Notwithstanding conflicting pressures, the Marković government has held to its position that anti-inflation measures cannot succeed without creating the legal foundation for a market economy and "material conditions" for the reforms. Piece by piece the scaffolding went up. Amendments to existing laws on enterprises, banks, and other financial institutions, and accounting; new laws on labor relations, foreign trade, commodity reserves, securities, and money and capital markets were fought through the assembly.

By the end of 1989, the laws on foreign currency, prices, and taxation before the federal assembly were deadlocked by republic and provincial disagreements. Nonetheless, Marković judged that sufficient preconditions had been met in order to take a great leap forward in the war against inflation.

Indeed, many of the economic indicators that the prime minister reported to the assembly were favorable. Exports were up; there was a $2.3 billion balance-of-payments surplus; foreign exchange reserves had reached $5.8 billion; and the foreign debt had dropped to $16.6 billion. Moreover, only 16 percent of the foreign currency went to debt servicing as compared to 45 percent "in the most difficult periods." Industrial production was up 1.9 percent, whereas agricultural production had grown by 6 percent.[67]

Marković advocated shock treatment in line with the theories of Harvard Professor Jeffery Sachs, or what in December 1989 might be called the Polish road to capitalism. The dinar was to become convertible, pegged to the deutschemark at a seven to one ratio (the U.S. dollar would be twelve to one) and not to be changed until June 1990. Yugoslavs would have the right to freely exchange dinars for foreign currency at the official rate.

Convertibility would be combined with a tight monetary policy, a balanced budget, a floating interest rate, and, for the most part, market-determined prices. An exception was made for some infrastructural services such as energy and utilities where prices would be frozen until June 1990. And most painful of all for the alienated, increasingly desperate Yugoslav population, wages were to be frozen at the November 1989 rate until June.

The Serbs immediately condemned the program, and the Slovenes resisted the taxation measures. Others had their complaints as well. Yet during the infighting that persisted until the new year, it became clear that Serbian detractors were largely isolated. Resorting to temporary, emergency measures when agreement could not be reached, the federal assembly gave Marković a green light. Among ordinary Yugoslavs who were being asked pay the price, there was relief that something was being done to deal with the estimated 2,500-percent inflation.[68]

Thus, in 1989 the Yugoslav government set out on what many viewed as the last chance to salvage the economy. By March 1990 the early indicators were favorable. Foreign currency reserves had risen to $7.5 billion, and most important, inflation had reportedly dropped to 8.4 percent in February.[69] The emphasis on "property pluralism," which can be seen as a code term for privatization, is expected to reduce the roughly 85 percent social property sector of the Yugoslav economy to an estimated 13 to 14 percent,[70] that is, reversing the existing ratio of social to private property over a five- to ten-year period. At a minimum we must say that this scenario will restructure the Yugoslav experiment with socialist self-management as a development strategy. It is a much needed step by federal politicians in facing the reality that Yugoslav workers, citizens, and housewives want bread, not political circuses. No matter how well crafted the Marković plan may be, his government cannot put it into place without republic and provincial cooperation.

In post-Tito Yugoslavia, attacking the center has become a national sport. It is not the answer, however. Regional politicians must realize that, like it or not, they have won. It is too late to pass the buck back to the federal government if Yugoslavia is not to slide rapidly backward as 1992 approaches. They are the center of power, and that victory carries with it certain responsibilities.

The republic and provincial politicians hold the key to economic stabilization. The federal center can only be as strong as they allow and as decisive as their willingness to implement agreed on measures even when it hurts. The official economy cannot become productive unless regional politicians cooperate and help get the grey economy, where much of the economic action is, under control. This requires defusing the atmosphere of polemical charges and counterattacks, as well as backing off from treating interrepublic relations as a soccer match.

In the end, for Yugoslavia as for other federal systems in the world, the legitimacy of wherever the barometer of federal-regional relations settles (participatory or centralized federalism) will be measured by performance.

At the Seventeenth LCY CC session, Joze Slokar warned prophetically, "The confidence that people have in us is expiring; if we do not make a bold turn to get out of this situation . . . the people itself will replace us. We shall not make any criteria, but the people will take the criteria in their hands."[71]

Yugoslavs, like the Poles, want a government that works. Such a government must respond to the domestic and foreign policy imperatives of today and look forward, not backward. It must meet the challenge of the scientific-technical revolution that will determine the international political economy of the twenty-first century. Yugoslav economists are well aware that, these days, overall Yugoslav development depends on using science and technology and competing effectively in the international economic system.[72] Yugoslav politicians cannot afford to look the other way.

Yugoslavs are justified to demand that their political leaders get their act together. If post–Tito politicians are to produce results, however, they need more help. Simply condemning the League of Communists is ineffective. Although the move in the direction of a multiparty system provides healthy political competition, at the moment the proliferating movements and parties do not have either political power or the answers.

To whatever degree increased productivity is needed to make the Yugoslav economy work, it will not happen until all Yugoslavs see not just the federal or regional scapegoat of the moment, but themselves as accountable and responsible. Perhaps that is what the survival of "real self-management" is all about.

Notes

1. See Vladimir Dedijer, *With Tito Through the War: Partisan Diary, 1941–1944* (London: A. Hamilton, 1951).

2. Ivan Avakumovich, *History of the Communist Party of Yugoslavia* (Aberdeen: Aberdeen University Press, 1964).

3. For the official Yugoslav version, see *White Book on Aggressive Activities by the Governments of the USSR, Poland, Czechoslovakia, Hungary, Rumania, Bulgaria and Albania Toward Yugoslavia* (Belgrade: Ministry of Foreign Affairs, 1951). See also Robert Bass and Elizabeth Marbury, eds., *The Soviet-Yugoslav Controversy, 1948–1958: A Documentary Record* (New York: Prospect Books, 1954).

4. Edvard Kardelj, *Self-Management and the Political System* (Belgrade: Socialist Thought and Practice, 1980).

5. Vladimir Dedijer, *Tito* (New York: Simon & Schuster, 1953), p. 428. For analysis, see George W. Hoffman and Fred Warner Neal, *Yugoslavia and the New Communism* (New York: Twentieth Century Fund, 1962), pp. 174–210.

6. Dennison Rusinow, *The Yugoslav Experiment 1948–1974* (Berkeley and Los Angeles: University of California Press, 1977), p. 74.

7. See Table 11 in Bogdan Denis Denitch, *The Legitimation of a Revolution: The Yugoslav Case* (New Haven and London: Yale University Press, 1976), p. 94.

8. Deborah D. Milenkovitch, *Plan and Market in Yugoslav Economic Thought* (New Haven and London: Yale University Press, 1971), p. 101.

9. See Svetozar Pejovich, *The Market-planned Economy of Yugoslavia* (Minneapolis: University of Minnesota Press, 1966).

10. Rusinow, *The Yugoslav Experiment*, p. 70.

11. Milenkovitch, *Plan and Market*, p. 122.

12. Z. Popov, "Zemlje najbrzim privrednim razvojom," *Ekonomska Analiza*, 1–2 (1967): 120. See Denitch, *The Legitimation of a Revolution*, p. 140. This was emphasized in the question and answer period following Prime Minister Kazimir Zivko Pregl's presentation at the Yugoslav ambassador's residence in Washington, D.C., February 21, 1990.

13. *Borba* (Belgrade), July 9, 1949.

14. Alvin Z. Rubinstein, *Yugoslavia and the Nonaligned World* (Princeton, N.J.: Princeton University Press, 1970), p. 328.

15. Edvard Kardelj, *Yugoslavia in International Relations and in the Nonaligned Movement* (Belgrade: Socialist Thought and Practice, 1979), p. 219. For more recent Western analysis, see Robin Alison Remington, "The Functions of Nonalignment in Post-Tito Yugoslavia: Domestic-Foreign Policy Linkages," *The Nonaligned World* (Delhi), 2, no. 1 (April–June 1984): 243–59, and William Zimmerman, *Open Borders, Nonalignment, and the Political Evolution of Yugoslavia* (Princeton, N.J.: Princeton University Press, 1987).

16. See Milenkovitch, *Plan and Market*, p. 175 ff. and Christopher Prout, *Market Socialism in Yugoslavia* (Oxford: Oxford University Press, 1985), p. 32ff.

17. Zvonko Lerotić, "Political Democracy and Federalism," in Dennison Rusinow, ed., *Yugoslavia: A Fractured Federalism* (Washington, D.C.: Wilson Center Press, 1988), p. 94.

18. See Rusinow, *The Yugoslav Experiment*, pp. 172–91, for detailed analysis of the political maneuvering that went on between reformers and their opponents.

19. Gerson S. Sher, *Praxis, Marxist Criticism and Dissent in Socialist Yugoslavia* (Bloomington and London: Indiana University Press, 1977), pp. 167–87.

20. *Borba* (Belgrade), September 22, 1969.

21. See Paul Shoup's classic study, *Communism and the Yugoslav National Question* (New York and London: Columbia University Press, 1968); see also Walter Connor, *The National Question in Marxist-Leninist Theory and Strategy* (Princeton, N.J.: Princeton University Press, 1984), p. 222 ff.

22. Ernst Halperin, *The Triumphant Heretic: Tito's Struggle Against Stalin* (New York: British Book Service, 1958) captures the drama of those days and is among the most readable of the prolific analyses of the Soviet-Yugoslav dispute.

23. See Vojislav Stanovčič, "History and Status of Ethnic Conflicts," in Rusinow, ed., *Yugoslavia: A Fractured Federalism* (Washington, D.C.: Wilson Center Press, 1988), p. 34.

24. Arend Lijphart, *Democracy in Plural Societies: A Comparative Exploration* (New Haven: Yale University Press, 1977). On Yugoslavia see also Jack C. Fisher, *Yugoslavia— Regional Differences and Administrative Responses* (San Francisco: Chandler Publishing Co., 1966) and Pedro Ramet, *Nationalism and Federalism in Yugoslavia, 1963–1983* (Bloomington: Indiana University Press, 1984).

25. Stephen E. Palmer and Robert R. King, *Yugoslav Communism and the Macedonian Question* (Hamden, Conn.: Shoe String Press, 1971).

26. Dennison I. Rusinow, "Yugoslavia's Muslim Nation," Universities Field Staff International (UFSI) Report, no. 8, Europe, 1982.

27. Peter Zwick, *National Communism* (Boulder, Colo.: Westview Press, 1983), p. 24.

28. *Vjesnik* (Zagreb), February 11, 1971.

29. For a detailed account, see Rusinow, *The Yugoslav Experiment*, p. 273 ff. and Ramet *Nationlism and Federation*, pp. 104–43.

30. In a recent analysis, Yugoslav authors refer to the "unrealistic assumption that the Yugoslav market was both unified and developed"; see Dragomir Vojnić, Rikard Lang, and Bozo Marendić, "The Socioeconomic Model of Socialist Self-Management," in George Macesich et al., eds., *Essays on the Yugoslav Economic Model* (Westport, Conn.: Praeger, 1989), p. 43. This analysis points out that to be unified a market must be developed, and it asserts that the market as an institution had remained underdeveloped within the framework of socialist self-management.

31. There is considerable evidence to support the conclusion that, much as John Lampe describes in terms of interwar Yugoslavia, communist Yugoslavia did not have what could be considered an integrated market. See Ivo Bićanić, "Fractured Economy" and John Burkett and Borislav Skegro, "Are Economic Fractures Widening?" in Rusinow, ed., *Yugoslavia: A Fractured Federalism*, pp. 120–55.

32. Laura D'Andrea Tyson, *The Yugoslav Economic System and Its Performance in the 1970's* (Berkeley: University of California, Institute of International Studies, 1980), p. 27.

33. Dennison I. Rusinow, "Yugoslavia and the World, 1978," *UFSI Report*, no. 43, 1978.

34. Tito's speech to the Eighth Congress of Trade Unions called for one-year terms for party presidents and secretaries in communes, republics, autonomous provinces, and at the top of the federal party. *Borba* (Belgrade), November 22, 1978.

35. This section expands on my earlier analysis, "Nation Versus Class in Yugoslavia," *Current History* (November 1987).

36. Najdan Pašić Open Letter to the LCY Presidium, *Politika* (Belgrade), September 29, 1982.

37. *Politika* (Belgrade), June 25, 1986.

38. Revised from the author's presentation on Yugoslavia between crisis and reform given to the Institut za Medjunarodni Radnicki Pokret, Belgrade, May 15, 1989.

39. D. Vojnić and M. Korošić, "Problemi Inflacije v Jugoslavija," *Ekonomiski Pregled*, 26, nos. 5–6 (1975), 241–50.

40. Rusinow, *The Yugoslav Experiment*, pp. 120–37.

41. Among the best Western analyses of this period is that of Chris Martin and Laura D'Andrea Tyson, "Can Titoism Survive Tito: Economic Problems and Policy Choices Confronting Tito's Successors," in Pedro Ramet, ed., *Yugoslavia in the 1980s* (Boulder, Colo.: Westview Press, 1985), pp. 184–200.

42. The Bosnian agro-industry that went bankrupt when its self-financing scheme of borrowing without collateral collapsed in 1987 with political repercussions that reached all the way to the Yugoslav state presidency.

43. Mikulić resignation speech, *Politika* (Belgrade), January 1, 1989.

44. M. George Zaninovich, *The Development of Socialist Yugoslavia* (Baltimore, Md.: Johns Hopkins University Press, 1968), p. 44 ff.

45. Quoted by Dennison I. Rusinow, "Yugoslavia's 1986 Party Congress: Did Anything Happen?" *UFSI Report*, no. 21 (1986): 4.

46. The similarity of some American and Yugoslav views on this issue was even more evident in the discussion at the September 4–6, 1986, international conference on Yugoslav federalism at the Wilson Center than in the subsequently published conference papers in Rusinow, ed., *Yugoslavia: A Fractured Federalism*.

47. Koštunica in Rusinow, *Yugoslavia: A Fractured Federalism*, p. 5.

48. Samuel P. Huntington, *Political Order in Changing Societies* (New Haven: Yale University Press, 1968), pp. 12–24.

49. For Croatian reservations, see *Danas* (Zagreb), April 4, 1989, pp. 7–8.

50. *Politika* (Belgrade), April 1, 1989.

51. Marković Program, *Politika* (Belgrade), January 29, 1989.

52. *The New York Times*, January 23, 1990.

53. For a much sounder academic analysis, see K. Krishna Moorthy, *After Tito What?* (New Delhi: Radiant Publishers, 1980).

54. The Marković program as presented to the federal assembly, *Borba* (Belgrade), December 19, 1989.

55. Laura D'Andrea Tyson, *The Yugoslav Economic System* concluded that, despite shocks in the international economic system, Yugoslav development throughout the 1970s was still above that of most middle-income and developing countries. For a substantially more negative assessment, see Ljubo Sirc, *The Yugoslav Economy Under Self-Management* (London: Macmillan, 1979).

56. Mikulić resignation speech, *Politika* (Belgrade), January 1, 1989.

57. *Politika* (Belgrade), December 10, 1986. For recent analysis, see Harold Lydall, *Yugoslavia in Crisis* (Oxford: Oxford University Press, 1989), p. 193ff.

58. This in turn led to increased Serbian police presence, although Western reporting of the relationship of federal, republic, and provincial security forces was confusing at best. *The New York Times*, March 25, 1990.

59. A Yugoslav parliamentary commission noted that 2,900 Albanians had been hospitalized in Kosovo complaining of lung and skin problems, but there was no evidence

of poisoning. An international team of doctors sent by Helsinki Watch, the human rights organization, reported that it found no evidence of poisoning. See *New York Times*, March 28, 1990, p. A6.

60. Statement by President of SFRY Presidency, Dr. Janez Drnovsek, to the emergency session of the federal assembly on the developments in Kosovo, February 6, 1990.

61. *The New York Times*, March 24, 1990.

62. This appears to have been the thrust of the Memorandum of the Serbian Academy of Sciences and Arts; see NIN, November 9, 1986.

63. *Tanjug* (Belgrade), March 12, 1990; FBIS, March 13, 1990.

64. *Vjesnik* (Zagreb), August 20, 1989.

65. Quoted in *Borba* (Belgrade), August 25, 1989.

66. *Christian Science Monitor*, May 16, 1989.

67. *Borba* (Belgrade), December 19, 1989.

68. Pregl, February 21, 1990.

69. Interview with Marković, *The New York Times*, March 5, 1990.

70. Pregl, February 21, 1990, statement, p. 9.

71. *Politika* (Belgrade), October 20, 1988.

72. Vojnić, Lang, and Marendić "The Socioeconomic Model," p. 12.

5

Development Through the Market in Greece: The State, Entrepreneurs, and Society

Gerasimos Augustinos

The Historical Conditioning of Underdevelopment

Greece began its existence as an independent nation-state with a legacy that reflected both the opportunities and the burdens of the Ottoman imperial world. Geography and the vicissitudes of voluntary and involuntary human movement had resulted in the dispersion and isolation of its people. The infrastructure needed to build a national economy was largely missing. Roads, port, and post facilities were in a primitive state. Banking services would take decades to develop, primarily through investment by Greeks from outside the country. Agriculture, the main productive sector of the economy, was handicapped by poor techniques, abandoned and undeveloped land, complicated and inexact legal relationships, fractionalized and insecure landholding, and a primitive distribution network that kept it localized. Industry was at the protoindustrial stage with small artisan and craft enterprises. Commercial wealth was to be found mostly outside the state frontiers among the Greek communities in the major urban centers of Europe and the Near East. The development of political life also reflected the historical conditions from which Greece emerged. Like other subject peoples who were part of the Ottoman imperial world, the Greeks had maintained limited contact with the political authorities through a few communal intermediary bodies controlled by their religious leaders and notables. Limited and distant contact through patrons became a characteristic feature of political life in the new state. A series of political relationships, linked through a group of families that established themselves socially and economically in the country, grew during the nineteenth century. Thus, political unification was achieved without social integration.

Building a national consensus was hampered by various social divisions such as those between "outsiders" (those who originated beyond the state frontiers) and "insiders" (those who came from within national territory), town versus the countryside, islanders versus mainlanders, and "old" wealth derived from the land as opposed to "new" elites that arose with the growth of urban life in private professions and public service. These divisions even affected the integrative nationalist vision for the completion of the nation's development through the instrument of the state. The *megali idea*, or the goal of enlarging the frontiers of the state to encompass "unredeemed" parts of the nation, served as the legitimizing epicenter of political culture until the end of World War I. To some Greeks the country could not effectively pursue this goal unless it first developed its social institutions and natural resources by turning to and emulating the West. Others believed that domestic development had to be subordinated to the rapid realization of the nationalist objective. Only by territorial expansion would the country's economic and political progress be fulfilled. The Greeks who espoused this view were distrustful of outsiders and saw themselves not as imitators of European ways, but as bearers of a unique folk culture embodied in the popular language and customs of the people. By the latter part of the nineteenth century, the growth of an indigenous middle class brought about the mingling of these two views as the effort to develop the country continued in the name of a national vision.[1]

The particular mode of development that Greece has undergone hinges on a few fundamental, historically conditioned, social factors. For centuries Greeks have coped with limited natural resources and an often unfriendly social environment. Security and stability in the public world have seemed possible only by relying on the closest of personal relations and trusting little to impersonal institutions. Furthermore, the dearth of favorable economic conditions in the country prompted the movement of individuals. Searching for better opportunities, Greeks in numbers have migrated from one region to another and from rural areas to urban centers. When economic prospects within the nation-state diminished, especially in the late nineteenth century and after World War II, they emigrated by the thousands to other countries on both a temporary and a permanent basis. These realities have complicated as well as facilitated the state's coordination and development of society at the national level.

Finally, in Greece corporate institutions to mediate between the individual and the state have been limited. Prior to independence the main intermediary institutions were the Orthodox Church and the local communities. Since then the essential social units for much of the modern Greek experience have been the individual and the family. The Greek national world, then, was forged around two poles of activity: individuals supported by a family structure and the state through its administrative mechanisms. The two sectors have moved along parallel courses. Interaction between the two has taken various forms, including guidance, intervention, opposition, and collaboration. Because the entrepreneurial class together with the capital it contributes has developed as much from outside as from within the country, other groups have not effectively challenged it economically or politically.[2]

From the late nineteenth century to the Great War, Greece tasted both the fruits of economic and territorial growth and the bitterness of small state limitations in the face of powerful, international political and economic forces. An ill-advised confrontation with the Ottoman Empire in 1897 ended in a humiliating defeat. National frustration over this fiasco was heightened when the country's poor financial condition led to the imposition of an International Financial Commission the following year, which continued to function during the interwar era as Greece negotiated new loans.[3]

These events only increased the growing middle class's distaste for what was seen as inept and self-serving leadership among both political leaders and the monarchy. Following the example of the Committee of Union and Progress, which organized the Young Turk revolt, a group of Greek Army officers formed a Military League in the spring of 1909, and in July they ousted the government. The leaders of the Goudi revolt were concerned mainly with perceived weaknesses in the military. They wisely withdrew from politics the following spring after agreeing that Eleftherios Venizelos form a new government and introduce reforms.

Venizelos and his political party, the *Komma Fileleftheron* or Liberal party, won a majority in parliament in the election held in 1910. Venizelos then embarked on a program of moderate reform that included a revision of the constitution, some social legislation, and a strengthened military through new equipment and training. His efforts at modernization on behalf of the nation won him support among the growing commercial and industrial interests and the general populace, which supported the irredentist goals of the *megali idea*. These modernizing measures paid off when Greece participated in the Balkan Wars of 1912–1913 against the Ottoman Empire. The new lands gained enlarged the territory and population of Greece by more than 60 percent and added fertile farming areas.

Even before the territorial and population gains of the Balkan Wars, the country had been gradually developing its export market. The production of commercial crops, including olives, currants, fruits, and tobacco, helped offset the nation's continued dependence on imported grains and stimulated the domestic market. Urban development accompanied the growth of trade. Businesses serving the state and the needs of the townspeople grew apace. Textile manufacturing, food processing, and leather working, as well as consumer industries, increased the size and diversity of urban society.

Some see in Venizelos's rise to power the ascendancy of the commercial and manufacturing class. Although the Cretan leader and his party were committed to reform, the program they undertook did not constitute a new developmental direction, nor did it dramatically affect the nation's productive capabilities.[4]

Venizelos was able to continue with his reform program until about 1915, when a growing dispute between him and King Constantine over Greece's stance in the Great War threw the country into political turmoil. By 1917 the leader of the Liberal party broke with the king and created a revolutionary government in Thessaloniki, the major city and leading port in the newly acquired territories. Although the "new" Greece supported Venizelos by and large, Constantine counted on the backing of the "old" Greece, those lands included in the state when it was created. Although Venizelos won a victory of sorts—Constantine was forced to step down under pressure from the Entente powers—political bickering continued.

Venizelos's wager on the side of the Entente powers seemed to have paid off as hostilities ended and peacemaking got under way. His supporters argued that the country could look forward to progress and prosperity by basing development on agriculture and the merchant marine. By careful planning in these two sectors, Greece might achieve much desired self-sufficiency in foodstuffs and increase needed foreign exchange. A progressive industrial and commercial policy completed the Liberals' economic proposals. Industries that survived only because of "prohibitive protectionism against foreign products and consequently are a burden on the country" ought not to be supported. The government had a responsibility to encourage industries that made use of the land's productive potential and the nation's natural resources. In true liberal fashion there was a call for lowered tariffs on manufactured goods needed by consumers whether domestically produced or imported. Yet the country might still attain a favorable trade balance because of the agricultural surpluses that would be produced and the remittances generated by the maritime industry.[5]

The dream of domestic buoyancy under the Liberal aegis foundered on the dangerous shoals of international affairs. Venizelos attempted to secure the position of the Hellenic world in Asia Minor by capitalizing on Greece's contribution to the Allied war effort. But the Greeks now faced the Turkish Nationalist forces galvanized and guided by Mustafa Kemal. In a stunning dénouement, the Greek armies were defeated, and the Turkish leader demanded an exchange of populations. In the aftermath of this tragic episode, Greece was overwhelmed by the inflow of a million and a quarter refugees. Postwar developmental possibilities for both politics and the economy were dramatically altered as a consequence.

The Interwar Era: Looking Inward, Dependent Outward

In the aftermath of the Great War and the Asia Minor debacle, self-interest dictated that Greece maintain its international ties as it strove for political security and economic growth. Increasingly, however, development was hindered as domestic crises arose and the international system destabilized. To add to its burden of coping with the great influx of refugees, Greece was in the unenviable position in the 1920s of being the only Balkan state with a trade balance deficit. Unable to produce enough to feed a greatly enlarged population, the country was forced to import large quantities of grain and foodstuffs, as well as fuel. In addition, with 336 inhabitants per square kilometer of cultivated land, its population density was about double that of the neighboring countries. Yet, already some one-third of the population lived in urban centers (5,000 or more inhabitants). Greece had no choice, therefore, but to try to develop *both* its industrial and agricultural sectors, while continuing its dependence on the international market for needed goods and capital.

Unfortunately, Greece still displayed all the characteristics of early development. The domestic market was neither very broad nor very strong. Its infrastructure, including the transportation system and the communications network, was far from adequate. Much of the agricultural sector was geared to self-sufficiency rather than the market so as to absorb as much employable labor as possible. Even then many agriculturalists did not possess adequate property to sustain a viable life on the land.

Industrial conditions were not much better. This sector was adversely affected by improperly applied state intervention. Established enterprises were protected even when the result was less efficiency and greater costs for the products. If the state was willing to regulate industry, this did not mean it provided financial support to encourage industrial development. Although the state did create an agricultural bank in 1929 to extend credit to farmers, a similar institution for industry was not established until 1954. The banks in the country were not much help at this time because of the general perception that native industry could not really compete with foreign firms. By and large, private investors preferred commercial enterprises and shipping firms where the risk was substantial, but so were the profits to be made on a short-term basis.[6]

Since the state's financial and administrative resources were inadequate to deal with the uprooted mass of newcomers, help was sought abroad. A Refugee Settlement Commission was created under the aegis of the League of Nations and began its work in Greece as an independent private organization in 1924. The commission resolved to place the refugees in new communities throughout the country and to provide as many as possible with land so that they could sustain themselves and eventually begin to earn a livelihood. Making land available to the refugees gave greater impetus to the state to carry out land reform.

Mindful that sweeping measures were required, the government in February 1923 decreed the turning over of public land for distribution and the expropriation of large private estates (except for land cultivated by the owners themselves), the houses of estate owners, and forests and manufacturing enterprises held by them. The 1917 decree setting up cooperatives to enable agriculturalists to purchase land was reinstated. Property owners were to be reimbursed at prewar land values with an increase of up to 40 percent allowed. The normal procedure for the expropriation of land, including measuring and valuing the property supervised by the courts, was set aside in favor of direct government intervention. By 1933, some 1,645 large estates, amounting to almost 7 million stremmata (1 stremma = 0.247 hectares), had been declared subject to expropriation. Of these properties a little over 4 million stremmata were distributed by that time. Land was given out by lot to propertyless agriculturalists aged twenty-one or over. Each plot was supposed to yield enough to feed a family. The amount an individual received depended on the fertility of the soil in the particular province. Properties distributed varied in size from 40 to 77 stremmata with the national average around 45.[7]

With the redistribution of land and the settlement of about half the refugees on agricultural property, the nature of the agrarian sector was defined and its benefits to the national economy were soon apparent. Much land that had not been cultivated, especially in Macedonia and Epiros, now was tilled. Smaller holdings, averaging less than 10 hectares, became predominant throughout the country. By 1928 around 28 percent of the refugees over the age of ten were engaged in agriculture, thus becoming a productive and stabilizing force in society. The refugee farmers made use of new agricultural methods and raised the amount of land under cultivation from 354,052 acres in 1923 to 622,820 acres in 1927. By 1927 three-fourths of the rural refugees were cultivating cereal grains while 14 percent raised tobacco. Their efforts helped decrease Greece's dependency on imported grains and boosted foreign earnings through the export of aromatic tobacco.[8]

The good fortune of those refugees who became agriculturalists was not unalloyed. In return for receiving land and services from their settlement, they had to compensate the state for the property and pay back the Refugee Settlement Commission for the implements and services it provided. When the commission ended its work in January 1930, it turned over to the Greek government all the promissory notes it held that were still outstanding. The state agreed to calculate what each refugee owed based on his debts to the commission and on the value of his property. This debt, totaling £9,440,377 (with currency stabilization under-taken in 1928 the drachma was fixed at 375 to the pound), was to be paid to the government with the newly founded Agricultural Bank handling the financial mat-ters.[9] The landed refugees then became debtors in their new homeland; they needed to be not just self-sufficient farmers but producers for the agricultural market.

About half the newly arrived refugees became part of the Greek urban world. Their impact on society was both profound and permanent. All the major cities experienced phenomenal population growth during the 1920s. Athens and the port of Piraeus alone accommodated almost one-quarter of all the newcomers. The strain on the state to provide housing and services was enormous. Yet, by way of putting this great burden on urban life in perspective, writers have pointed up the benefits the refugees provided to the country's economy. The newcomers from Asia Minor became a major source of skilled labor in manufacturing and commerce. Their craftsmanship in ceramics and carpet weaving added much to those industries. Such a large influx of people also greatly enlarged the consumer market of the country in the years following their arrival. Construction increased significantly as part of the effort to house the refugees.

One cannot make too much of the early experience of the refugees. On the eve of the great world economic crisis, half the male and female refugee popula-tion was unemployed. Males as a group fared better with 18 percent unemployed. While men more readily found jobs in industry and trade, women were often employed as servants, waitresses, and help in hotels. Even then numbers of Greeks migrated to Athens, attracted by the hope of an easier and more prosperous future. But the mobility of the refugees, including those in the capital, was more cir-cumscribed. At least in the first years after their coming, their lives were more dependent on the settlement policies carried out by the state.[10] The refugees did add to the growing manufacturing sector. By and large, however, they did so in the form of small, family undertakings that could not transform the country into an industrialized nation.

Whatever optimism there had been at the close of World War I about increasing trade and agriculture was tempered by the refugee problem and the need to recover from the economic toll of the long conflict. By 1927, when a liberal coalition government was formed, some political leaders were eager to create a national program that would commit the state's resources to the agriculturalists. In their view in the past the peasants had been taken advantage of by merchants, large landowners, usurers, and the state that overtaxed them. A laissez-faire economy for agriculturalists meant only misery and exploitation. What was needed was a progressive government that would intervene in a positive fashion to create the favorable institutional, technical, and market basis for the eventual attainment of agricultural self-sufficiency.[11]

The government was to aid in five areas: completing land reform, including the settling of all landless peasants and dealing with refugee debts; increasing productivity by bringing more land under cultivation and improving agricultural efficiency; supplying technical and educational assistance to help promote efficiency; establishing institutions specifically to provide credit to agriculturalists; and helping farmers increase their profits by encouraging a better distribution network and the judicious employment of protective measures.[12]

Those who supported the agricultural reform recognized that it was counterproductive in terms of rationalizing cultivation and marketing produce. But the reform's positive results were deemed to outweigh the negative impact. In any case, the large estates had not been particularly well run in the past. By owning their own land, the peasant property holders would be more committed to farming. As propertied citizens, they also would form a solid citizenry loyal to the state. Furthermore, settling families on the land was a good way to provide the large amount of labor needed to manage the country's labor-intensive crops such as vineyards, orchards, and vegetable gardens.[13]

To offset the inefficiency and weakness in the market associated with small holdings, governments in the interwar era encouraged the formation of agricultural cooperatives. It was clear from the beginning, however, that the state would oversee these organizations. In 1917, Venizelos's government created a supervisory body within the Ministry of Agriculture to watch over the development of the cooperatives. When the Agricultural Bank was created in 1929, the personnel supervising the cooperatives in the ministry were assigned to it. In the government's well-meaning attempt to keep politics out of the affairs of cooperatives, a law passed in 1930 banned political figures from serving on the governing boards of the agricultural organizations. They were also limited geographically by the stipulation that a cooperative could not encompass more than one *deme* or two neighboring communities.[14]

Less than ideal physical and climatic conditions for growing grains had led governments in the nineteenth century to protect domestic producers by imposing tariffs on imports of wheat, corn, and barley. Spurred by the insufficiency of domestic production, the government implemented even stronger measures in 1927. Tariffs on imported grains were raised yet again. Subsequently, the government funded an organization for the concentration of wheat through the National Bank. Specific collection centers for the domestic wheat crop were designated by the state, which purchased the grain at a price higher than that which was imported. Millers and warehousers agreed to buy wheat at the government-fixed price and to guarantee that the flour they produced would contain a minimum of 25 percent domestic grain. During the next three years, however, local harvests were poor, and farmers made no headway in paying off their debts to the state.[15]

Those debts were supervised by the Agricultural Bank, which had begun operating in 1930. Loans were extended to individuals and cooperatives to enable them to acquire needed items such as machinery, seed, and fertilizer. The bank also endeavored to aid farmers in marketing their products both locally and abroad. But the worldwide economic downturn was already taking its toll. In its first year of operation the bank experienced late payments on 29 percent of its loans. By 1932, the rate had climbed to 60 percent. Hopes for increasing agricultural productivity through modernization did not materialize. Little modern machinery was bought during this period, except for some of the large properties in Macedonia and Thessaly, as the small farmers continued to rely on traditional implements.[16]

With poor harvests in 1929 and 1930 and the onset of the depression, the government was forced to intervene and provide financial relief to farmers. Until this time the state had continued tapping the agricultural sector as a source of revenue. Agricultural products for export as well as goods imported for farmers were taxed. By 1932, the government abolished export taxes on products such as tobacco and cheese. The tax on livestock such as goats, sheep, and pigs was replaced by one on slaughtered animals. Cooperatives were now allowed to export their products and to import needed goods duty free.[17]

These measures were palliatives rather than remedies for the great disease that afflicted the country's peasant farmers—the financial debt incurred as part of the agrarian reform and refugee settlement. To keep financially troubled farmers from losing their land, in June 1932 the government made it more difficult to initiate legal proceedings against them. This was only temporary relief, however. In parliament some deputies called for full-scale reform and reorganization in the agricultural sector. Proposals were made to write off the debt which the refugees owed to the Resettlement Commission, lower the interest on notes for expropriated land from 8 percent to 6 percent, forgive up to half the debts owed to the National Bank, transform short-term debts owed to the Agricultural Bank into long-term obligations, waive penalties for late payments on debts, and reduce by 30 percent debts owed by farmers to private individuals. It was the authoritarian Metaxas regime in the late 1930s that eventually acted to forgive the obligations of agriculturalists.[18]

When industry began to develop in Greece after the mid-nineteenth century, the enterprises that were established, such as flour mills, textile plants, shipyards, tanneries, and mining firms, reflected the nation's natural assets. Many of these firms evolved from handicraft industries and were transformed into manufacturing establishments as capital and equipment were acquired. Later, other industries, including glass, paper, and cement factories, and sugar and cloth-making firms, were established with technologies and skilled labor from abroad.[19]

During the interwar period several factors restrained industrial progress. Even with the influx of the refugees, there was a limited consumer market for manufactured goods. The agriculturalists' standard of living made little demand on the consumer market, and they took care of many of their needs themselves. Manufactured goods were often not competitive on the international market because of the high cost of the raw materials produced locally, and so they remained oriented to the small domestic economy. The country's transport and communication infrastructure was rudimentary and insufficient for rapid growth. In addition, Greece relied very heavily on imported coal to fuel its railroad, shipping, and power industries. As with many nations attempting to industrialize at the time, Greece was seen to lack two basic assets—a skilled labor force and a ready supply of capital.[20]

Given the country's needs after World War I, public officials and administrators sought to create larger manufacturing enterprises, especially in heavy industry. A law passed in 1922 offered incentives toward this goal. There were tax breaks on net income for firms with a capital value of more than 5 million drachmas, discounts on the cost of public transportation and raw materials, tariff reductions on machinery and building materials used to create new enterprises, and state expropriation of land for industrial plants. As a result, a number of corporations were formed during the 1920s and early 1930s to take advantage of these incentives. However, most of the enterprises that were incorporated were already existing private firms, which sought to benefit from the development laws.[21] Overall, the large majority of manufacturing enterprises that operated at the time were small firms, employing fewer than five workers. Many of these were established by the Asia Minor refugees, who formed a major new supply of labor.

Because of the war and the refugee settlement, Greece's indebtedness had increased significantly. By the mid-1920s the government of the Republic had undertaken several measures to restore economic confidence. Budget reductions for a number of ministries were ordered, greater efforts were made to collect taxes more systematically, and the government raised duties on imported goods. In addition, by 1928 the drachma was stabilized against the major foreign currencies. Negotiations were undertaken with Britain in early 1927, which resulted in reducing Greece's war debts from £21,441,000 to £6,950,000 and spreading out the payments over a sixty-two-year period. Under the agreement that was reached, Britain agreed to raise its veto on external loans to Greece which it had put into effect through an accord signed in 1918.

At the end of 1927 arrangements were completed for loans from both Britain and the United States. The British authorized a reconstruction loan for £9 million, to be used equally to liquidate outstanding liabilities, strengthen a new central bank in Greece and its currency issue, and provide funds for the establishment of the refugees. In a similar fashion, the United States agreed to provide a loan of £2 million on favorable terms to be used to help settle the refugees. Both loans were under the auspices of the League of Nations. For its part, Greece agreed to establish a new bank of issue, the Bank of Greece, which, unlike the private National Bank of Greece, would serve as the country's central banking institution. It centralized the money transactions of the state and limited its loans to state institutions. The loans were a welcome financial boost to the country, though the government's fiscal restraint had an adverse impact on consumers and retailers.[22]

The other part of the government's "strategy" to bolster the country's economic growth was to undertake a series of major public works projects. The "new" territories of Macedonia promised wealth and productivity if the land was developed. By the late 1920s, the government had contracted with several foreign firms to improve the physical environment. The major rivers—Axios (Vardar), Struma, and Aliakmon—were to be controlled to prevent flooding, and the marshy areas around them were to be drained and opened up to farming. Some 135,000 acres were to become cultivable, and another 150,000 would be protected from floods once work on the Axios was completed. The Struma project was to provide another 200,000 acres of protected land in the Serres and Drama plains. A road network, sanitation, and water works were also envisioned. Work proceeded gradually because the cost was impossible to bear all at one time, and several loans were negotiated by the government. These large projects provided work for numbers of the country's unemployed and underemployed population. They also demanded a major commitment by the state to finance economic growth by relying on foreign credits.[23]

In the interwar period agricultural and industrial productivity did not expand sufficiently to produce a favorable trade balance for Greece. Even though the value of industrial production rose by 30 percent in the decade after 1921, and industry contributed some 18 percent of national income and employed 15 percent of the total working population by the eve of World War II, this sector was constrained by the inhibiting factors noted above. Although valuable agricultural exports, especially tobacco, helped the country's balance of trade, Greece continued to import about twice the value in goods and foodstuffs (flour and wheat accounted for a quarter of these) as it exported. To offset the unfavorable trade balance the nation counted on income from its merchant marine, the remittances of emigrants, funds provided by loans to settle the refugees, and growing tourism. These sources could not resolve the perennial trade deficit, however.[24]

The onset of the Great Depression took its toll on the country. Invisible revenues fell dramatically as the world economy faltered. Remittances by emigrants in 1933 amounted to only a third of what they were just three years before. Shipping also suffered from the economic crisis. For some time the industry had been undergoing significant changes. The total number of vessels increased during the interwar era. Sail gave way to steam as the size of the ships grew. A plethora of shipping companies carried on both an international and a coastal trade, hauling cargo and passengers. From Piraeus ships sailed to 153 places and represented 118 lines in 1927. However, the growth of economic nationalism brought a contraction in the Greek merchant marine and shipping communities along the Black Sea and the Danube.

Tourism was still an infant industry and could make only limited contributions to Greek revenues. In the early 1920s, the tourist trade suffered because of the political instability and the great refugee inflow. It was not until 1929 that the Greek Tourist Association was organized as a coordinating agency for all state and private services relating to tourism, such as hotels, tourist offices, and railroads. The government estimated that by 1930 the country was earning about £1 million from tourism. In the early 1930s many foreigners were stopping off on their way to Egypt, apparently attracted by the depreciating drachma. Because of the depression, the director of the Tourist Organization could only "propose" the building of "modern hotels in Athens, Salonica and in some of the provinces and in the archaeological districts." In any event it was left to the private sector to actually undertake any such projects.[25]

With state revenues down appreciably, the government was forced into a partial default on the public debt in April 1932. That same month Greece abandoned the gold standard following the example of Britain, which had done so the previous September. As might be expected, when the country went off the gold standard, the drachma began to depreciate rapidly. To minimize the financial consequences of these actions, the government at the same time passed laws that applied to foreign exchange. By a decree on April 26, 1932, the export of foreign exchange was to be restricted and carefully controlled. On July 29, a further law arbitrarily converted all deposits of foreign exchange in Greek banks into drachmas. However, the International Financial Commission continued to collect duties for the service of loans that it controlled.[26]

Faced with a financial crisis, the government attempted to deal with the economic ills besetting the country. An effort was made to reduce public spending. Expenditures for public works projects were scaled back considerably by 1933. In a stopgap measure, the government temporarily suspended payments on the public debt, pending negotiations with the bondholders. In a more positive vein, the government endeavored to increase state revenues. New taxes were instituted on tobacco and other items that already were directly assessed. An innovation in revenue gathering was the introduction of a turnover tax. A levy of 1.5 percent was placed on the value of imported goods and manufacturers' sales, while banks and other financial institutions were required to pay 0.5 percent on their gross earnings.[27]

A combination of negative and positive stimuli was applied to the economy in an effort at national salvation. In 1932 the importation of goods was placed under a quota system. Using the preceding three years as a guideline, importers were given specific allocations. For those who dealt in necessary goods, the amount they could import was as high as 95 percent. Importers of luxury items and products that competed with those manufactured locally were allowed only 20 percent of the quantities they had previously brought in. Needed raw materials such as wool, cotton, and crude oils were not affected. Conversely, the government worked to increase domestic production and exports. Since the country still was not self-sufficient in foodstuffs, an attempt was made to stimulate wheat production through the imposition of protective duties, which were borne by consumers. As for exports, the government recognized that its main products—tobacco, currants, oil, wines, and figs—were luxury goods. To deal with this drawback, the government was willing to negotiate barter and compensation agreements with countries as politically and economically diverse as Germany, the USSR, Sweden, Turkey, Switzerland, and France.[28]

In the midst of the depression (1934), a national system of social security— IKA (Idryma Koinonikon Asfaliseon)—was created to provide protection to workers, and to a lesser degree their dependents, for sickness, maternity, disability, unemployment, and old age. All salaried employees and wage earners were required to contribute, and the program was funded entirely by contributions from their employers. Although the program was established at a time when unemployment had started to decline somewhat, the upward trend resumed again by 1937. In the early 1930s, there were over 200,000 officially unemployed persons in the trades and manufacturing. The figure dropped to less than 100,000 in 1936 but climbed steadily afterward, reaching half a million by the start of World War II. This does not take into account the underemployment in the country's agricultural sector.

By the end of the 1930s, the liberal vision of development, embodied in parliamentary government and the competitive international market had proven untenable. Agriculturalists still made up the largest portion of the labor force, yet the state could not hope to meet the population's basic nutritional needs. Greece remained in a weak position in the matter of trade and foreign investment. Whatever industrial growth there was had foundered in the Great Depression. Moreover, it had not brought about the needed sectoral restructuring in the economy. Finally, the bitterness and divisions in political life had opened the way for authoritarian rule under Metaxas, supported by the now returned monarch, George II.[29]

War, Resistance, and Recovery: Challenge for Development

After Greece was defeated by the Axis powers in April 1941, the occupation that followed defeat brought unparalleled dislocation and destruction to the nation's society and economy. The price of basic comestibles increased enormously as the production of these goods fell precipitously. The figures in Table 5.1 attest to the growing crisis in the country because of inflation. During these difficult years the Bank of Greece estimated that wheat production in the country, excluding eastern Macedonia and western Thrace, fell to approximately 390,000

Table 5.1
Prices of Goods (Drachmas)

Commodity	1938-39	Oct. 41	May 42	Dec. 42	Feb. 43
Bread (kg)	9	500	3,000	7,000	5,000
Butter	150	--	7,500	45,000	45,000
Dry beans	20-24	550	4,200	8,000	
Olive oil	46	800	4,500	9,500	
Sugar	21	1,000	6,000	13,000	

Source: Xydis, 16.

tons a year on average compared to 668,000 tons in the period just before World War II. Olive oil production dropped to 89,000 tons in 1941 and to 83,000 in the two years following from a prewar average of 129,000 tons. The amount of butter produced in 1946 was only 48 percent of that in 1938. Tobacco cultivation came to only 3,900 tons in 1942 and 9,000 tons in 1943 and 1944, as land was left idle or used to grow other more needed crops.[30] For the Greeks the economic difficulties resulting from the scissors effect on prices and production were compounded by the problem of distribution. By November 1941 the Axis powers instituted a system of barter between the various zones of occupation. Within the various zones strict prohibitions were placed on the movement of goods, and foodstuffs were forbidden to be transported from rural to urban areas. This allowed the occupiers to requisition goods as they needed them.[31]

These conditions produced great hardship among the people. In the capital, in particular, they eventually resulted in starvation as the Germans failed to take necessary measures to relieve the food shortages. The war years brought a drastic decline in the general standard of living. Not until November 1941 were the first measures taken to make adjustments to the worsening financial position of salaried employees. To cope with the inflationary spiral of prices, workers received not only a 50 percent raise in wages but also were given their monthly salary every twenty days. By the summer of 1942 governmental employees began receiving cost-of-living allowances, which varied from 150 percent to 300 percent of their base pay, in inverse proportion to their salaries. When this was deemed inadequate to keep up with inflation, the collaborationist government began giving out food as well. By the fall of 1943 public employees were receiving eighty times their prewar wages, private workers were getting up to one hundred times their pay, while pensioners only saw their income go up by a multiple of forty. Yet the prices of goods had risen one thousand times from their prewar level. Thus, at best, the people's standard of living was about one-half of that before the war, while many were much worse off.[32]

Just as significant for the nation was the demographic toll of the war and the civil war that followed. Before World War II Greece had a population rate of increase of 13.7 per thousand. In 1940 the population of the country was 7,344,850. It was estimated to be 7,257,000 in 1946 as civil war tore at the nation. By 1951 the figure has risen to only 7,511,321. In addition to the falling rate of population increase, there was a significant loss of life in the 1940s because of the world war and the civil war. During this terrible era other demographically important developments occurred. In the interwar period the rural population decreased by only 2.1 percent. Between 1940 and 1951, however, the rate rose to 4.9 percent.[33]

After the Axis forces left and the country was liberated, villagers who had fled their homes began to return in 1945. When fighting between the leftist forces and the government troops started in 1946, an even more dramatic movement of population occurred. Much of the fighting took place in the northern provinces of Epiros and Macedonia. Tens of thousands of people left their villages in the mountains for the relative safety of the cities in the plains below, where they became refugees in their own country. The Greek National Army promoted this flow of humanity through the tactic of evacuating people from areas of leftist strength to deny the enemy support. By 1949, when the fighting ended, more than half a million people had been displaced either willingly or by government order. In addition, close to 50,000 people, mostly from the countryside, went into the mountains to fight with the communists. Many were joined by their families, so that by war's end some 150,000 people either were dead or had fled across the border to communist states.[34]

The social consequences of these developments were far-reaching and to a large extent permanent. Villagers were displaced from their homes and moved to towns controlled by the government, where they had to adjust to new ways. Since they were away from their land, they were forced to depend on the government for their subsistence. By leaving their villages much land went uncultivated, forcing the national authorities to depend on outside aid to provide for the peoples' basic needs. During their stay in the provincial cities, the displaced persons made the best of things by finding jobs where they could. Many became accustomed to the urban scene with its greater amenities and decided not to return to their often isolated villages. Others found neither place satisfying and chose instead to emigrate or to migrate to the capital in search of a better life. The factors that were to dramatically alter society in the late 1950s and 1960s were already present.[35]

With the liberation of the country, a government of national unity, headed by the Venizelist politician George Papandreou, arrived in Athens on October 18, 1944. Recognized by King George II and his hosts, the British, the government gave the appearance rather than the reality of a legitimate national regime. But the real issue was not the particular political makeup of the government, something that had preoccupied leaders during the war. Rather, it was whether the political culture that had functioned before the war could meet and survive the radical challenge in a disrupted society. This was resolved only after four years of bitter political and military struggle with the defeat of the communists by the fall of 1949.

With inflation out of hand and the need to distribute supplies to the population, the Papandreou government initiated a number of measures, which were mostly temporary. Coal shipments brought in by the Allies were given to the coal importer's cooperative to distribute. Workers were to help manage some industrial firms in Athens, such as textile mills and small shipyards. In an effort to coordinate economic policies and minimize political influence on long-term planning, the government attempted to vest responsibility in a small ministerial committee. To combat inflation a new drachma, with much greater value against the old currency, was introduced, and gold was allowed to circulate as a measure of confidence in the new drachma. Attempts were made to protect industrial workers against layoffs, and there was talk of imposing a war profits tax on industrialists who benefited from the occupation. The latter proposal was not acted on as the Papandreou government collapsed in the face of the crisis in the capital in December 1944.[36]

There was no lack of ideas for the recovery of the economy. On the left, the communists called for reorganizing the economy through nationalization and a greater role for workers through unions and cooperatives. Ultimately, the very basis of the economy was to be changed by turning to heavy industry. They believed the economic transformation of the country was feasible because it possessed favorable technical conditions and the basic resources for key industries such as iron and steel, chemicals, aluminum, and electric power. The hope was that society and political life would be restructured in the process and that Greece would gain its independence from foreign financial and economic markets, while accumulating needed wealth domestically. While the leftists believed their economic ideas were realistic, the political realities were something else. Their ideas were not effective in meeting the war-torn country's short-term problems, and the governments of Greece from 1945 on did not turn to them.[37]

Instead of structural change in society and the economy, as the left desired, the immediate postwar governments pursued policies along more traditional lines that were also acceptable to Britain, the most influential power in Greece at the time. In January 1946 the government of Emmanuel Tsouderos, the Venizelist who favored political reform, obtained a loan from Britain. In return, Greece agreed to foreign financial intervention. The International Financial Commission, which had existed since 1898, was abolished. It was replaced by the Currency Control Commission, whose British and American members could veto any monetary policy proposed by the Greek government or the banks. The Tsouderos government's attempt to use state authority to protect industrial workers proved ineffective.[38]

The uneasy truce between the left and the right fell apart in the spring of 1946 as the first elections since the Metaxas regime brought the rightist People's party to power in March. By the summer, the "Third Round" had commenced as leftist forces attacked government outposts.

Intervention, Stability, and the State

When the responsibility for supplying economic and military aid to Greece shifted from Britain to the United States in the spring of 1947, a new era commenced. With it developmental policies and practices that Greek governments had already attempted earlier were revived and strengthened. American military and economic intervention beginning with the Truman Doctrine greatly influenced several vital developments in the next five years. The civil war that now wracked the country was decided in favor of the government forces. Economic recovery picked up as American aid stimulated both agriculture and industry in the country. Many villagers who were displaced from their homes found employment on public works projects and were exposed to new ways. Finally, after the left was crushed in 1949, political stability was eventually established when General Alexander Papagos, leader of the Greek Rally, became head of the government at the end of 1952.

Aid from the United States was conditioned on Greece accepting American oversight and expertise, which was formalized in an agreement signed in June 1947. The Greek government thereby acknowledged that it was unable to administer the country during such difficult times. But the state's interventionist role in the economy was soon revived, and with it the entrepreneurial class came to realize that this could be to its benefit. By the late 1940s, Greece had committed itself to a "market economy, with a heavy state intervention under the tutelage of the sole foreign lender, the U.S. Government."[39]

The American mission to Greece, AMAG, arrived in the summer of 1947, and supplies soon followed. With Greece eligible for aid under the Marshall Plan the next year, American advisers began to think in terms of more than the rehabilitation of the country. The American mission hoped to promote the maximum possible development by obtaining the maximum possible credits from the U.S. Congress and setting up a four-year plan similar to plans devised for other Western European states. However, fighting in Greece prevented any real economic development for almost two years, and it took second place to the military mission. With so much of the population displaced and living as refugees by 1949, the United States provided aid and, as part of the resettlement program to get people back to their homes, housing materials, farm equipment and seeds, and livestock were made available.[40]

In the aftermath of the civil war, the country's economy was in dire circumstances. Public finances, credit, and the nation's balance-of-payments deficit were all in a serious condition. More important, the production of necessary foodstuffs was inadequate. In April 1950 the government published a plan to address the country's long-term problems. It called for the rehabilitation of the monetary and credit system, managing the balance-of-payments deficit, fully developing the nation's natural resources, increasing employment, and raising the standard of living. The state's most notable efforts toward promoting recovery were made in the first two areas.[41]

The bulk of American economic aid was appropriated between the fiscal years of 1947 and 1951. Planning and administration were carried out by U.S. experts assigned to work with the government of Greece, a situation accepted by the host nation because of the exceptional conditions. Funding and contracts were handled through the Greek state agencies. The Ministry of Coordination was created at this time expressly to cooperate with the American mission in supervising the investment program.[42]

With the defeat of the communist forces, the American mission saw an opportunity to promote capital projects that would enhance Greece's long-term industrial development. The country was energy poor in the production and consumption of power by European standards. Consumption per capita in 1951 was one-eighteenth that of Norway. At the time almost 80 percent of the electricity produced was for the Athens–Piraeus area. The American mission recommended a series of electric-generating plants, mostly hydroelectric and some lignite powered, to be built throughout the country. Facilities were created in Macedonia, Epiros, Euboea, the Peloponnesos, and eventually Thessaly. Because of a cut in U.S. aid only about one-half the proposed generating capacity was actually built. By the early 1950s the power grid in the north was connected with that in the south and put under the Public Power Corporation (DEI).[43]

Public projects like road building continued to be carried out with American aid from 1948 until the early 1950s. In addition, the Greek government began planning major reclamation and irrigation projects that eventually added several hundred thousand acres of arable land. Besides strengthening the country's economic infrastructure, these projects enabled the government to provide employment for thousands. Supported by American economic and military aid, the projects enabled the government to play a greater role in the countryside. Whether these methods helped keep the villagers on the land or induced greater movement is debatable.[44]

With the United States pumping millions of dollars into Greece, economic recovery proceeded into the 1950s, but it was founded on controls and constraints exercised by both the Americans and the Greek government. The rationing and controls on goods in effect during the war were continued through the civil war. Some easing did occur eventually, but it only fueled inflation and benefited just a few. The state tried to protect the domestic economy and kept the drachma higher than its real value against other currencies. An aggravating and seemingly unending state budget deficit was covered in part by U.S. aid. When American economic aid was curtailed beginning with the 1951–1952 fiscal year, new measures from the government were needed.[45]

In the spring of 1953 the Papagos government undertook a long-needed devaluation, setting the drachma at 30,000 to the dollar (later the 1,000 was dropped), a 50 percent reduction in value. Intended to promote stability in the currency and the prices of goods, the measure only fueled inflation as the productive capacity of the country could not yet meet domestic demand or compete on the foreign markets. With the approval of the U.S. advisers, the government also attempted to attract investments from abroad. In November 1953, an investment law was passed that granted privileges for the importation of capital as well as machinery, materials, and technology. The law guaranteed the repatriation of capital, on a fixed annual percentage, for approved projects and offered inducements to Greek shipowners if they re-registered their vessels under the Greek flag. State approval through the Ministry of Coordination was required for the importation of capital, however. Over the next few years some German and French capital was secured for large projects, while U.S. investors indicated their interest in hotels, mining operations, and industrial projects. Even so, foreigners remained concerned about the stability of the drachma and protection against future increases in tax rates.[46]

The prescription for Greece's postwar development, as summed up by a British official, echoed the view espoused by Greeks after the First World War. "As a predominantly agricultural, shipping and trading economy, Greece has the strongest possible interest in open-door commercial policies and the free flow of international trade."[47] In the early 1950s, the country attempted to follow this prescription by easing controls on the export trade and aligning its economy with the international market by joining several transnational organizations. Greece became a member of the Economic Commission for Europe, the International Labor Organization, and the European Payments Union. It also participated in the General Agreement on Tariffs and Trade, but only by requesting special consideration as a developing nation. Its entry into NATO brought benefits through common infrastructure projects in the country.

Greece's trade pattern remained similar to that in the interwar era in the types of goods exported and imported, as well as in a continuing trade deficit. Tobacco, which had represented 40 to 50 percent of the total value of exports before World War II, regained its importance, accounting for 42 percent of the total by 1955. Traditionally valuable dried fruit export crops like currants and sultanas, which were declining in importance, were replaced by new lines of products such as fresh grapes and citrus fruits. Textiles, chemicals, and cement became increasingly valuable exports. While Greece reduced its dependence on imported wheat, it still relied on the foreign market for light and heavy manufactures, iron, and textiles. There was also a growing reliance on petroleum, which replaced coal as the main imported fuel.[48]

The important role of trade notwithstanding, agriculture continued to be the main economic sector in terms of national income generated and the number of persons employed. In addition, at that time, industry was hampered by difficulties in obtaining raw materials, fuels, and power, while manufactured goods were deemed noncompetitive on the world market. American advisers in the early 1950s, therefore, emphasized aid to agriculture because it promised a greater return on investment.

Agricultural development strategy rested on two premises. Until the Second World War agriculture was geared to the production of specialized goods such as tobacco, raisins, and olives for the export market while needed grain was imported. This approach now seemed flawed, for it assumed a dependency on trade in semiluxury goods and vulnerability in basic foodstuffs. Much as the government had attempted to do just before the war, an effort was made to increase domestic production in food supplies and thus decrease the country's dependency on imported grains. In addition, in the long run it seemed sensible to expand and diversify the agricultural production of needed goods such as meat and dairy products, olives, vegetables, and fruits. Both aspects of the agricultural strategy required improving the arable land and strengthening technical development. American agricultural aid, therefore, emphasized providing advice through technical agents and supplying production-raising materials like fertilizers, livestock, and improved seeds.[49]

In certain ways the agricultural strategy succeeded by the mid-1950s. Large-scale land reclamation in the river valleys of Macedonia, Thrace, and Thessaly significantly enlarged the wheat-growing area. This, coupled with increased irrigation and mechanization, the greater use of fertilizers, and improved transport facilities enabled farmers to double the total crop output in 1954 from the average of the mid- to late 1930s. By 1950 the prewar annual wheat crop average of 800,000 tons was surpassed and continued to rise in the next few years. But since the consumption of bread was very high, amounting to 250 pounds per person a year and providing half the calories in the Greek diet, the country still was not self-sufficient. As for tobacco, by the mid-1950s the amount of acreage devoted to this crop and the quantity produced had exceeded those of the best prewar years.[50]

Behind the impressive production statistics loomed disconcerting social and economic realities. Agriculture remained the least prosperous sector in the nation. Although 60 percent of the working population was engaged in agriculture in 1954, it produced only a little over one-third the net national income. Cultivation was still overwhelmingly in the hands of the peasant farmers. Small farms were the norm, and nearly 90 percent of agricultural holdings were less than 5 hectares. The peasants managed to survive by joining cooperatives through which they obtained needed supplies and sold their crops. To acquire the new technology, machines, livestock, and fertilizers, the farmers, individually and as members of cooperatives, relied on the Agricultural Bank for loans, thus continuing their indebtedness.[51]

Perhaps most problematical of all was the shifting labor situation on the land. Until the mid-1950s, it was still possible to speak of a labor surplus in agriculture amounting to 2 to 3 percent of the workforce or about 60,000 to 90,000 persons. But the exodus from the countryside into the cities surged in the late 1950s and 1960s. This, combined with an increase in the production of labor-intensive crops like cotton, fruits, and vegetables, a growth in acreage under cultivation, and larger crop yields requiring more workers, turned the agricultural labor surplus into a shortage.[52] The government's role in these significant social shifts remained largely passive.

Tangible as the benefits of economic aid to agriculture were, there was a need to strengthen and enlarge the industrial sector. Yet both Greeks and the U.S.

advisers were unwilling to alter the private basis of the economy. Aid for public works was channeled through the Greek state apparatus, which supervised the projects. Capital for businesses was handled by the Economic Development Finance Organization (EDFO). Since most manufacturing was in the Athens area, the capital was favored. The efficacy, value, and functioning of the loan program generated mixed reviews. Some businessmen delayed repaying them and used their own capital in other ways, which did not benefit their firms. Many recipients of loans, however, complained that they were required to pay them back in dollar equivalents and at current prices, putting them in financial difficulty. Because so many delayed making payments and the loans went into default, monies dried up, and the EDFO did not have the capital to make new loans.[53]

Aid to businesses did have a salutary effect as the figures in Table 5.2 indicate. Textiles provided 30 percent of industrial output in 1954, with chemicals and foodstuffs following closely behind. But growth began to slow after the mid-1950s, owing in part to the high cost of credit which made industrial production expensive. In addition, local firms were facing increased competition from imported goods. The Papagos government attempted to increase the competitiveness of Greek firms by exposing them to the demands of the international market. However, textile mill owners and other manufacturers demanded higher tariffs. When Constantine Karamanlis became premier upon the death of Papagos in 1955, the government reverted to the traditional policy of protection.

The Greek merchant marine, which suffered devastating losses in the war, made a recovery and again became a pillar of the economy. By the mid-1950s shipping was providing $28 million in invisible receipts and employing more than 35,000 sailors. Because of the rapid increase in the Greek-owned and -registered merchant fleet, support facilities were needed. Several shipping magnates undertook to build or reconstruct shipyards at Skaramanga, Suda Bay, and Syros to repair and manufacture vessels. About one-third of the funds for these projects were to be furnished by the EDFO.[54]

Table 5.2
Industrial Production Index (1939 = 100)

	1950	1954
Textiles	107	149
Chemicals	90	160
Foodstuffs	107	152
Metallurgy	79	194
Building Materials	100	232

Source: Munkman, 149.

American aid to Greece helped the country rebuild its economic infrastructure. After 1952, material support from the United States lessened significantly, but the close material ties between the two countries continued. With the emergence of a bipolar world, Greece was seen as necessary to the American-sponsored, Western European military alliance system. Even without the burden of expanded military preparedness, Greece's state budget was running in the red. Therefore, to support the state budget the government continued to depend on the United States for grants, arguing that this was the only way it could continue to shoulder its military responsibility in the alliance.

Where did the Greek economy stand by the end of the 1950s? After an impressive spurt in the early 1950s, industrial growth settled in at around 5 percent a year. There was a sectoral shift in the gross domestic product as agriculture's share dropped from a pre-World War II high of almost 40 percent to around 30 percent. Conversely, the share of manufactures in the GDP rose to just under 20 percent. But these changes did not reflect a transformation to an industrialized society. Most of the business investment went into housing construction, transport, and communications enterprises. Investment in manufacturing fell from 20 percent of the gross total in 1950 to about 8 percent in 1960.[55] Manufacturing could not absorb the growing tide of migrants to the cities from the countryside. The result was urban underemployment and a growing petit bourgeois class. Greece recovered during the 1950s, but without a major restructuring of the economy or the state addressing the long-term developmental issues stemming from conditions in the countryside.

Planned Development and Unplanned Developments

With the postwar recovery, Greece had committed itself to a system "founded on free enterprise and trade with the rest of the world."[56] It was an economy that some associated with an underdeveloped country characterized by "the predominance of agriculture, low real income per capita as a result of a fundamental disequilibrium between population and resource development, underemployment of capital assets, inferior technology and dependence on a few highly specialized farm products for foreign trade."[57] How then was Greece to be transformed into a modern, economically advanced nation? From the experience of the late 1940s and 1950s, government officials thought in terms of a rational, well-conceived long-term plan, prepared and implemented by the public sector to promote the rapid industrial growth needed for modernization

In the spring of 1960, the Ministry of Coordination unveiled its five-year (1960–1964) economic development program. The plan called for greater public investment to aid industry, restructuring agriculture to make it more productive and competitive, encouraging capital formation, providing more technical education, promoting regional development, and enhancing the country's infrastructure. At this time the Industrial Development Corporation (OVA), later renamed the Hellenic Industrial Development Bank (ETVA), was created. Despite the carefully delineated areas of activity in the plan, there was a lack of specific policy analysis in implementing it, with only a small staff to work on the program.[58]

It was clear from the beginning that no matter how detailed and technically advanced the planning became, leading circles in government and finance were opposed to the state taking a directing or controlling role in the economy. Their strategy, which accommodated governmental planning, was to attract foreign financial and productive investment through monetary stability, to build up the industrial sector, thereby dealing with the problems of under- and unemployment in the country, to promote exports by supporting the most productive enterprises, and to force inefficient firms to become competitive or face elimination.

The pivotal factor in this scheme, for both domestic and foreign goals, was the maintenance of monetary stability. A start had been made in 1953 with the devaluation of the drachma. It was hoped that devaluation would stimulate industrial growth and increase exports, while domestic prices would remain stable. If aggregate demand was balanced against the productive capacity of the economy, inflation could be avoided and confidence ensured. Another objective was to promote savings, which would provide needed investment capital for the private sector. To encourage savings, interest on savings deposits was raised in 1956. Maintaining monetary stability was seen as promoting foreign capital inflow and aiding the attainment of an acceptable balance-of-payments equilibrium. There was even a social benefit to following this policy. The "weaker economic classes (farmers, workers, wage earners)" could experience a "continued and permanent rise in their real incomes."[59] By the mid-1960s, however, it was clear that the relative stability in prices had not greatly benefited the country's exports, although invisible income and capital imports had increased significantly.[60]

Greek economists and financial administrators in the 1960s hoped for a breakthrough to an industrially developed society. The private sector was to be the driving force in achieving this transformation. "In a free democratic economy, the organization, modernization and expansion of production should be chiefly on private initiative."[61] That initiative was to emanate mainly from the industrial sector. Government planners recognized the problem behind this policy, however. In the early 1960s, industrial goods contributed only 3 percent of the total value of the country's exports. The cause was identified as government protection of industry, which allowed it to remain noncompetitive. The remedy was to open up the country to the foreign market and allow more competition for manufactured goods. The Karamanlis government indicated its serious intentions by seeking associate membership in the European Economic Community in 1961.[62]

To achieve the needed breakthrough, the state was to nurture industrial development rather than direct it. Foreign investment in capital and enterprises was to be encouraged. Exports would be stimulated by allowing Greek manufacturing firms to deduct more of their gross earnings from taxable income. Long-term loans were to be available through the Industrial Development Corporation. The state would do its part by continuing to support large public works projects such as land reclamation and the construction of power plants. Rates for public services

such as transportation and utilities were to be reduced for export-oriented industries. Industrial development in the country needed to be rationalized by creating specific zones to maximize investment and resources. Modern industry needed
skilled labor and effective public sector support. The state would supply both
by improving educational facilities and increasing the efficiency of the civil service through training.[63]

Despite the planning, neither the state nor the private sector fulfilled its assigned
task. Private investment in industry did not rise sufficiently to bring about the
desired rapid development. Manufacturing was increasingly geared to consumer
goods rather than intermediate and capital goods industries. Scores of new entrepreneurs, primarily from merchant and craft families, embarked on industrial
ventures. Yet the traditional pattern in manufacturing continued. The overwhelming majority of industrial firms, employing a majority of the workers, remained
small, individually owned businesses with fewer than nine workers (see Table
5.3). Geographically rationalized development ("decentralization") failed to
materialize, as most industry remained centered in the Athens area, while
Thessaloniki and Patras experienced some growth. For its part, the state did not
come through with sufficient investment in support sectors such as education,
and its financial backing of the private sector was not selective enough to induce
the hoped for structural changes in industry. Most aggravating of all, the balance-
of-payments deficit grew as demand for imported consumer goods increased.[64]

At the time the groundwork for the technocratic apparatus to developmental
planning was being laid. With funds from the United States and the Greek government, the Center for Planning and Economic Research (KEPE) was established.
Andreas Papandreou became its director. He quickly set the tone of the Center's
work by addressing the issue of whether the economy should be planned or function as a decentralized, market system. For Papandreou "the question is *not*, to
Plan or not to Plan; it is How to Plan." His professional experience and political
temperament prompted Papandreou to note two broad "universal imperfections"

Table 5.3
Industrial Firms by Employment Size and Number Employed

No. Persons Emp.	1970	1980	No. Empl. 1980
1-4	106,190	108,648	209,554
5-9	9,169	10,910	64,896
10-19	3,193	4,602	56,020
20-29	1,076	1,331	31,293
30-49	744	1,118	42,096
50-over	897	1,500	254,183

Source: Adapted from Annual Industrial Survey for the Year 1970,
Annual Industrial Survey for the Year 1980.

that all less developed countries faced. They had to confront the influence of "external economics" and the exploitation that was associated with it. In addition, the need to manage their nation's resources on a large scale and in a relatively short time posed problems of efficacy in market-type economies.[65]

Since Greece had begun its association with the Common Market, looking to full membership in a couple of decades, Papandreou argued that the country needed to accomplish several basic objectives during that time. The rate of economic growth had to equal or improve on that of the 1950s. Resources had to be redistributed on a sectoral basis in order to improve the share that manufacturing held in the total economy. To accomplish this the economy had to become more efficient and competitive. All "arbitrary interference of government activity must give way to rational control and planned promotional activity, while the market mechanism is given a freer hand (where appropriate) in the process of resource allocation." The country's social needs were addressed in the demand that unemployment be reduced, especially in the countryside, and the standard of living raised so that personal and regional income inequalities could be ameliorated. The formulation of public policies, in Papandreou's thinking, needed to be based on efficiency, market competitiveness, and rational public management and to embody social considerations in resource allocation. With the electoral victory of George Papandreou in 1964, KEPE was poised to play a leading role in the formulation of economic policies.[66]

Behind the imperative that there be rapid economic growth and a sectoral restructuring toward manufacturing and industry lay the long-standing problem of rural labor. In the early 1960s more than half the country's working population was engaged in agriculture. But it was not simply a matter of excess numbers. As Greece turned its economy more toward the international market, the movement of labor would be an increasingly significant factor. With a declining birth rate and a death rate that had reached its lowest point, the labor supply was certain to be affected and, in turn, would affect industrialization plans. In addition, given the nature of Greece's agricultural economy, which was labor intensive for only part of the year, seasonal fluctuations in worker demand was a problem.[67]

Several planning solutions were broached to deal with these issues. One suggestion was to smooth out the peaks and valleys in seasonal labor through mechanization, multiple crops, and employment of people already in the countryside, who were not regularly involved in farming at times of peak labor demand. Another idea was to create nonagrarian employment opportunities in the countryside such as the handicraft industry and food processing plants. This offered a triple benefit. Rural workers could remain in the countryside in the number that was needed, they would find employment that supplemented and supported the rural economy, and regional development would be enhanced.[68]

Rather than follow a state-sponsored solution, the people in the countryside dealt with their problems in their own way. A longstanding lack of employment opportunities combined with a booming labor market in Europe, especially West Germany, and a rising standard of living in the cities to produce a major flow from the least developed rural provinces to the capital and abroad (see Table 5.4).

Table 5.4
Emigration by Country of Destination (thousands)

Country	1955-59	1960-64	1965-69	1970-74	1975-76
FRG	7,964	240,176	215,443	153,117	14,167
Australia	32,848	57,154	59,371	23,062	2,168
USA	24,083	18,946	49,308	38,757	8,747
Canada	21,003	20,857	27,041	13,983	2,875
Belgium	15,041	10,607	2,005	1,191	429
Italy	5,896	9,235	8,143	3,076	2,223

Source: Adapted from The Population of Greece in the Second Half of the 20th Century.

Emigration produced both unfavorable consequences and positive results. To begin with, the country was losing its healthier and more active population. Those aged fifteen to forty-five years accounted for 85 percent of the emigrants. The outflow from the provinces created a human resource shortage, which was considered detrimental to the development of the economy. With the birth rate declining, emigration was bound to have a serious impact on the country's demographic makeup. The loss of the younger, reproductive population could seriously affect the continued regeneration of the nation and put regions important to national interests, like Thrace and the Aegean islands, at risk.[69]

Nevertheless, emigration took care of underutilized labor. As the government knew, the emigrants substantially aided the country's perennial balance-of-payments deficit by their remittances. And since they were leaving for developed countries, where they gained valuable training and experience, it was assumed that the nation would soon have a pool of skilled labor once the emigrants returned. Because the government was not able to deal with the conditions that promoted emigration, it sanctioned the movement and sought to manage and gain benefits from it.[70]

The assumptions and projections of the planners regarding emigration were only partly realized (see Table 5.5). Many who experienced the trials and uprooting of *xeniteia*, foreign journeying, did not return home like Odysseus. Those who were repatriated did not necessarily fulfill the roles expected of them. Generally, the returnees did not become a major new source of capital for industrial development. Many with factory experience abroad did not pursue similar work when they returned. Instead, they invested their hard-earned wealth in small enterprises and real estate, thereby enlarging the middle and lower middle classes. Expectations and fears about the influx of a class-conscious proletariat, ready to alter the political and social dynamics of Greece, failed to materialize.

Table 5.5
Migrants Returning to Greece (thousands)

Country	W.Germany	Australia	USA	Canada
1968	8,867	2,322	967	636
1969	9,093	2,025	1,500	807
1970	11,553	3,165	1,963	1,035
1971	11,803	4,165	1,819	1,297
1972	13,535	4,247	1,945	1,201
1973	11,539	3,082	1,542	870
1974	15,414	1,323	1,497	605
1975	24,534	1,109	1,927	781
1976	22,436	1,225	1,928	1,059
1977 (Sept.) total all countries		12,572	903	

Source: Adapted from The Population of Greece in the Second Half of the 20th Century, Concise Statistical Yearbook of Greece 1985-86.

The other major development, which resulted in the social and demographic transformation of Greece, was the large movement of people from the countryside to urban centers in the 1960s and 1970s. Most of the provincial towns experienced substantial growth with the arrival of new dwellers. At the same time, already established residents were leaving for the capital. Overall, the provinces were losing population, with only a few showing increases. By 1963 the balance between the rural and urban sector shifted in favor of the urban. Athens remained far and away the leading attractive pole for the internal migrants. In the 1950s, the majority of newcomers to the capital came from the nearby provinces in "old Greece," the Peloponnesos and central Greece. The migrants found employment mainly in industry, construction, and services, areas in which there was growth and that were not difficult to enter. Commerce remained mostly in the hands of established residents. This same employment pattern held for the rest of the cities in Greece as well. As with emigration, the state was unable to manage this unprecedented phenomenon. The explosive growth of greater Athens overwhelmed attempts at planning and available services. Development in this case had become a runaway engine without an engineer.[71] For some, however, it was a success that needed to be encouraged, and they used it politically.

Development Upstaged: Dictatorship and Recession

The rising standard of living in the early 1960s and the coming to power of the Center Union in 1964 fed expectations in the country for continued economic growth and political liberalization. A dark cloud threatened this rosy vision, however, when the young King Constantine and the veteran politician, George Papandreou, clashed over whether parliament or monarch had control of the military. As the confrontation turned to crisis, a group of army officers, led by the ultranationalist Colonel George Papadopoulos, seized control of the government. They proclaimed they were guarding the interests of the nation, but the conspirators were looking after their own careers as well. The colonels proceeded to establish themselves in power.

The military-dominated regime curbed civil liberties and employed retrograde and reprehensible tactics against its opponents. Such conduct earned it the opprobrium of other governments, and the country paid a heavy price. The association agreement with the EEC was limited to existing administrative relations, and millions of dollars in funds earmarked for Greece to help it make the transition to full membership were withheld. In the initial political uncertainty following the takeover, tourism fell and with it foreign earnings that the country counted on.

Papadopoulos and his associates countered that they had inaugurated a new era of morality and strength in the nation. In an era of unprecedented political and social ferment in the United States and Europe, the colonels boasted of stability and calm in Greece. They offered a haven for tourists and foreign investors and golden opportunities for domestic business. With little popular support to count on, the regime of the 21st of April enunciated a series of policies intended for maximum appeal to the less advantaged economic strata. In the spring of 1968, farmers were told that their debts to the Agricultural Bank would be canceled. At a time when thousands were streaming to the capital, urban workers were promised low-income housing. The goal of many parents—a full education for their children—was to be more accessible through free education, with the state taking care of tuition and textbooks. There was another side to these populist policies, of course. Through its appointees, the regime took care to control local government, the trade unions, and agricultural cooperatives.[72]

To gain the support of the populace and strengthen its hold on the country, the colonels' regime counted on the expansion of the economy in order to ensure prosperity and fulfill consumer demands. As with earlier plans, the developmental goals the regime promulgated in 1968 were predicated on continuing two policies: monetary stability was to be maintained and reinforced, and economic growth had to remain high and even increase to an annual rate of about 8 percent a year. Under the military dictatorship the country reached a high mark in laissez-faire economics.[73]

Projects needed to support the industrial sector, but lacking private investment, would be handled by the Hellenic Industrial Development Bank with the cooperation of Greek and foreign firms. Modernization of the country's infrastructure would be managed as "complexes of fully harmonized projects instead of isolated and functionally unrelated ones." Financing for the development program was to be taken care of through domestic savings, which were to cover 90 percent of the total investment. The public sector would provide only 13.3 percent of the funds required. These projections assumed that savings activity would remain at least at 20 percent and even increase over the next few years.[74]

Although the development plan promulgated by the dictatorship followed the previous scheme in many instances, certain differences in emphasis are worth noting. Both plans called for an increase in the merchant marine by inducing shipowners to register more of their vessels in Greece. The 1968 development plan, however, went further. It sought the removal of "various technical and institutional barriers, which fostered the heavy concentration of the head offices of Greek shipping companies abroad." To get the companies to return, the dictatorship was willing to provide "low rents and reductions of general expenses for the establishment of head offices of shipping . . . combined with a tax exemption for shipping businesses established in Greece on profits realised abroad."[75]

Tourism, already a significant industry and a major source of invisible revenue, became a darling of the military. The dictatorship hoped to accelerate the increase in tourism and make it a prime sector for private investment. A law was approved that provided "special incentives for the attraction of private enterprise to the new areas selected for tourist development." Those willing to invest in tourist-related businesses were given reduced rates for electricity and the installation of telephone services, could make smaller payments to Social Security and the Hotel Employee's Fund, and enjoyed a 50 percent reduction on taxable profits, not distributed to shareholders. Another law in 1972 again lowered tax rates for social insurance, while dividing the country into development zones for tourism much as had been done for industry. The years of the military were a heyday of untrammeled growth in the building and running of hotels.[76]

The laissez-faire attitude of the dictatorship was also evident in its attitude toward employment, including emigration and labor. Although the government talked about increasing employment opportunities, it assumed certain trends and encouraged others. Greece's employment problem would be ameliorated by a declining rate of population growth and continued emigration. In the guise of improving occupational mobility, the government was willing to reorganize the labor exchanges, "to free enterprises . . . from the restrictions concerning the dismissal of surplus personnel . . . and to open restricted occupations."[77]

Perhaps most indicative of the military regime's preoccupation with the allure of a free-wheeling, foreign-financed, growth-oriented, private initiative economy was its investment policy. Already in the late 1950s the government of then Prime Minister Karamanlis had issued legislation intended to encourage the creation of investment capital for the construction of large projects in mining, industry, and handicrafts. Depending on the location, a firm could take a 100 percent allowance on its investment from its undistributed profit at various rates over several years. During the dictatorship, the emergency laws passed in 1967 and 1968 went even further. Not only were firms exempted from income taxes, but as an added incentive to industrial, hotel, mining, and utilities enterprises, the state was ready to help by "partially covering their burden from interest, bond issues, and credits or loans granted by banking institutions in Greece."[78]

In a rush to promote economic activity, in order to claim that it was doing more for the nation than the now-ousted parliamentary parties, the military regime was uncritical and arbitrary in its development policies. There was growth in total productivity, but it was unbalanced and not necessarily beneficial to the country's fiscal health.

By 1972 industrial production made up almost 23 percent of the total income generated. Foreign investment and credit in manufacturing had grown substantially, but so also had the balance-of-payments deficit. Exports of manufactured goods had failed to offset the importation of capital and goods. Enterprises still relied heavily on banks for funding rather than on private venture capital. Much investment had gone into the construction business as the housing market soared. The unprecedented growth in this sector did not, however, benefit the overall structure of the economy. Allocating resources to the building sector was not producing a developed economy. The demand in the housing market and the profits derived from it created inflationary pressures that put a strain on the sacred policy of monetary stability. Labor costs rose as the rapidly expanding construction industry placed a premium on workers.[79]

Even more significant for the economy was the poor record of the agricultural sector. Part of the slow growth could be attributed to poor weather conditions. Certainly, however, the large movement from the countryside to the cities and out of the country had had serious repercussions on productivity for Greece's labor-intensive crops. There was already talk of crop restructuring and the need to turn to more "dynamic" crops such as sugar beets, cotton, and citrus fruits. These were more amenable to mechanization and new technology as well as producing more return on investment. But the regime had devoted more effort in the countryside to propaganda and controlling the productive mechanisms like the cooperatives to do much good.[80]

During the last year of the dictatorship economic activity began to slow in reaction to domestic policies and unfavorable world conditions. By this time, however, the military regime was riven by internal feuding. A miscalculated gambit in Cyprus in July 1974 resulted in a crisis that brought about the downfall of the dictatorial government, the withdrawal of the military from politics, and the return of democracy. The years of the dictatorship had been harmful to political and economic life in Greece. Development policies and projects were instituted without proper consideration and rationalization. The criteria employed in setting policies did not take social and economic implications into proper account. As a result, the economy was skewed by excessive consumer-driven growth, compounded by heavy investment in enterprises low in productivity and noncompetitive on foreign markets.[81]

Greece and the West: National Autonomy and Internationalism

The new government headed by Constantine Karamanlis, who returned from abroad, confronted the deleterious legacy of the dictatorship and the difficulties that had mounted in the world economy. After the October War (1973) in the Middle East, oil prices rose swiftly to quadruple their previous level. The Cyprus problem brought relations between Greece and Turkey to a crisis point. To protect its perceived national interests, the government significantly increased the purchase of military equipment, such as jet fighters. In the meantime invisible earnings from tourism and Greeks living abroad declined considerably as a result of the Cyprus crisis and the world recession.[82]

To counter the downturn in the economy that had resulted from the confluence of these developments, the Karamanlis government initiated some short-term policies that were intended to restore confidence in the economy and to help end the recession. Credit was once again liberalized to encourage development. Inflation had hurt the lower income strata including wage earners, civil servants, farmers, and pensioners. To restore the purchasing power of these groups, wages and pensions were increased. Agriculturalists were aided when the government raised the prices they received for their products and provided subsidies to support their incomes. The purchasing power of these groups was also enhanced by reducing income tax rates, increasing allowances on family income, and raising the maximum deductible on earned income. Although banking circles showed concern that these "reflation" measures would set off a new round of inflation, they were continued into 1975.[83]

Renewed economic confidence was coupled with the return of public assurance in the political system, especially as exemplified by Karamanlis. Calling for elections, his New Democracy party—the right regrouped—won a resounding victory in the popular vote and parliamentary representation in November 1974. Moving with the times and reacting to the negative popular feelings over U.S. attitudes toward Greece in the Cyprus crisis, Karamanlis withdrew the Greek armed forces from the NATO wing, legalized the Communist party, and eliminated many of the repressive rules that had been fastened on society in the aftermath of the civil war.

The liberalizing and opening up continued with the formulation of policies for economic development. It was time, so the argument went, to change tactics from those employed in the 1950s and 1960s. In the two decades that preceded the dictatorship, economic development had focused on a few strategic sectors like tourism and shipping. Domestic industries were nurtured not only by providing state protection, but also by taking away the risk involved in making them competitive enterprises. The state's most visible activities in the economy had been those of control and intervention. As a result, private initiative and competitive modernizing development had been held back. Current conditions demanded a different approach. The Greek economy needed to debouch from the confines of the domestic market ringed by protection out onto the open fields of the international economy. "The possibilities for creating a broader and competitive industrial base exist."[84]

Leading economic planners believed that development policy itself had to change. In an era when consumer demand could not be easily reined in and manipulated and fiscal stability was fragile, the state's role in fostering restructuring in the economy was seen in socially and financially prudent terms. The state was to turn away from negative intervention, watching over prices and making arrangements with industries at the consumer's expense. Such tactics were to be replaced in favor of those that encouraged investment and productivity in a competitive business environment. It was not that these were new ideas, but rather the voicing of a demand that they actually be realized. In effect, it was hoped that the state could elicit new responses from established practices and institutions.[85]

In view of Greece's impending accession to full membership in the EEC, problems relating to the nature and purpose of industrial production needed to be addressed. To begin with, many of the industrial firms established in the postwar era engaged primarily in the finishing of goods. These enterprises were often heavily dependent on imported materials either in a semifinished or an almost completed condition. This type of firm only drove up the import payment bill. In addition, the state's drive to increase exports often led to the granting of incentives without discriminating between enterprises that finished off goods and those that engaged in the total manufacturing process. On the other hand, many firms were still geared to the domestic market. Protected and subsidized, they had little incentive to become more technologically advanced and efficient.

The question, therefore, was whether national autonomy ought to be fostered and the import bill lowered by concentrating on import substitution, or whether the emphasis should be placed on exports with manufacturing directed to the foreign market. An investment incentive law passed in 1978 brought tax incentive practices in the country into agreement with those of the European Community. Rather than subsidies, as originally proposed, the law offered interest-free loans to businesses. All areas of industry were reviewed to determine which would need aid to meet the expected competition once Greece became a full member. An attempt was made to rationalize the granting of incentives. They were to be based on an industrial grading system with consideration for the location of the firm, and its effort to reduce pollution, save energy, and create research facilities. All of this was an implicit recognition that the country needed to attract foreign investment capital for industry.[86]

As with industry, agriculture served both the domestic and foreign needs of the nation. Because of its continued importance in the total economy, agriculture was considered an important lever in dealing with the intractable balance-of-payments problem. The thrust of development policy, therefore, was to rationalize the agriculture sector, gearing decisions to the perceived needs of the market. This meant inducing farmers to produce those crops that would increase the value of the country's exports and also meet domestic needs, thereby lessening the reliance on imported products. Currants, for example, which had experienced a significant decline in production, were no longer considered a highly desirable market crop. On the other hand, sugar beets, tobacco, fruits, and olive oil were commended as "dynamic crops" whose cultivation should be fostered.

To achieve higher productivity and competitiveness, restructuring the agricultural sector was also regarded as necessary. The state was expected to intervene in the setting of prices and the marketing of produce and to discriminate in the type and size of agricultural enterprises it supported. State subsidies and price supports were to promote solid, middle-level farms. Marginal agricultural holdings were not to be protected, but large-scale operations were not to be overprotected either. Agriculture was to be treated as a business, and the state's task was to encourage it.[87]

Desirable as the goals of competitiveness and efficiency in the economy were, mounting fiscally related problems in the mid-1970s made it impossible to find solutions that were both rational and politically popular. Although a little behind in economic trends than other Western European countries, Greece again experienced growing inflation as the government promoted an expansionist economic policy to overcome the recession in 1974. In the wake of inflation the inequality of incomes also increased. Those whose manufacturing firms had little competition, middlemen, and the self-employed in the service sector were able to adjust their prices so that their profits gained on inflation. Farmers, civil servants, salaried employees, and, to some extent, wage earners suffered a setback in their living standard relative to the cost of living. Equally disconcerting was the deteriorating savings situation. Bank deposits as well as investment in housing had decreased because of the unsettled condition of the economy. Many chose to hedge their bets on inflation by buying imported durable goods or saving only until they had enough to purchase housing. This tendency was troublesome because savings deposits had become a major source of funds, which the central bank used to finance key sectors of the economy including shipping, tourism, agriculture, and industry.[88]

The state's possible fiscal responses were encumbered by problems over their feasibility and efficaciousness. Because of increased tension in the Aegean with neighboring Turkey, expenditures for military defense grew. As a consequence of mismanagement during the dictatorship, the public demand for more and better services heightened. In 1976, for example, compulsory education was raised to nine years, and an effort was made to provide greater opportunities for university and technical education. Similar problems arose when it came to better managing revenue gathering. Many recognized that the burden needed to be lifted from the shoulders of the lower income groups through a progressive income tax policy. Implementing this policy, however, required addressing the equally traditional practice of tax evasion. There was talk of rationalizing the system to get rid of exemptions for businesses that were not beneficial to the economy and setting "tax rates at levels better suited to the country's present stage of economic development, without adverse effects on tax revenue." Even though the fiscal problems had been recognized, this was only a small step in offsetting the continuing increase in social spending and the trade imbalance.[89]

Nevertheless, Karamanlis was determined to strengthen Greece's political and economic ties with the developed world even more. He was motivated as much by political as economic reasons. Indeed, issues of economic development were bound up with the desire for international support in confronting Turkey over problems in the eastern Mediterranean and maintaining a more independent stance vis-à-vis the United States. There was opposition in parliament from the left, including the communists and PASOK (the Panhellenic Socialist Movement), formed and dominated by Andreas Papandreou. Nonetheless, the treaty of accession was ratified, and Greece became the tenth member of the EEC on January 1, 1981.

As premier, Karamanlis could point to a number of accomplishments. Political democracy had been restored to the country, and relations with neighboring states in the Balkans, with the exception of Turkey, had improved substantially. Greece's entry into the Common Market was assured by 1979. Taking advantage of the political luster that accrued from these accomplishments, Karamanlis sought and gained the presidency of the Republic in 1979. His achievements did not transfer to the benefit of his party. Andreas Papandreou, having forged the Panhellenic Socialist Movement, shrewdly promised broad but nonthreatening "change" for Greek society. His popularly crafted appeals to national independence, social labor, and popular local self-government persuaded many that a new era was at hand. In October 1981, PASOK won a comfortable majority in parliament, along with 48 percent of the popular vote.

The Panhellenic Socialist Movement rolled into power, however, at a moment when the country was in the midst of economic doldrums. It was experiencing "slow economic growth, high inflation, and a widening current external deficit," popularly termed stagflation. When the second energy crisis of the 1970s struck in 1979, Greece's economy was affected by the world economic downturn even more than other European countries.[90]

For Greece the problems had been growing since the mid-1970s, after the first energy crisis set in. Not only had productive growth slowed, but also what there was of it was being increasingly provided by the third sector of the economy— services. The increase in the number of people in private services such as tourism could be justified by the productivity that accompanied it. The same case could not reasonably be made for the public sector. In 1978 the deficit for this sector was 68.2 billion drachmas, and by 1980 it had ballooned to 158 billion. Just as significant, industrial productivity as a share of the gross domestic product (GDP) fell as investment declined. Ironically, this was partly attributed to the prospect of Greece's accession to the EEC. With businessmen uncertain about the future, they were reluctant to invest.[91]

During these years, the New Democracy government had pursued an expansionary fiscal and incomes policy. Consumer demand grew while national income increased by an annual average of 5 percent. Inflation also jumped, at the rate of at least 12 percent a year. To boost exports and attract foreign investment, the drachma was unlinked from parity with the dollar in 1975. The depreciation that followed only fueled inflation to the detriment of low-income groups. After the energy crisis of 1979 and until PASOK came to power in the fall of 1981, the government reversed its economic tactics and tightened access to money and credit. The depreciation of the drachma was slowed, but inflation persisted.[92]

In its initial effort to deal with the economic malaise, the Papandreou government followed a policy that fitted in with promises made during the campaign.
It chose to stimulate productivity through the tested method of fiscal initiatives.
Real income in the private and public sectors, which had fallen in the preceding
two years, was increased by an automatic cost-of-living indexation scheme for
employees. The demand that was stimulated as a result of this policy was filled
not by local industries but by foreign manufactures, which now could not be
restricted beyond certain limits. Domestic manufacturers, uncertain whether they
could recover their costs at home or abroad if they expanded production, hesitated
to step up investment. As a result, this strategy hampered economic recovery
as higher inflation stalked the country and labor costs went up.[93]

The failure of fiscal intervention to straighten out the economy through a demand incentive strategy posed both economic and ideological issues for the Papandreou government. With their leader supporting their views, PASOK technocrats
tackled the problem by arguing for an economic course that reflected both their
ideological and technical predilections. They argued that in the postwar era the
Greek economy had become dependent on external economic forces with its internationally oriented sectors—tourism, shipping, emigration—functioning only
as intermediaries. Now, however, the country faced great challenges: a world
economic crisis, technological revolution, the devaluation of the quality of life,
and social restructuring. To survive in a world of entangling forces, Greece needed
to assert its national independence. This could only be achieved by pursuing
autonomous economic development, which they considered different from autar-
chic development.[94]

Turning rhetoric into policy boiled down to taking a few basic measures. In
the past the state was seen as indiscriminately protecting industries, especially
large ones that supplied primarily the domestic market. Now the emphasis was
to be on incentives for medium-sized businesses that embraced new technologies,
adopted efficient operating methods, were export oriented, and were capable of
withstanding the competitive forces of domestic and foreign markets. It was to
be a wager on a new generation of entrepreneurs as opposed to those from previous
decades who were not "capable of dealing with present problems." To make
Greek goods more attractive on the world market, the government was willing
to allow the drachma to find an appropriate level. In August 1983, the drachma's
tie-in with the U.S. dollar was again broken, and it depreciated still further. In
order for industries to be more competitive and efficient, the government would
try to keep wage increases down and use its power to promote "harmonious"
relations between the two "social partners," labor and business.[95]

As part of its campaign promise to promote worker participation in the management of private enterprises, the government called for "social control" and
"self-management" for certain companies. Not clearly defined, this policy was
applied in a limited number of instances involving financially troubled ("problematic") firms, whose continued operation was in the government's interest vis-à-
vis the workers' jobs at stake. In practice, it meant coordinating activities between

the government, the management of the enterprise, and the banks. Workers were to receive representation on the company board. It was as much a means for the government to intervene in industry as a benefit to workers.[96]

On the whole, the socialist government shied away from any radical changes in developmental policies. It was willing to continue aiding large manufacturing enterprises, even if they were in financial difficulties. It also recognized the continuing importance of key sectors like shipping and tourism, and it was willing to support them in upgrading their services in order to strengthen their productive capacity.[97]

Greece's relations with the European Community further underscore how seeming contradictions between ideological positions and developmental interests were accommodated in the policies of the Papandreou government. Before coming to power, the socialist leader had argued that Greece would find itself in a dependent relationship and be taken advantage of, and the only real alternative was autonomous economic development by building up the domestic markets in agriculture and industry.[98]

When Papandreou took power, however, he did not take up the attack on Greece's membership in the EEC. Instead, the socialists sought to negotiate a special status for Greece. The Greek government argued that the European Community was divided between advanced and peripheral countries. Greece, as a less developed nation, could not become fully integrated quickly. As a remedy, Papandreou called on the EEC to redistribute resources from the wealthy to the poorer regions of the Community, thereby promoting the convergence of the various economies. The Greek government also sought to keep up agricultural prices. The EEC responded by arguing that it would be better to speed up Greece's integration into the European Community and promote the competition of goods. At the same time, however, a regional program was created, and in 1983 Greece began receiving aid in the form of net transfers that would run for five years.[99]

As the end of Papandreou's first term approached, payments from the EEC providentially flowed in. Aiding farmers, among others, they amounted to 21.4 percent of the total invisible receipts, in which they were classified, by 1985. A timely increase in public spending also benefited civil servants, teachers, and pensioners. When elections were held in June 1985, Papandreou easily won a second term. The borrowing necessitated by the public spending now totaled 18 percent of GDP (1985). The demand that it fueled only drove inflation and the payments deficit spiral still higher as consumers bought up foreign goods.

The gradualist mix of fiscal and monetarist policies had proved ineffective against double digit inflation, sluggish industrial productivity, and unemployment that was approaching 10 percent. An economic stabilization program was enacted in October 1985 in an attempt to quickly bring down inflation and the balance-of-payments deficit. Some of the measures were seen as having a developmental dimension because they were designed to encourage exports and limit imports. This included devaluing the drachma again by 15 percent. Importers were required to make a six-month advance deposit on certain categories of goods ranging from

40 to 80 percent of the value of the item imported. The wage indexation plan was modified so that wages were adjusted on what the government forecast inflation to be rather than actual rates in the past. Other measures were intended to help knock down inflation. The prices of agricultural products were adjusted at a rate lower than actual inflation. An attempt was made to curb public sector borrowing by cutting public expenditures, increasing the price of goods and services provided by the public sector, and boosting public revenues by broadening the tax base and cutting down on tax evasion. Finally, the growth of money and credit was restricted, and short-term interest rates were increased.[100] These measures were a reaction to the problems of promoting steady growth. They were also an admission that the policies of the past three decades were no longer effective.

In the 1980s the confident march of economic progress became discomfiting as leading indicators turned negative, even allowing for the worldwide recession. Consumer demand continued strong as people desperately tried to keep abreast or even gain on inflation. As a consequence, the cost to the country of maintaining and financing the standard of living mounted. Greece benefited from full membership in the EEC, receiving favored treatment in its agricultural sector and economic aid. With trade barriers falling, however, imports steadily increased to fill domestic demands for durable goods as housing and vehicles became prohibitively expensive for many. On the other hand, some Greek products lost their competitiveness in the face of rising labor costs and the failure to implement cost-cutting production measures.[101]

The "peculiarities" in the economy that helped development in past decades could not be counted on to the same extent in the 1980s. Emigrant remittances leveled off as some sojourners abroad found fewer employment opportunities and began to return (see Table 5.5). In other cases the ties to the homeland weakened as the years passed. Shipping receipts reached a peak in 1980–1981, but then fell to half that in 1985 because of the world crisis in shipping and the subsequent contraction of the Greek fleet. Earnings from tourism, which had risen dramatically in the preceding two decades, declined in value relative to the number of visitors. In addition, much tourist income remained unaccountable to the state.[102]

Most significant of all was what happened to the overall economic and demographic character of the country as it was transformed from a largely rural and agrarian society to an urban and industrial one. By the end of the 1970s, the contribution of the agricultural sector to the total domestic economic product ceased to decline and stabilized at around 17 percent. At the same time agriculture continued to take up about 30 percent of the total employment force. These were relatively high percentages among developed nations. Furthermore, farmers gained significantly from EEC payments, as part of its regional development program. As their economic status improved, so did their social benefits from the PASOK-dominated government. But farmers continued to pay almost no taxes, thus depriving the state of a reasonable need for revenues.

Concomitantly, the share of employment in manufacturing rose to almost 30 percent. Yet it was not matched by growth in productivity. Manufacturing output grew at the rate of about 10 percent a year in the postwar years—a respectable showing. In contrast, it flattened out in the 1980s to the point where it was barely above the peak reached in 1979. Several reasons have been offered to explain this phenomenon. A considerable portion of the manufacturing sector continues to be made up of small enterprises (see Table 5.3). Nearly two-thirds of those employed in industry, producing nearly 60 percent of manufactures, are in traditional but not necessarily dynamic trades such as food, textiles, leather goods, cement, and tobacco products. In the early 1980s, as industries in other European countries reacted to the recession by lowering production costs, Greece went in the opposite direction. Although workers' wages needed to be improved, they did so faster than the concurrent growth in productivity, especially in the early years of the socialist government. From 1979 to 1985, the cumulative increase in unit labor costs was 26 percent. During these years the state strengthened controls on the prices of manufactured goods and the profit margins of the enterprises. Medium and large-scale firms were affected more than small businesses, which could more easily get around the controls. By the time the government turned to a policy of restraint in 1985, Greek products had lost a good deal of their competitiveness. As a result, imported goods, especially from the EEC countries, increased their share of total sales from 11.3 percent in 1980 to 18.9 percent in 1985.[103]

The driving consumer demand behind the rising tide of imports was symptomatic of the growth in the material and social expectations of the populace. A sense that individual well-being took precedence over the developmental needs of the nation became prevalent in society in the 1980s. It was fueled by the strong inflow of foreign exchange in the form of invisibles, including large payments by the EEC, as well as the social welfare policies of the socialist government in the early 1980s. PASOK contributed to this trend by increasing direct subsidies and transfers and by keeping the cost of public services like transportation down. The lower economic groups benefited most by policies such as cost-of-living indexing for workers, increased payments to pensioners, and expanded numbers of those so covered. As a consequence, the government increasingly resorted to borrowing to meet these public sector expenses, rather than gaining the needed revenue to pay for them from a growing economy as had happened in the past.[104]

Development: The Elusive Goal

Development in Greece has been bound up with a society characterized by entrepreneurs who operate small-sized private businesses, protected and "guided," in a legalistic sense, by state mechanisms, and with a political system that gradually has become pluralistic with parties that are still compounds of personalities and patronage organizations. The "peculiarities" in this development enabled the country to solve, at least temporarily, its domestic problems from without. Labor surpluses and unemployment were controlled by large-scale emigration. Satisfactory amounts of capital and revenues to promote economic growth were provided by the emigrants as well as a flourishing shipping trade and tourist industry. This brought a rising standard of living and the attributes of modernity to what had become a consumer-driven society. The state aided industries through protectionist duties and subsidies. In the process, much private capital and public investment went into small, domestic-oriented firms and residential construction to meet the demands of a rapidly urbanizing population. Greece's economy thus enjoyed a respectable rate of growth during the decades up to 1980, but it lagged in the structural and technical changes that were needed for economic modernization.

More recently, development became mired in national politics as parties vied for power by claiming to best understand the interests and demands of society. Since the days of the military dictatorship, political leaders on the left and the right have offered the people social improvement through Western-oriented development. While the right embraced outward-directed development through market competitiveness and economic ties with the West, the left charted a path emphasizing national sovereignty and the people's social welfare in its dealings with the developed world. In the process, problems arose from implementing policies that reflected these two views. The right's commitment to state-supported economic growth tied to the international market produced a consumer-oriented society with little concern about the long-term requirements of the national economy. The left's notions of ''social rights'' resulted in a state plagued by an inflated public sector financed by a growing public deficit. The advantages of the two socioeconomic perspectives that should have accrued to the nation turned to disadvantages.

In the past there were tensions between the state, with its instruments of control—the bureaucracy and formal culture—that benefited a few, and the general populace. Today large segments of the population see the state as the guarantor of social services and benefits, while industrialists speak of the need for less state interference.

Greece has attained many aspects of a modern nation, which no one wishes to jeopardize. Yet uncertainty over whether the country's economy can become and remain competitive is palpable and justifiably so.[105] Many now argue that the country's institutional structures and productive mechanisms need to be made responsive and competitive as the integration of the European Community proceeds, while the nation continues to create a secure position for itself, politically and economically, in the region.[106]

Pessimists in Greece fear the country will not be able to meet the challenge. Optimists believe that, with the support of the EEC, the nation will be able to implement needed fiscal and structural changes and gradually integrate into the larger Western economic community. More to the point, however, Greece must confront the very factors that have shaped its society in the twentieth century: an individualist social culture, skewed demographic development, the dominance of the commercial and service sector, weakness in the generative capabilities of manufacturing, and the unproductive aspects of the state. Governments have been pressed to find ways to create incentives for business investment while better regulating the corporations that provide public services. Developing the country's productive capabilities has meant reconciling the need to enhance the conditions for market-driven economic growth and lessening dependence on the public sector with the widespread popular support for the continued provision of services and employment through public corporations. Development is not merely a question of exploiting limited means to the fullest. There must be confidence in the nation and its institutions as well as a consensus on how to achieve integration with the Western developed world. Given the developments since the mid-1970s, these issues have not yet been clearly resolved.

Notes

The author wishes to thank Byron Kotzamanis and Elias Athanasiades for their help in gathering material while he was in Athens.

1. Augustinos (1977), chaps. 1–2
2. On industrial developoment, see Agriantoni (1986) and Zolotas (1966), pp. 26–27.
3. Turner (1928), 19. Financial obligations undertaken by successive governments were a loan in 1914, the refugee loan of 1924, and a new reconstruction loan in 1928.
4. Mavrogordatos (1983), pp. 121–27; Dertilis (1977), pp. 220–45.
5. Tsouderos (1919), 102–103.
6. Westebbe (1980), pp. 269–70.
7. Sideris (1934), pp. 176–81; Cumberbatch (1934), pp. 35–36, 38; Turner (1928), p. 20; Kotzamanis (1987), pp. 188–89.
8. Sandis (1973), pp. 160, 162–63; Turner, p. 20; *Financial News* (1931), p. 13.
9. Sideris, pp. 221–26.
10. Sandis, pp. 94, 98–99, 160, 167–168, 171–172; Turner, pp. 20–21.
11. Sideris, pp. 361–361.
12. Ibid., pp. 265, 369; Kostis (1987), pp. 110–30, 252.
13. Sideris, pp. 181–83.
14. Ibid., pp. 165–68, 286–88, 308–309. In 1920 there were 1,171 cooperatives with 58,000 members; by 1930, there were 2,800 with 168,000 members; and in 1938 there were 4,862 cooperatives with 359,000 members. See Bandaloukas (1984), p. 573.
15. Sideris, pp. 275–79; Cumberbatch, pp. 36–37.
16. Sideris, pp. 295–303; Cumberbatch, p. 37.
17. Sideris, pp. 293 94.
18. Ibid., pp. 305–306.
19. Zolotas, pp. 26–27.
20. Cumberbatch, pp. 29–34; Mason (1956), pp. 34–35; Zolotas, p. 139.
21. Zolotas, pp. 138–139; Turner, p. 23; Cumberbatch, p. 29.
22. Turner, pp. 5–13; Kostis, p. 255.
23. *Financial News*, pp. 5, 11; Kostis, pp. 254–255.
24. Turner, pp. 6–8, 30–32.
25. *Financial News*, p. 14; Cumberbatch, p. 49.
26. Cumberbatch, pp. 10–16.
27. Ibid., p. 18.
28. Ibid., p. 10, 18, 26; U.S. Embassy map.

29. Diomidis (1935), pp. 11–13, 21, 26; Mason, pp. 64–65; Bandaloukas, pp. 564–565; Kostis, p. 249.

30. *Report* for 1941, 1944, 1945, and 1946, pp. 68–69, 72, 75.

31. Xydis (1945), p. 1.

32. Ibid., pp. 37–38, 41.

33. Laiou (1987), 95–101.

34. Ibid., pp. 60–77.

35. Ibid., pp. 97–102; Kotzamanis, pp. 213–14.

36. Hadziiossif (1987), pp. 26–28; U.S. Embassy Map.

37. Batsi (1977), pp. 195–96, 204–205, 213, 375.

38. Hadziiossif, pp. 38–39.

39. Ibid., pp. 24, 40.

40. Munkman (1958), pp. 55–58; McNeill (1957), pp. 33–84.

41. Papandreou (1962), pp. 18–19; Westebbe (1980), p. 270; Mason, p. 1.

42. Munkman, pp. 72–73.

43. Ibid., pp. 55–57, 77–78; Mason, p. 16.

44. Mason, p. 18; Kotzamanis, pp. 213–17.

45. Mason, p. 14–15; Munkman, pp. 63–64; U.S. Embassy Map.

46. Mason, pp. 14, 20–21, 67–69.

47. Ibid., pp. 1–2.

48. Ibid., pp. 2, 54–58.

49. Munkman, p. 73; McNeill, pp. 55–56.

50. Mason, pp. 23–24.

51. Ibid., pp. 4–5, 21–23.

52. Pepelasis (1962), pp. 41–42.

53. Mason, pp. 11–12; Munkman, pp. 143–51; McNeill, 52–53.

54. Mason, pp. 18–19, 44–45.

55. Papandreou, pp. 23–24; Mason, pp. 5–6.

56. *Report* for 1961, p. 15.

57. Coutsoumaris, pp. 20–21; Nugent (1966), pp. 33–34.

58. *Report* for 1959, p. 18; *Report* for 1960, pp. 15–17; Ward (1963), pp. 135–36; Candilis (1968), pp. 168–79; Germidis (1975), p. 39.

59. *Report* for 1961, pp. 14–16; *Report* for 1963, pp. 17–18.

60. Kartsaklis (1980), p. 322.

61. *Report* for 1961, p. 79.

62. *Report* for 1961, p. 19; *Report* for 1963, pp. 46, 49.

63. *Report* for 1961, pp. 20–22; Germidis, p. 39.

64. *Report* for 1963, pp. 15–18, 45–46; Germidis, pp. 194–99; Alexander (1964), pp. 29–30, 46, 65; Nugent, pp. 33–34; Angelopoulos (1974), I, 597–598.

65. Papandreou, pp. 5, 29–31.

66. Ibid., pp. 14, 102–105.

67. Pepelasis, pp. 20–21; Angelopoulos (1974), II, 598.

68. Pepelasis, pp. 43, 53; Ward, pp. 140–41.

69. Angelopoulos (1967), pp. 3–5, 24–25.

70. Ibid., pp. 5–6.

71. Kayser (1968), pp. 91–116.

72. Clogg (1971), pp. 77, 109–26.

73. Ministry of Coordination (1968), pp. 9–10; Center of Planning (1965), p. 80.

74. Ministry, pp. 9–10, 45, 81.

75. Center, p. 80; Ministry, pp. 38–39.

76. Center, pp. 70–71; Ministry, pp. 33–34; Lemonias (1985), pp. 39–41.

77. Ministry, p. 16.

78. Lemonias, pp. 26, 30–31, 34–36; Ministry, pp. 17–18.

79. *Report* for 1972, pp. 14–15, 17, 51; OECD (1975), pp. 6, 8, 16–17, 38; OECD (1976), p. 10.

80. *Report* for 1972, pp. 36–37.

81. *Report* for 1974, p. 17; *Report* for 1975, p. 20; Lemonias, p. 44; OECD (1975), pp. 6–8.

82. *Report* for 1974, p. 12.

83. Ibid., pp. 12–13, 18.

84. Ibid., pp. 19, 28.

85. *Report* for 1974, pp. 19, 21, 25–28.

86. *Report* for 1974, p. 25; Germidis, p. 198; Lemonias, pp. 48–50; Grothusen (1980), p. 234. In the wake of the Cyprus crisis, the areas of the country closest to Turkey were seen as in need of special treatment to boost development and keep up morale. See Lemonias, pp. 45–47

87. Yotopoulos (1967), pp. 219–24; OECD (1978), pp. 15–16; *Report* for 1974, p. 21, 28–29; *Report* for 1975, pp. 30–31.

88. *Report* for 1975, pp. 11, 20–21; *Report* for 1974, pp. 15–16; Germidis, pp. 194–95; OECD (1977), passim; OECD (1976), p. 32.

89. *Report* for 1975, p. 19; *Report* for 1976, pp. 20–21; OECD (1977), pp. 23–25; Lambiri-Dimaki (1971), p. 62; OECD (1978), p. 23.

90. OECD (1981–1982), p. 8; *Report* for 1980, p. 9.

91. OECD (1981–1982), pp. 8–17; *Report* for 1980, pp. 20–22; *Report* for 1983, p. 11.

92. *Report* for 1983, pp. 11, 22–23; *Report* for 1980, p. 12; *Report* for 1976, p. 11; Kartsaklis, (1980b), p. 322.

93. Spourdalakis (1988), pp. 225–26; *Report* for 1984, p. 16; In 1982, hourly wages rose by 33.5 percent, weekly earnings by 30.3 percent, and monthly pay 22.5 percent. In 1983 the wage indexing scheme was deferred for four months, nevertheless, hourly earnings rose 19.4 percent, weekly wages grew 19.2 percent, and monthly pay went up 14.3 percent. Labor costs in manufacturing, which now concerned PASOK's economic administrators, rose 37.6 percent in 1982. See *Report* for 1983, pp. 39–41.

94. Vouli (1983), pp. 7–10.

95. *Report* for 1984, pp. 13–18; *Report* for 1983, pp. 22–23; *Report* for 1985, p. 14; Spourdalakis (1988), pp. 227, 229–33, 238–39.

96. Vouli, p. 10; Lemonias, pp. 68–69; Smokovitis (1984), pp. 74–78, 91, 99–108; Lyrintzis (1987), pp. 678–679.

97. Vouli, p. 11; *Report* for 1984, pp. 14–15.

98. Triantis (1965), pp. 40–41, 53, 58, 227–31; *Report* for 1963, pp. 22–26; Kartsaklis, (1980b), pp. 319, 337–39; Westebbe, pp. 283–84; Verney (1987), pp. 253–56.

99. Verney, pp. 265–67.

100. *Report* for 1985, pp. 10–11, 15–17; OECD (1985–1986), p. 43; OECD (1986–1987), pp. 7–11, 51–52.

101. OECD (1985–1986), passim; *Report* for 1980, pp. 23–24; *Report* for 1983, pp. 12–13; *Report* for 1987, p. 15; Kazakos and Stefanou (1987), pp. 17–129.

102. *Report* for 1983, p. 13; *Report* for 1985, pp. 120–25; *Report* for 1986, pp. 15–17; *Report* for 1987, pp. 16–17; Westebbe, p. 287.

103. *Report* for 1984, p. 14; *Report* for 1986, pp. 12, 14, 17–18; OECD (1986–1987), pp. 26–31.

104. *Report* for 1986, p. 14; OECD (1986–1987), pp. 37–45; *Report* for 1985, p. 11.

105. A study of the manufacturing sector in 1980, by KEPE researchers, advised that some 40 percent of Greek firms would be vulnerable to foreign manufacturers once the country became a full member of the EEC. The management efficiency of Greek enterprises was estimated to be only half that which prevailed in the EEC countries. See Skoumal and Kazis (1985), pp. 18, 80. Greek businessmen's concerns about the country's preparedness for the integration of the EEC countries are noted in *Oikonomikos Tahidromos*, November 17, 1988, pp. 8–9.

106. Some possible economic scenarios for Greece's development in the coming integration of the EEC are posited in Hristodoulakis. See also Skoumal and Kazis's recommendations for improving the productivity and competitiveness of the manufacturing sector, pp. 80–81.

References

Agriantoni, Hristina. *Oi aparhes tis ekviomihanisis stin Ellada ton 19 aiona*. Athens, 1986.
Aigidis, A. I. *I Ellas horis tous Prosfigas*. Athens, 1934.
Alexander, Alec. P. *Greek Industrialists, An Economic and Social Analysis*. Athens, 1964.
Andreades, Andreas M. *Elliniki polemiki kai metapolemiki dimosia oikonomia, 1912–1925*. Athens, 1927.
Andreades, A., G. Charitakis, D. Kallitsounakis, et al. *Les effets socio-économiques de la guerre en Grèce*. Paris/New Haven, 1928.
Angelopoulos, Angelos. *To oikonomiko provlima tis Ellados*. Athens, 1945.
_____ . *Oikonomika: arthra kai meletes 1946–67*. 2 vols. Athens, 1974.
_____ . et al. *Essays on Greek Migration*. Athens, 1967.
Augustinos, Gerasimos. *Consciousness and History: Nationalist Critics of Greek Society 1897–1914*. Boulder Colo., 1977.
Baerentzen, Lars, John Iatrides, and Ole Smith, eds. *Studies in the History of the Greek Civil War 1945–1949*. Copenhagen, 1987.
Bandaloukas, Klaodios. "I elliniki oikonomia 1923–1940 Sintomos statistiki skiagrafisis," *Spoudai* 34 (July–December 1984), 561–625.
Bank of Greece. *Report* for 1928–1988.
_____ . *I Elliniki Oikonomia*. 3 vols. Athens, 1980.
Batsi, Dim. *I vareia viomihania stin Ellada*. 2nd ed. Athens, 1977.
Bernaris, Ant. *Ta dimosia oikonomika 1932–1935*. n.p., 1936.
Candilis, Wray. *The Economy of Greece, 1944–1966*. New York, 1968.
Center of Planning and Economic Research. *Draft of the Five Year Economic Development Plan for Greece 1966–1970*. Athens, 1965.
Clogg, Richard, and George Yannopoulos. *Greece Under Military Rule*. New York, 1971.
Collaros, Titsa, and Loukia M. Moussourou. *The Return Home*. Athens, 1978.
Coutsoumaris, G. *The Morphology of Greek Industry*. Athens, 1963.

_____ . *Analysis and Assessment of the Economic Effects of the U.S. PL 480 Program in Greece*. Athens, 1965.

Crockett, Jean. *Consumer Expenditures and Incomes in Greece*. Athens, 1967.

Cumberbatch, A. N. *Economic Conditions in Greece, 1932–33*. London, 1934.

Delivani, Maria. *Analisi tis Ellinikis oikonomias*. 2nd ed. Athens, 1981.

Dertilis, Giorgos. *Koinonikos metaschimatismos kai stratiotiki epemvasi*. Athens, 1977.

Diomidis, Alexandros N. *To provlima tou oikonomikou mas mellontos*. Athens, 1935.

[Doxiadis, K. A., et al.]. *I epiviosis tou Ellinikou laou Eisigisis eis ton organismon anasigrotiseos*. 2 vols. Athens, 1947.

Eliadis, Evangelos Ap. *Stabilization of the Greek Economy and the 1953 Devaluation of the Drachma*. Washington, D.C., 1954.

Ellis, Howard, et al. *Industrial Capital in Greek Development*. Athens, 1964.

Featherstone, Kevin, and Dimitrios Katsoudas, eds. *Political Change in Greece Before and After the Colonels*. London, 1987.

The Financial News. "Greece," March 23, 1931.

Germidis, D. A., and Maria Negreponti-Delivanis. *Industrialization, Employment and Income Distribution in Greece*. Paris, 1975.

Grothusen, Klaus-Detlev, ed. *Südosteuropa—Handbuch, Bd. III, Griechenland*, Göttingen, 1980.

Hadziiossif, Christos. "Economic Stabilization and Political Unrest: Greece 1944–1947," in *Studies in the History of the Greek Civil War 1945–1949*. Edited by L. Baerentzen. Copenhagen, 1987.

Halikias, D. I. *Oikonomiki anaptixi tis Ellados kai isozigiou pliromon*. Athens, 1963.

Hatzivasileiou, N. I. *I Ellas apenanti tou oikonomikou provlimatos tis kentrikis Evropis*. Athens, 1935.

Hill, Henry A. *The Economy of Greece*. New York, 1943(?).

Hristodoulakis, Nikos. "Ta krisima oikonomika provlimata tis horas mas tha parameinoun kai to 1992." *Oikonomikos Tahidromos*, June 1, 1989, 25–26, 84.

Kanellopoulos, Athanasios. *I oikonomia anamesa chthes kai sto simera*. Athens, 1980.

Kartsaklis, George A. B. "Economic System," in *Südosteuropa—Handbuch, Band III, Griechenland*. Edited by K. Grothusen. Göttingen, 1980a.

_____ . "Foreign Economic Relations," in *Südosteuropa-Handbuch, Band III, Griechenland*. Edited by K. Grothusen. Göttingen, 1980b.

Katakouzinos, Dim. *Ginetai viosimos i simerini Ellada?* Athens, 1946.

Katsanevas, Theodore. *Trade Unions in Greece*. Athens, 1984.

Kayser, Bernard. *Anthropo-Geografia tis Ellados*. Athens, 1968.

Kayser, Bernard, P. Pechaux, and M. Sivignon. *Exode rural et attraction urbaine en Grèce*. Athens, 1971.

Kazakos, P., and K. Stefanou. *I Ellada stin Evropaiki Koinotita: I proti pentaetia*. Athens, 1987.

Klimis, A. N. *I agrotiki oikonomia pro kai meta tin idrisin tis A.T.E., 1924–1954*. Athens, 1961.

Kostis, Kostas. *Agrotiki oikonomia kai Georgiki Trapeza*. Athens, 1987.

Kotzamanis, Byron. "Le mouvement migratoire dans la Grèce de l'apres-guerre." Ph.D. thesis. Paris, 1987.

Laiou, Angeliki E. "Population Movements in the Greek Countryside During the Civil War," in *Studies in the History of the Greek Civil War*. Edited by L. Baerentzen. Copenhagen, 1987.

Lambiri-Dimaki, Jane. "Democratization of Education in Contemporary Greece." *The Greek Review of Social Research*, No. 1 (1977), 55–64.

Lemonias, E. *Anaptixiaka kinitra stin Ellada kai stin EOK*. Athens, 1985.

Lianos, Theodore P. *Aspects of Income Distribution in Greece*. Athens, 1974.

Lyrintzis, Christos. "The Power of Populism: The Greek Case," *European Journal of Political Research* 15 (1987), 667–86.

Manologlou, Evdokia, and Ariadni Mihalakopoulou. "Oikonomika haraktiristika mias agrotikis koinotitas." *The Greek Review of Social Research* 58 (1985), 73–91.

Mason, F. C. *Greece: Economic and Commercial Conditions in Greece*. London, 1956.

Mavrogordatos, George Th. *Stillborn Republic*. Berkeley, 1983.

McNeill, William. *Greece: American Aid in Action 1947–1956*. New York, 1957.

Ministry of Coordination, Greece. *Economic Development Plan for Greece 1968–1972*. Athens, 1968.

Munkman, C. A. *American Aid to Greece*. New York, 1958.

National Statistical Service of Greece. *Statistical Yearbook of Greece 1974*. Athens, 1975.

———. *Annual Industrial Survey for the Year 1970*. Athens, 1975.

———. *Annual Industrial Survey for the Year 1980*. Athens, 1986.

———. *Concise Statistical Yearbook of Greece 1982*. Athens, 1983.

———. *Concise Statistical Yearbook of Greece 1985–1986*. Athens, 1987.

———. *The Population of Greece in the Second Half of the 20th Century*. Athens, 1980.

Nugent, Jeffrey B. *Programming the Optimal Development of the Greek Economy, 1954–1961*. Athens, 1966.

Organization for Economic Cooperation and Development. *Economic Surveys Greece*, 1975–1987.

Papandreou, Andreas G. *A Strategy for Greek Economic Development*. Athens, 1962.

Pepelasis, Adam A., and Pan A. Yotopoulos. *Surplus Labor in Greek Agriculture 1953–1960*. Athens, 1962.

Protecdicos, D. E. *Greece, Economic and Financial*. London, 1924.

Sandis, Eva E. *Refugees and Economic Migrants in Greater Athens*. Athens, 1973.

Sideris, A. D. *Ai georgikai politikai tis Ellados kata tin lixasan ekatontaetian*. Athens, 1934.

Skoumal, S., and D. A. Kazis. *Innovation in Greek Manufacturing*. Athens, 1985.

Smokovitis, Litsa N., and Severyn T. Bruyn. "The Social Structure of Self Managed Firms in Greece." *Spoudai* 34 (January–March 1984), 73–108.

Spourdalakis, Michalis. *The Rise of the Greek Socialist Party*. London, 1988.

Stefanidis, Dimosthenis S. *Ai katefthitirioi grammai tis oikonomikis mas anasingrotiseos*. Athens, 1947.

Sweet-Escott, Bickham. *Greece: A Political and Economic Survey, 1939–1953*. London, 1954.

Thomadakis, Stavros. "The Truman Doctrine: Was There a Development Agenda?" *Journal of Modern Hellenism* 5 (Autumn 1988), 23–51.

Thompson, Kenneth. *Farm Fragmentation in Greece*. Athens, 1963.

Triantis, Stephen G. *Common Market and Economic Development*. Athens, 1965.

Tsouderos, Emmanuel. *Le relevement economique de la Grèce*. Paris, 1919.

Turner, R.M.A. *Report on Economic Conditions in Greece*. London, 1928.

U.S. Embassy, Athens. *A General Economic Map of Greece*. Athens, 1947.

Verney, Susannah. "Greece and the European Community," in *Political Change in Greece Before and After the Colonels*. Edited by K. Featherstone and D. Katsoudas. London, 1987.

[Vouli ton Ellinon]. *Pentaetis programma oikonomikis kai koinonikis anaptixis 1983–1987.* Athens, 1983.

Ward, Benjamin. *Problems of Greek Regional Development*. Athens, 1963.

Westebbe, Richard M. "Industry, Handicraft and Tourism," in *Südosteuropa Handbuch, Band III, Griechenland*. Edited by K. Grothusen. Göttingen, 1980.

Xydis, Stephen G. *The Economy and Finances of Greece Under Occupation*. New York, 1945(?).

Yotopoulos, Pan A. *Allocative Efficiency in Economic Development*. Athens, 1967.

Zolotas, Xenophon. *I Ellas eis to stadion tis ekviomihaniseos*. 2d ed. Athens, 1966.

6

Politics, Nationalism, and Development in Romania

Mary Ellen Fischer

Romanians, like the inhabitants of all the Balkan countries, have been tossed repeatedly from waves of great optimism to depths of dashed expectations. The years following 1989 should prove no exception. A small Balkan state once bordered by major empires, Romania has been a pawn of its neighbors, Austria-Hungary, Russia, and the Ottomans, and also of more distant powers. All too often, the hopes of Romanians for political unity and autonomy were shattered as the country was victimized by wars and the vagaries of European diplomacy. As a result of this legacy of outside interference and indirect domination by imperial powers, overall the population mistrusts and is hostile toward political authority. In addition, because local elites have often exercised power on behalf of more distant sovereigns, Romanians have frequently tried to avoid rather than outwardly resist that authority.

A major break in the pattern of avoidance occurred in December 1989 when spontaneous demonstrations, provoked by the repressive dictatorship of Nicolae Ceauşescu and inspired by events elsewhere in Eastern Europe, resulted in the violent overthrow of the communist regime and the beginning of what appears to be a new era in Romanian development. Despite the radical changes that have taken place since the death of Ceauşescu, the dilemma that has emerged in Bucharest is familiar: how to create a political system with the capacity to bring about economic and social development.

Until recently, the socioeconomic order in Romania, as in the rest of the Balkans, has rested on agriculture, and the export of agricultural products usually has created a surplus for the local elites. By forming an alliance with the state bureaucracy, landowning families maintained control over those working the land and extracted the surplus. The nature of this alliance between the dominant economic interests and political officials has changed radically from one historical period to the next as the basis of power has moved from one class to another. Nonetheless, the alliance has continued in effect, usually to the detriment of most of the population. For example, after World War I economic power shifted from landowners to commercial and business interests, and after World War II to the Romanian Communist party (RCP). Despite these changes in the dominant economic interests, the process of cooperation between them and the state bureaucracy continued and in large part was responsible for the failure of Romania to realize its significant foreign trade and agricultural potential.

Development implies a process of economic and technological change, a transformation of institutions and values in such a way as to increase the capacities of all members of society, and it can often be measured by socioeconomic data. Because development implies growth in the mental and physical capacities of most citizens, it can also be defined in terms of positive change in educational levels, productive power, vocational opportunities, access to resources, and living standards. These improvements must be in absolute terms and at a rate to keep up with the citizens' expectations in order to maintain political and economic stability.

A developed political system must have the ability not only to maintain order, but also to do so while allowing, and initiating if necessary, the processes that develop citizens' capacities in accordance with their goals and expectations. Political development thus needs to be a continuing process, not merely a stage in the evolution of a system. The governing elites must establish and maintain an accommodation with nonelites through concrete achievements, including economic growth, rising living standards, and cultural enlightenment based on education and the creative arts. This means cooperation with various economic sectors and strata and with the intelligentsia. In the Balkans political development also means finding a way to resolve the various divisions and rivalries within society—the splits between urban and rural interests and among economic strata, for example, as well as the even more open hostility among ethnic groups. The pre–World War II elites in Romania clearly failed to maintain order, to develop most citizens' opportunities to improve their lives, or to heal social and ethnic divisions. Yet even the communist elites, if we measure their achievements by these demanding criteria, failed to keep up with citizens' expectations or to reduce social and ethnic tensions, particularly in the 1980s under Nicolae Ceauşsescu.

In order to explore and evaluate the attempts of successive regimes to accomplish significant and long-lasting development, we will first turn to the background that produced the political, economic, and social institutions of twentieth-century Romania. Next, we will examine the attempts to change the socioeconomic order by improving agriculture and developing industry in the first part of this century, attempts interrupted by two world wars and foreign occupation. Then we will turn to the communist experience since 1945 and evaluate the successes and failures of that period. Finally, we will try to assess the potential for political development in Romania now that Ceauşescu has left the scene.

The Baseline: Romania Before 1900

Each of the Balkan nations looks to its own history to glorify its origins and to defend its territorial ambitions at the expense of its neighbors.[1] The Romanians trace their origins to the Geto-Dacians who, they assert, by the first century B.C. had established a slaveowning culture over much of contemporary Romania, including the Danubian plain and parts of Transylvania.[2] The Roman legions reached the Danube in 74 B.C., but it was not until A.D. 106 that the Roman Emperor Trajan defeated the Geto-Dacians and their ruler, Decebal, and made Dacia a Roman province. The intensive Romanization in the years that followed produced a Daco-Roman population speaking a Latin language, the ancestors of contemporary Romanians.[3]

The history of the Daco-Romans after the withdrawal of the legions from north of the Danube in the late third century is a matter of controversy. Romanian historians assert that they continued to inhabit Transylvania as well as the Danubian plain (later Wallachia); this would give their claims historical precedence over those of other nationalities. In contrast, Hungarian historians claim that the Romanians' ancestors retreated south of the Danube and returned only later, after the Hungarians had arrived in Transylvania during the ninth century.

This pedantic disagreement among historians would be irrelevant and largely forgotten had politicians in both countries not seized on it to justify possession of Transylvania. The territorial dispute was decided by international agreements following World War I, when the area was awarded to Romania largely on the basis of population. Many Hungarians have never accepted the loss, however, and the Romanians have defended their control of the province, and their view of history, with a tenacity and passion born of their insecurity.

Later developments have generated less controversy but no less hostility. Transylvania came under Hungarian control during the eleventh century and was ruled at least indirectly from Budapest or Vienna until 1918, except for periodic incursions by Mongols or Ottomans. To defend the territory, Hungarian rulers encouraged German or Hungarian military colonists to settle along its borders (in the center of what is now Romania) and rewarded them with land and privileges. The Romanian population had neither. Indeed, it was not even included as a recognized nation in medieval Transylvania, in the fifteenth-century Union of Three Nations, or in the Constitution of 1542.[4]

The other two major regions of contemporary Romania, Moldavia and Wallachia, managed to avoid Hungarian control because of the Mongol invasion in the mid-thirteenth century. After the Mongols withdrew, two small states appeared on the trade routes to the Black Sea and Constantinople. As the Ottomans' power grew during the fourteenth and fifteenth centuries, the principalities were forced to accept their suzerainty, and from the sixteenth to the mid-nineteenth century they were ruled indirectly by the Ottomans. Two princes who proved exceptions to the general decline were Stephen the Great of Moldavia (1457-1504), the builder of monasteries, and Michael the Brave of Wallachia (1593-1601), who for a few months in 1600 was able to unite Wallachia, Moldavia, and Tran-sylvania under his rule.[5] A small aristocracy did develop in the two principalities, in contrast to Transylvania under the Hapsburgs (or elsewhere in the Balkans where the Ottomans ruled directly), but the landed Romanian nobles were heavi-ly dependent on the state for their economic privileges and many princes were outsiders appointed by the Turks.[6]

The decline of the Ottoman Empire produced nationalist sentiment in Romania, as in the other Balkan states. In 1821 a confused series of events loosely con-nected to Greek revolutionary movements turned into an abortive revolt led by a minor Wallachian noble, Tudor Vladimirescu. He expected support from Russia against the Turks, but it did not materialize, and Vladimirescu was executed. One of his major goals was achieved, however, as the Porte thereafter appointed native princes to rule both provinces.[7] In any case, the reassertion of Ottoman control was only temporary, for Russia was becoming the dominant power in the region. After a brief war between the Russians and the Turks in 1828, Russia occupied the Danubian principalities for six years and under General Paul Kiselev reor-ganized and codified their internal political structure in a series of detailed ad-ministrative regulations known as the Organic Statutes. The occupation brought a number of improvements in administration, communications, transport, and finances. It also strengthened the power of the upper aristocracy and the prince at the expense of the lower gentry and the peasants, a result, as Barbara Jelavich has observed, "fully consonant with the desires of the conservative Russian regime."[8] In addition, as Daniel Chirot has demonstrated, "the period of Rus-sian rule was a typical example of 'indirect colonial rule' in which a local land-controlling aristocracy profited from the colonial situation."[9]

In subsequent decades the rural economy in Wallachia shifted from pastoral to cereal-cultivating, increasing the food supply and allowing a population ex-plosion. The increased power of the large landowners, the growing subjection of the peasants, the opening of grain markets in the West, and the profits from cereal exports produced a situation in which as much grain as possible was sqeezed from the peasants to provide exports to support the urban and cosmopolitan life-style of the nobility as well as the agents who collected from the peasants.[10] An 1864 land reform only made the peasants' situation worse by clarifying the nobles' (boyars) outright ownership of land and requiring the peasants to pay for whatever land they received, which in most cases was too little for self-sufficiency. As they had neither capital nor the economic freedom to experiment with new tech-niques, their wheat and corn yields remained low. Growth in production was ac-complished extensively by adding land under cultivation[11] and increasing the labor force. Not until the very last years of the century did agricultural techniques begin to change. By then, pressure to shift from animals to cereals had been so successful and rural living standards had fallen so low that the peasants' diet con-sisted almost entirely of grain, resulting in widespread pellagra.[12] Even the minor improvements in agricultural production that began to occur at the turn of the century were soon interrupted by a great peasant revolt in 1907.

Meanwhile, international events had brought major political changes. In 1848 rising national consciousness (especially among the educated but economically marginal nobility in the principalities and the Orthodox peasants in Transylvania) produced separate unsuccessful revolts in the three provinces. Their goals differed—mainly unification in the principalities and national recognition in Transylvania—but all were put down by the direct or indirect intervention of the Russian Army (and in Wallachia by Russia and Turkey jointly).[13] Change was postponed but not for long. "Protected" by Russia since 1829, yet ostensibly under Ottoman suzerainty, the Danubian principalities once again became pawns of international diplomacy in the Crimean War. Negotiations among the major European powers in 1856–1858 prevented Russian expansion but weakened Turkish rule still further by allowing an assembly in each principality to choose its own prince for life. Membership in the assemblies was restricted almost entirely to the several hundred richest noble families, and so their domination of the political and social system continued. Much to the surprise of the great powers, in 1859 both assemblies elected the same prince, Alexandru Ioan Cuza, an act which in effect joined the two principalities into a new Romanian state (in theory still subject to the Ottomans).

Cuza moved quickly to gain international recognition for the united principalities under the name Romania, but his internal reformism brought him into frequent conflict with the National Assembly, still dominated by the upper nobility. In May 1864 he overthrew the constitution and called a national plebiscite, using his control of the state administration to win the election by a huge margin—an example that would be copied by his successors. Cuza then pushed through the land reform, which was intended to create a prosperous, landed peasantry. But the tenacity of the boyars in holding on to their best lands and powers combined with a population explosion to worsen the condition of the peasantry in the second half of the nineteenth century. Elite opposition to Cuza and his reforms led to his overthrow in 1866. Unable to agree on an internal candidate as ruler, the Romanian nobles imported Charles Hohenzollern to become King Carol I.

The new constitution drawn up in 1866 provided for a bicameral parliament that shared power with the king, but the complicated electoral system continued to restrict political influence to the rural and urban propertied classes. Just as important as the new constitution was the rapid growth of a new state bureaucracy, modeled on the centralized French administrative system, whose powers of regulation, enforcement, and tax collection produced a sudden shift in influence from local landowners to local administrators and their superiors in the capital of Bucharest. Local prefects learned how to turn out electoral majorities with considerable ease, and soon only a token opposition existed in the legislature. In addition, because the king managed to gain control of the bureaucracy from the parliamentary leaders after 1886, he "could make and unmake governments" with the help of the bureaucrats.[14] Under Carol this translated into alternating governments of the Conservative and Liberal parties, the Conservative composed mainly of large landowners and the Liberal dominated by businessmen, professionals, bureaucrats, and small landowners. In the last decades of the nineteenth century, the propertied classes again cooperated with political officials in order to maintain their joint domination of Romania.

From 1890 to 1945

At the beginning of the twentieth century, the Romanian kingdom was an agrarian society lacking most of the accepted prerequisites for economic development. In 1899 only 15 percent of Romanian citizens were literate, and about 17 percent of the population lived in urban areas.[15] To make matters worse, the disparity in land distribution between large and small holdings was the greatest in Europe, including Russia: in 1907 over 95 percent of the holdings were crowded onto 40 percent of the land. More than 60 percent of the peasant holdings were below even bare subsistence (3 hectares), and another 25 percent were marginal (below 5 hectares).[16] In addition, the direction of change was not encouraging: the average peasant holding in 1864 had been 4.6 hectares; by 1896 it was 3.4, and by 1905, 3.2.[17] In 1870 peasants delivered an average of 20 to 33 percent of the produce from rented land to the owner, depending on the region; by 1906 the rent was often 50 percent.[18]

Given this background, it should not be surprising that in March 1907 a violent peasant revolt broke out in northern Moldavia and spread rapidly south and west into much of the country. The king dismissed the Conservative government, and a Liberal government then took strong measures that protected Bucharest, put down the rising within a month, and killed about 11,000 peasants.[19] The revolt frightened the government into passing a number of laws on behalf of the peasants regulating contracts, creating a Rural Office, and establishing cooperatives to rent land. These paternalistic policies were given wide publicity as a new form of *socialism de stat*, but they barely "scratched the surface of the problem."[20] Daniel Chirot has argued that Romanian agriculture was beginning to shift toward intensive growth strategies at the turn of the century, at least on owner-managed larger holdings, and that yields were rising. Over time, he speculates, mechanization could have pushed excess labor off the land (presumably into industry), and the landlords might have changed from "dues collectors to rational capitalist producers."[21] The changes were too little too late, however, as the peasant violence and then the effects of World War I led the government to defend the small, inefficient producer, first with the bandaid laws following the 1907 revolt and then in 1918 with the most extensive land reform in interwar Europe (excluding the Soviet Union).

Although the deteriorating situation in agriculture so clearly revealed in 1907 provided the general background to the land reform of 1918–1921, its immediate causes were varied.[22] The Liberals had promised such a reform in 1913 during a successful election campaign. King Ferdinand (who had succeeded to the throne in 1914 on the death of his uncle, Carol I) made the same promise in 1917 to motivate his peasant army to fight despite severe military defeats.[23] After the war, growing fear of Bolshevism stimulated the government to keep those promises. The reform turned over 40 percent of all arable land to peasant owners[24] and, in effect, destroyed the political and economic power of the landowning elites and the Conservative party. Unfortunately, however, it did little to increase the size of farming units or to consolidate the holdings. Even worse, the frequent delays in settling ownership rights discouraged both investment and the purchase and consolidation of the land by more efficient farmers.[25] Many of the landholdings remained too small and scattered to be economically viable, and the Romanian peasants exacerbated the problem by the tradition of dividing their land among male children. The average yield of cereals per hectare dropped about 24 percent, consumption rose, and exports declined, thus ending the Liberals' hopes that industrialization could be financed internally by agricultural savings.[26] Although the agrarian reform destroyed the old landowners, it led to rural overpopulation, underemployment, and low productivity. It also failed to produce savings for investment and therefore actually delayed the painful transformation of poor or landless peasants into industrial workers.

A major purpose of the 1918–1921 land reform, however, had not been to improve the social and economic situation of the peasants but rather to prevent their conversion to political radicalism. Political stability was of more immediate importance to the Romanian elites than economic development. This fear of instability stemmed from the 1907 revolt, from the threat of Bolshevism, and from the fragility of national unity and independence in the postwar era. Romania's late entry into World War I had been a major gamble that had led to devastating losses in 1916 but had brought windfall profits after the war. The small Kingdom of Romania, which until 1918, consisted of Wallachia and Moldavia, more than doubled in size and population with the addition of the following territories: Transylvania, the Banat, and Bucovina from Austria-Hungary; Bessarabia from Russia; and Northern Dobrogea (Dobrudja) from Bulgaria. Along with these new territories, Romania acquired substantial numbers of national minorities. The 1930 census showed that almost 30 percent of the population of the new Greater Romania (*România Mare*, as the new political entity was called) was not ethnically Romanian, and many of these other ethnic groups were by no means reconciled to Romanian rule. The political unity and internal stability of the new state were therefore threatened by ethnic tensions.

In addition, the almost simultaneous collapse of the Ottoman, Austro-Hungarian, and Russian empires as a result of the war led to the creation in Eastern Europe of a number of small states with minority populations inside Romania. Given the hostility of these new neighbors, it is not surprising that Romanian nationalism in defense of the newly acquired territories played a major role in the country's domestic and foreign policies in the interwar years. In fact, nationalism was so pervasive that many observers of Romanian affairs have concluded that the "overriding motive force" in Romanian history has been nationalism.[27]

As we know, the cleavages in Romanian society were not only ethnic but also involved elite-mass relations. What Michael Shafir has termed the most striking feature of Romanian society and politics was the contrast between the *pays légal* and the *pays réel*: Western constitutional forms (*pays légal* grafted onto a corporate, patriarchal, and status-based society (*pays réel*).[28] Not only was there a contrast in Romania between political form and substance, but also the country consisted of two separate worlds differing in political, economic, social, educational, and cultural experiences and values: the rural Romanian peasantry, most of whom eked out a living on below-subsistence holdings, and an urbanized aristocracy that was "probably the most cosmopolitan in Eastern Europe."[29] Both the land reform and the stress on nationalism were attempts to mitigate the insecurity of the Romanian elites by emphasizing the ties among ethnic Romanians of all social strata.

Perhaps the major effect of these cleavages in Romanian society on the political process was an electoral system so corrupt as to guarantee the election of the party in power. United by their joint fear of any real exercise of power by the masses, the political elites—through the interior minister and state bureaucrats at both central and local levels—simply ensured that the proper candidates won. The eclipse of the Conservatives, combined with King Ferdinand's support for the Liberal party under Ion Brătianu, allowed the Liberals to use the techniques that Carol I had evolved to assure the outcome of elections. In other words, until his death in 1927 Brătianu dominated the electoral process with the silent cooperation of the state bureaucracy. Rather than being responsible to the voters, the elected government and the civil service in effect united to dominate them.[30]

The political system was not only corrupt, but it was also personalized. The parties revolved around personalities and clans. The Brătianu family controlled the Liberals, for example, and the other party that evolved to oppose the Liberals—the National Peasant party, a combination of the old National party of Transylvania and the Peasant Party—was led by individuals such as Iuliu Maniu, Ion Mihalache, Alexandru Vaida-Voevod, and Constantin Stere, each with his own loyalists. As Joseph Rothschild has described the situation, "A leader was followed for the sake of the power, influence, and positions he could command and distribute, and so his death would entail a severe crisis for his party, and perhaps even dissolution."[31]

In 1925 King Ferdinand's son and heir to the throne, Carol, renounced his rights to succession for personal reasons: his desire to live with Magda Lupescu rather than with his wife, Princess Helen. He then went into exile, and in 1927 his six-year old son Michael assumed the throne under a regency when Ferdinand died. That same year Prime Minister Brătianu also died; the Liberals never recovered from the deaths of these two men. They lost control of the electoral process, and in 1928 the National Peasants under Iuliu Maniu gained power in the one interwar Romanian election that is generally regarded as free from political manipulation. By 1930, however, Romania was facing the consequences of the international economic crisis, and Carol abruptly returned to Romania, ended the regency, and took the throne. Prime Minister Maniu agreed provisionally to Carol's return, but when Carol was not reconciled with his wife and brought back

Lupescu instead, Maniu resigned. From then until 1940 Romanian politics at the top level were largely dominated by Carol who, although he did lend state support to industrial projects and important growth was achieved in some areas, was no more successful in bridging the gap between *pays légal* and *pays réel* or improving the economic situation than the party politicians had been.

What was needed to end the stagnation was a crash program of industrialization, and the Romanian elites of the early twentieth century did not fail to recognize the importance of industry. Indeed, disputes among Romanian politicians and academics throughout this century have focused on *how*, not *whether*, to industrialize. There were bitter quarrels over the issue of protectionism between Liberals and Conservatives before World War I, and among Liberals, Social-Democrats, and National Peasant leaders in the interwar period, but all these parties assumed the necessity of industrialization. The Liberal party, when it governed from 1922 to 1928, was an avid protector of Romanian Capital and infant industries. Even the National Peasant party (NPP), which might have been expected to introduce policies to stimulate agricultural investment at the expense of industry, "was not very 'peasantist' either in its composition or in its activities."[32] When it assumed power in 1928, the NPP welcomed investment by foreign capitalists and adopted agrarian legislation that laid the party open to the charge of favoring the richer peasants and village bourgeoisie. Not even the leader of the fascist Iron Guard, Corneliu Zelea Codreanu, was totally hostile to industrialization. On the contrary, this leader of what was essentially an antibourgeois protest movement based on national rebirth "praised industry" and called on his fellow Romanians to develop "the art of entrepreneurship."[33]

Despite the widespread consensus on the need for industry, the Romanian elites were not able to achieve rapid industrial growth before World War II. In part this failure stemmed from the historical absence of a native bourgeoisie. Although the Danubian principalities originally gained considerable wealth through commerce, during the Ottoman period the commercial classes were usually non-Romanians—Greeks or Armenians—while the Romanians formed the peasantry and the small native aristocracy. During the tremendous increase in foreign trade in the nineteenth century, much of the new commercial class was again foreign—this time largely Jewish—because the Romanian peasants were tied to the land by economic obligations and the marginal gentry who needed income preferred the state administration: "The costs and risks of entrepreneurship far outweighed those of administrative office. To become and entrepreneur required [for an aristocrat] a sacrifice of social status."[34]

The absence of a Romanian middle class did not prevent the government from encouraging the growth of industry, and starting in the 1880s, a series of laws established a system of subsidies and tariff protection.[35] Indeed, the Liberal government was trying to finance industrialization internally "on the backs of the peasants" by changing the tax structure to take "four times more from the peasantry than from landlords."[36] Some large-scale enterprises were established, mostly in textiles and petroleum, but despite the government's efforts, they tended to result from foreign investment.

In 1899 about two-thirds of industrial capital in Romania was foreign, although the Liberals' protectionism would reduce that to 52 percent by 1912–1913 and 36 percent by 1929.[37] There was some industrial growth in Romania before World War I, but as late as 1913, 81 percent of the population of the Romanian Kingdom was employed in agriculture, and only about 3 percent of the labor force could be considered industrial workers.[38]

After World War I the political leaders, especially the Liberals, promised to stimulate industrialization, but again the search for stability intervened. Grain exports were heavily taxed to keep domestic prices low. The results were unfortunate for a number of reasons. Romania fell from fifth to tenth in world ranking of cereal exporters, the agricultural sector lost capital, rural consumption of urban products dropped, and both sectors suffered.[3] Manufacturing had been devastated by the war. Production in 1921 was only 47.2 percent of 1913, and the prewar level was not achieved until 1926. Production climbed to 136.9 percent of the 1913 level by 1929,[40] in part because of protectionist policies: tariffs and subsidies were increased, natural resources were nationalized to protect them from foreigners, foreign capital was limited to 40 percent in any company, and any board of directors had to be three-quarters Romanian.[41] The important petroleum industry, however, remained largely under foreign control and somewhat separate from the rest of the economy.[42]

One of the difficulties in the interwar Romanian economy was its disjointed nature. Not only was there the need to incorporate the various new territories into Greater Romania, but also state intervention in the form of subsidies and tariffs produced growth in certain sectors unrelated to the costs or demands of the market. During the 1920s Romania's overall industrial growth rates were notably lower than those of its Balkan neighbors, and by 1929 per capita gross material product had barely reached the levels of 1913.[43] Meanwhile, the huge rural sector faced deteriorating productivity and depressed consumption.

When the National Peasant party came to power in 1928, its leaders attempted to ease the lot of the peasants by attracting foreign investment, thus reversing the Liberals' protection of domestic industries. Unfortunately, the onset of the international depression reduced the availability of foreign capital, and Romania's grain exports—over 19 million lei in 1929—dropped to just over 3 million in 1932. Per capita income fell by almost 50 percent and by 1937 had not yet returned to 1927 levels.[44] Carol II and his minister of finance, Mihai Manoilescu, were convinced that strong state support for industrialization was the only solution. Protective tariffs were introduced once again, and rapid growth in certain areas such as steel and armaments began. This did not translate into benefits for the population, however: "Romania was the slowest of the East European states to recover from the material declines of the depression. As late as 1940 the standard of living was estimated to be between 33 and 64 percent lower than in 1916."[45]

Social conditions in Romania at the time present some surprising contrasts. Michael Kaser has painted a horrifying picture of health conditions. In 1932, for example, life expectancy was about the same as in Albania and Yugoslavia (forty-two years), but infant mortality was much higher: 179 deaths per 1,000 live births, compared to 133 and 100 in the other two countries. In 1938 Romania had the highest mortality rate in Europe (except for Spain, which was then in the middle of a civil war) and the highest death rate from pellagra in Europe. About a tenth of the deaths were from tuberculosis, and typhus, typhoid, and malaria were barely under control. Physicians, pharmacies, and hospital beds were scarce and unevenly distributed. As Kaser observed, "No country in Europe between the two World Wars had conditions of health that were worse than the Romanian."[46] One estimate asserts that Romania's standard of living in 1930 was roughly comparable to that of England in 1648 or France in 1789,[47] and yet the literacy rate was equivalent to the English in 1860 or the French in 1870.[48]

As in the rest of Eastern Europe, the one area in which the Romanian interwar governments achieved remarkable success was in education, both the spread of mass literacy and increased opportunities for higher education. Ironically, these successes in themselves contributed to instability because the newly literate masses could not only recognize their misery but also formulate and express demands. In addition, the new university graduates swelled an already huge and badly paid bureaucracy, or, if they failed to find employment that they considered suitable to their new status, they joined the growing numbers of citizens who were discontented but politically conscious and articulate.[49]

The deteriorating economic situation throughout Eastern Europe during the 1930s contributed to the growth of radical protest movements, and many of their adherents came from among those discontented students or university graduates. Romania was no exception. The fascist leader, Corneliu Zelea Codreanu, saw a vision of the Archangel Michael calling on him to save his nation and named his organization the League of the Archangel Michael. It was a protest movement of the radical right, appealing to the nationalism and religious mysticism of Romanian peasants and intellectuals. The Legion's overt anti-Semitism and xenophobia found support in the political environment of interwar Romania and interwar Europe, and its increasing use of violence gave it political influence far beyond its electoral support (16 percent in 1937).[50]

A political stalemate resulted from the 1937 elections, and King Carol took advantage of the situation to establish a royal dictatorship. During 1938 he dissolved the political parties, including the Legion, and even managed to rid himself of Codreanu, who was arrested, tried, imprisoned, and shot in what was reported to be an escape attempt. A year later, in September 1939, the Legion retaliated by assassinating Carol's prime minister, Armand Călinescu, and the king in turn carried out mass reprisals. Carol appeared to dominate the internal situation, but he could not prevent the Soviet seizure of Bessarabia in June 1940 or Hitler's decision later that summer in the Vienna Diktat to give northern Transylvania back to Hungary. The discontent in Romania over the country's dismemberment was so great that in September Carol was forced to abdicate in favor of his son, Michael. Real power, however, lay with General (later Marshal) Ion Antonescu, who in effect established a military dictatorship with the support of the Legion and the Germans. Then in January 1941 Antonescu forcibly suppressed the Legionaries, many of whom fled to Germany or abroad. Hitler, who wanted an effective military ally with an efficient economy, acquiesced in the destruction of the Legion, and Romania remained a German ally until August 1944.

One party or regime after another—parliamentary, royal, fascist, military—failed to achieve its goals for Romania during the first half of the twentieth century. First, the fragile national unity of Greater Romania was never solidified, and the country was dismembered during and after 1940. Second, like the other small states of Eastern Europe, Romania saw its independence in international affairs destroyed by the rise of two new empires. Germany and later the Soviet Union occupied the small state and forced it into a close alliance as Hitler and then Stalin sought to control the country's natural resources. Third, industrial growth and agricultural development were stifled for a variety of domestic and international reasons. The power of the Conservative landowners had been shattered by the 1918–1921 land reform, but the Liberals were unable to solve the agrarian issue or develop industry sufficiently to maintain, let alone raise, living standards. Small-scale peasant agriculture continued to dominate the Romanian economy until after World War II, and the spurt of industrial growth in the 1930s did not strengthen the country sufficiently to prevent its disintegration in the face of internal and external hostility.

The inability of successive Romanian governments to preserve national unity and independence and to implement a program of industrial development was matched by their failure to regularize constitutional procedures. Romania was not unusual in this respect, as many young parliamentary systems in Europe and elsewhere succumbed to economic difficulties during the 1930s. The deep gulf between the elites and the rest of society induced politicians in Romania to fear instability above all else. This fear created alliances among various elite groups and also stimulated electoral corruption to exclude nonelites from attaining power. Yet the frustrated expectations of the interwar decades intensified the desire of many Romanians for the basic national goals of unity, independence, and economic growth. Failure to make significant progress toward these goals had widened the gap between elites and nonelites before 1945 and prevented any evolution toward an open and institutionalized political process. Although the international environment in the 1930s—the depression and then the war—had precipitated Romania's collapse, the indigenous elites had not been able to make significant progress on the path of political development in the 1920s following World War I. The aftermath of World War II would be different.

The Communist Experience I: Gheorghiu-Dej

The communist era in Romanian development can be divided roughly into two periods: the first two decades following World War II, when the Romanian Communist Party (RCP) was led by Gheorghe Gheorghiu-Dej, and the Ceauşescu era beginning in 1965 when Nicolae Ceauşescu became party leader on the death of his predecessor. Table 6.1 gives the official figures on economic growth during those years, but these data cannot be considered accurate, especially during the last half of Ceauşescu's rule. For example, the grain harvest in 1989 was originally reported as 60 million tons; after the December 1989 revolution, the new government announced that the real figure had been 17 million. Indeed, specialists in the Directorate of Statistics complained bitterly in *Adevărul* as early as December 26 that official data given out by the "odious dictatorship" on industrial and agricultural production, national income, and other matters were not based on actual calculations but were simply made up at the whim of the dictator. A great many figures were released in early 1990, but an accurate picture of the economic situation had not appeared by late spring.[51]

The Ceauşescu data show the priority given to heavy industry under both Gheorghiu-Dej and his successor, and the resulting shift in the structure of the labor force (see Table 6.2). From 1950 to 1986 the percentage employed in agriculture fell dramatically, in contrast to that in industry and construction. Foreign trade also showed considerable change, both in growth (although the volume dropped significantly after 1981) and in structure. Table 6.3 reveals an impressive rise in machinery exports, for example. If we measure Romania's economic development by such socioeconomic indicators, we must conclude that the communist era produced some impressive results in promoting industrialization, especially in the period before 1980.[52]

Communism in Romania did not have a promising beginning. The Romanian Communist party was probably the weakest in Eastern Europe during the interwar period,[53] in part because the country had only a tiny industrial proletariat. The many Romanian peasants supported the National Peasant party and later, if they became radicalized in the 1930s, gravitated toward fascism. To make matters worse, the RCP was outlawed in 1924 and thereafter had to build a new, underground organization. Much RCP support came from the non-Romanian population, in part because of Comintern insistence that the RCP support the demands of the ethnic minorities to secede, and in part because these minorities were not attracted to the traditional parties or to the Romanian nationalism of the Legionary movement. As a result, in the minds of most ethnic Romanians the RCP became identified with national enemies: the minority nationalities and the Russian Bolsheviks who had seized Bessarabia. Factional struggles within the party also weakened it, and these were exacerbated by the interference of the Comintern. Indeed, one of Ceauşescu's first major speeches, just a year after he became party leader, denounced the Comintern for having caused serious "harm" to Romania's "revolutionary struggles."[54]

Table 6.1
Romania: Principal Growth Indicators

	1965	1950 = 100 1970	1975	1980	1986
Population	116.7	124.2	130.3	136.1	139.9
Working Population	115.6	117.9	121.2	123.6	127.4
National Income	413	599	1000	1500	1900
Per Capita					
National Income	354	482	784	1100	1400
Industrial Production	649	1100	2100	3300	4300
Group A	823	1500	2900	4700	6100
Group B	457	728	1200	1800	2400
Agricultural Production	193	212	289	349	468

Sources: Anuarul statistic al RSR 1981 (Bucharest: Directia centrală de statistică, 1981), Table 31, p.93; Anuarul statistic al RSR 1986 (Bucharest: Directia centrală de statistică, 1987), Table 3, p. 5.

Table 6.2
Romania: Working Population by Sector

	1938	1950	1965	1980	1985	1986
Total	100.0	100.0	100.0	100.0	100.0	100.0
Industry	9.2	12.0	19.2	35.5	37.1	37.3
Construction	1.3	2.2	6.3	8.3	7.4	7.4
Agriculture	76.4	74.1	56.5	29.4	28.5	28.3
Forestry	*	0.2	0.2	0.4	0.4	0.4
Transport	1.1	1.9	3.1	6.1	6.0	6.1
Telecommunications	*	0.3	0.6	0.8	0.8	0.8
Internal Trade	3.5	2.5	4.0	6.0	5.8	5.8
Local Services	*	0.7	2.1	3.8	4.1	4.2
Education, Culture	*	2.3	3.5	4.2	3.9	3.8
Science	*	0.2	0.5	0.9	1.3	1.3
Health and Social Services	*	1.1	2.0	2.7	2.7	2.7
Administration	*	1.7	1.0	0.6	0.5	0.5
Other	*	0.8	1.0	1.3	1.5	1.4

*No figure given.
Note: All figures are percentages.

Source: Anuarul statistic al RSR (Bucharest: Direcţia centrală de statistică, 1987), Table 18, p. 20.

The defeat of Germany and the Soviet occupation of Romania at the end of World War II changed the situation completely. With Soviet backing, the RCP leaders were able to defeat their political rivals such as the Liberal and National Peasant politicians, force King Michael to abdicate, and establish a monopoly over the political system by 1948. Meanwhile, a land reform in 1945 destroyed any remnants of the large landowning class, a currency reform in 1947 ruined the middle classes, and in 1948 expropriation of large industrial properties began so that, by 1950, 90 percent of industrial production was state-owned. Between 1948 and 1953 commerce was also taken over: the percentage of privately owned shops dropped from 90 to 14. Kenneth Jowitt calls this the period of "breakthrough," when the revolutionary elite destroyed the old elites in the name of progress.[55]

The peasants were handled more cautiously, in part because they were the overwhelming majority of the population, and in part because the country was already short of food as a result of the war and a subsequent drought. The 1945 land distribution had not alleviated the fundamental problem of tiny plots, but it had helped to stifle overt discontent until the leaders of the National Peasant party had been arrested or forced into exile. In 1949 a collectivization campaign began,

Table 6.3
Romania: Structure of Foreign Trade

	1950	1965	1975	1980	1985	1986
Total	100.0	100.0	100.0	100.0	100.0	100.0
X	100.0	100.0	100.0	100.0	100.0	100.0
M	100.0	100.0	100.0	100.0	100.0	100.0
Machinery and Equipment						
Total	22.4	29.2	30.0	24.7	31.1	33.3
X	4.2	18.8	25.3	24.9	34.7	36.9
M	38.3	39.9	34.7	24.6	26.7	29.1
Fuels, Minerals, Metals						
Total	28.3	28.2	30.3	40.6	36.5	34.6
X	33.8	25.1	22.3	29.5	24.9	22.0
M	23.5	31.4	38.2	50.3	51.0	48.9
Chemical Products, Fertilizers, Rubber						
Total	3.2	6.4	8.6	7.9	8.3	7.6
X	1.7	6.4	10.8	9.7	9.8	8.9
M	4.5	6.3	6.5	6.4	6.4	6.1
Construction Materials						
Total	2.7	2.4	2.0	1.6	1.3	1.2
X	4.4	3.4	2.9	2.2	1.8	1.6
M	1.1	1.4	1.1	1.0	0.7	0.8
Raw Materials and Semi-Fabricates - Non-Food						
Total	24.8	12.4	7.3	5.3	4.9	4.9
X	28.9	13.8	6.3	4.8	4.4	4.4
M	21.4	11.1	8.4	5.7	5.6	5.4
Live Animals						
Total	*	*	0.1	0.1	*	*
X	*	*	*	*	*	*
M	*	*	0.1	0.1	*	*
Raw Materials - Food						
Total	5.7	4.3	5.3	5.0	2.1	2.2
X	11.6	7.6	5.7	4.2	1.2	1.3
M	0.7	0.8	5.0	5.7	3.1	3.4
Processed Foods						
Total	6.8	8.2	6.4	5.7	4.5	4.9
X	14.1	13.9	10.6	8.5	6.3	7.6
M	0.3	2.4	2.2	3.2	2.3	1.8
Consumer Goods						
Total	6.1	8.9	10.0	9.1	11.3	11.3
X	1.3.	11.0	16.1	16.2	16.9	17.3
M	10.2	6.7	3.8	3.0	4.2	4.5

*No figure given.   X - Exports   M - Imports

Note: All figures are percentages.

Source: Anuarul statistic al RSR (Bucharest: Direcția
centrală de statistică, 1987), Table 4, p. 80.

but there was considerable resistance (evidently over 80,000 peasants were arrested), and by the end of 1950 only 2.6 percent of agricultural land had been collectivized. A halt was called for a year, and the program was resumed from time to time over the next few years. However, by the end of 1957 private farms still occupied over half the arable land. In 1958 the second phase of collectivization began, and by the end of 1962 only 3.5 percent of arable land was in private hands.[56] Gheorghiu-Dej could announce proudly that collectivization was complete.

Central planning started in 1949 and 1950 with one-year plans, and the first Five-Year Plan began in 1951. From 1950 to 1953, when the plan was abandoned, the ratio of investment to national income rose from 19 to 34 percent, with over half going to industry and construction, about 10 percent to agriculture, and only 3.2 percent to housing.[57] The economic dislocation caused by such extreme measures, combined with Stalin's death in March 1953 and Moscow's subsequent New Course, led the Romanian leaders to initiate their own New Course—a period of relative relaxation when more investment went to agriculture, consumer goods, and housing.

Meanwhile, Gheorghiu-Dej had already consolidated his control over the party. In the immediate postwar years he had shared power with Ana Pauker and Vasile Luca, both of whom had spent the war in the Soviet Union. Pauker was Jewish, and Luca Hungarian. In 1952 they were removed from the leadership, and Gheorghiu-Dej both then and later blamed them for the excesses of 1949–1953. A year after Stalin's death, the RCP leader executed Lucretiu Pătrăşcanu, who had been the other leading ethnic Romanian in the RCP at the end of the war and had then been arrested in 1948 as a Titoist. The unity of the RCP would henceforth be challenged only by subordinates, not colleagues, and they would never pose a serious threat to the party leader.[58]

Danger to Gheorghiu-Dej's control would come not from inside the RCP but from Moscow. Just as the original strategy of rapid industrialization and collectivized agriculture had owed much to Stalin's influence as to the presence of Pauker and Luca, so the economic relaxation was in part the result of demands from Moscow. These demands also included collective leadership: Gheorghiu-Dej was forced to give up one of the two top positions, head of party or state, in 1954, and he chose to remain head of state. A year later, however, he exchanged his job for head of the party, acknowledging where the real power lay. When the Soviet leadership rejected Malenkov's light industry for Khrushchev's defense of previous priorities, the Romanian leader did the same. The pace of industrialization in Romania had picked up by 1955, and the initial version of the 1956–1960 plan envisioned high investments, mostly in industry. The dramatic developments in Poland and Hungary in 1956 then led to new concessions, again to mollify not only the Romanian population, but also Moscow: "Compulsory agricultural deliveries were abolished, and worker's wages were increased by 15 percent[;] . . . the years between 1956 and 1958 were among the best experienced by Romanians since the end of the war."[59]

This period was not so positive for Gheorghiu-Dej, however. He could deflect Khrushchev's criticism of Stalin from himself by claiming to have removed Romania's Stalinists, Pauker and Luca, in 1952. But the ploy was not completely credible, and members of his own Political Bureau criticized him and had to be removed in 1957.[60] He was able to maintain party unity, but he had learned that he must rely on his own levers of power and not depend on Moscow. Soviet support had brought the RCP to power and had enabled the party to destroy its opponents and the old political and social structure of Romania. Moscow's support was still necessary to ensure communist rule, but after 1957 Gheorghiu-Dej would tolerate no internal interference in Romanian affairs from Khrushchev.

In 1958 Gheorghiu-Dej appeared to be the ideal Soviet ally. In foreign policy he had always followed Moscow's lead and, although in domestic affairs he was reluctant to adopt the reformist policies advocated first by Malenkov and then by Khrushchev, he had avoided the crises that had occurred elsewhere in Eastern Europe. Partly as a reward for loyalty, partly to indicate confidence in the Romanians as allies, and partly to fulfill promises made in the aftermath of the Hungarian uprising in 1956, Khrushchev removed Soviet troops from Romania in 1958. Almost simultaneously, the RCP leadership introduced a plan for rapid and broadly based industrialization: a return to the high investment rates and emphasis on heavy industry of the early 1950s. Then in 1959 the campaign to collectivize agriculture was resumed, and during the crucial 1960–1965 plan, 74 percent of state investment went into industry or energy development and only 10 percent into light industry and food processing.[61]

At first, there appeared to be no serious discrepancy between Soviet goals for Romania and those of its own leaders. The Soviets apparently acquiesced in the new industrialization plans, and relations between Khrushchev and Gheorghiu-Dej remained cordial, if not warm. Khrushchev, however, had concluded from the troubles in Poland and Hungary in 1956 that Stalinist coercion of the USSR's allies should be replaced by the more effective tie of economic integration within Comecon, the economic community of Eastern Europe. He thus began to pursue joint preparation of national plans by these small countries at the formulation stage, with increased specialization by each Comecon member in certain types of production. For Romania this would mean focusing on agriculture and related food industries, as well as petroleum and petrochemical products, rather than continuing the RCP's chosen path of stressing heavy industry. Recognizing that the proposed planning process would threaten their own control and the country's economic sovereignty, the Romanian leaders began to oppose the integration plans within Comecon.[62] The years from 1960, when the conflict between Khrushchev and Gheorghiu-Dej became apparent to both leaders, until 1964, when Gheorghiu-Dej emerged at least temporarily victorious in his resistance, reveal gradually increasing friction between the two allies and, simultaneously, a growing rapprochement between the Romanian government and its citizens.

In this respect, nationalism was crucial. The regime began to deemphasize its cultural ties with the USSR, downgrading the celebration of Soviet holidays and changing the names of streets, buildings, stores, and other institutions from Russian to Romanian. Cultural contacts and trade with the West increased dramatically, and a new emphasis on Romanian political and cultural traditions appeared. During 1964 the dispute in Comecon came to a head, and in April the RCP issued a statement that became known as Romania's "Declaration of Independence," calling for close unity among bloc members but rejecting interference in their internal affairs.[63] All these measures were greeted with great enthusiasm in Romania, and for the first time Gheorghiu-Dej had a taste of genuine popular support—despite the harsh economic policies. The Soviet leaders were not very happy about the Romanian actions, but they chose to do very little about them. Two days after Khrushchev's removal from office in October 1964, the new leaders in Moscow formally acquiesced in the Romanian industrialization plans by signing an agreement for extensive technical assistance.

Gheorghiu-Dej had little time to reflect on his growing popularity, for in March 1965 he died after a short bout with cancer. During the two decades that he led the Romanian communist movement, the accomplishments of his regime were considerable. First, the RCP with Soviet support brought about fundamental changes in the politics, economics, and social structure of the country, destroying the old elites and establishing a new basis for elite status in accordance with its definitions of Marxist development. The regime used considerable force, however, to maintain itself in power, ruling by coercion rather than consent, and its strategies of economic growth emphasized high investment in heavy industry to the exclusion of food, housing, and consumer goods, thus depressing the standard of living. As in the past, the political and economic elites (now RCP officials and the state bureaucracy) cooperated to maintain themselves in power at the expense of the general population. Second, when the RCP leaders disagreed with Soviet interpretations of Romania's needs, they started their party and their country on the path to autonomy. This new attitude toward the USSR then created the potential for a different relationship between the Romanian Communist party and the Romanian population in which coercion could be replaced at least in part by voluntary acceptance.

The Communist Experience II: Ceauşescu

When Gheorghiu-Dej died in March 1965, Ceauşescu was immediately elected first secretary, but he functioned for the next several years as the chief spokesman for a collective leadership that promised caution and compromise in domestic affairs, continuity in foreign policy, military strength to defend the country, and increased consumer satisfaction. In other words, during this period of regime weakness and transition, the new leaders acted so as to preempt the opposition of groups outside the party and even sought approval from the citizenry. They made overtures to various social and occupational categories inside the country—workers, peasants, intellectuals, economic managers, party administrators, the national minorities—and used promises instead of threats.[64]

Ceauşescu had been Central Committee secretary for cadres for over a decade and had considerable support within the apparatus, but he was surrounded by colleagues in the top leadership with considerably more prestige. As a result, he needed over four years to establish his dominance over the political system by a shrewd combination of four techniques: (1) manipulation of personnel and of organizational responsibilities to enhance his power in the party and the party's power in society; (2) policy compromise within the new collective leadership and policy ambiguity toward outside constituencies; (3) pledged to ensure socialist legality and to institutionalize the political process; and (4) populist appeals to the Romanian masses, promising broad participation in politics and emphasizing Romanian traditions and nationalism.

Personnel manipulation would eventually allow Ceauşescu to impose his own priorities on the party and the entire political system. Meanwhile, he needed to generate agreement among his colleagues and induce compliance from the population, and policy compromise and ambiguity were crucial in these attempts. The third and fourth techniques revealed his desire for cooperation—not just obedience—from the general population. His promises of legality were first used as a weapon against Alexandru Drǎghici, a major rival and former minister of internal affairs, who was ousted from the party leadership in 1968. However, by legality Ceauşescu also meant codifying procedures in dozens of sectors such as cooperative agriculture, criminal justice, press and culture, and education. In many cases this new legislation would merely multiply the rules regulating behavior and invade the privacy of Romanian citizens, reducing rather than improving efficiency, and leading many people to ignore them in practice. Thus, during the 1970s corruption and illegality actually increased.

Ceauşescu's participatory techniques showed no better results in the long run. They included increased "consultation" with groups in many sectors and at all levels, greater power for legislative bodies, and even multicandidate elections to the Grand National Assembly. As implemented, however, these consultative procedures rarely gave citizens that sense of efficacy and regime responsiveness that would make the effort of participation worthwhile. Huge conferences were not forums for genuine discussion and participation, but rather became opportunities for the ritualized worship of Ceauşescu in a leadership cult so extreme as to rival those of Stalin and Mao. The party continued to dominate the state legislative bodies, and the multicandidate elections were so carefully controlled during the nomination process that the voters had no real alternatives. As a result, these forms of participation in the 1970s became coerced and formalized, and produced cynicism and boredom.[65]

In fact, Ceauşescu's participatory techniques placed him squarely in the tradition of other Marxist-Leninist rulers, who have used high levels of mobilized participation to engender and demonstrate loyalty to the regime and to improve policy implementation.[66] As society develops, however, what Donald Schulz has called the "participation crisis" occurs: "Previously, citizen involvement had been defined predominantly in terms of mobilization for the purpose of policy intelligence and implementation and political socialization and recruitment. Now, however, issues of autonomy, interest articulation, and even elite selection and accountability [arise]."[67] In other words, the nature and function of participation change as the system becomes more highly developed and moves from the "mobilization" stage to the "inclusion" stage, when "manipulation rather than domination becomes the defining relationship between regime and society."[68]

During the 1960s Romania under Ceauşescu and the collective leadership seemed to be shifting toward inclusion, but such a shift would bring participation of "previously excluded, distrusted sectors of the population" and "the admission of a wide range of social elites to consultative status in sociopolitical activities."[69] However, the functions that Ceauşescu wanted participation to fulfill were to be limited to policy implementation and political socialization. As early as 1971, he became disillusioned with specialists because they told him what he did not want to hear about the economy and other issues. He wanted to encourage the specialized elites and other groups in society to help find ways to implement regime policies (and in doing so to develop a commitment to those policies), but he did not want voluntary and effective participation that could easily become "antisystemic or elite challenging" and begin to serve "policy input functions."[70]

As a result, in 1971 he began to change his strategies of rule, and thereafter his calls for participation were more clearly limited to mobilized participation. He initiated an ideological campaign, intensified the leadership cult, and began gradually to retreat from inclusion back to mobilization, from manipulation to coercion.[71] He returned to the economic policies of the early 1950s and early 1960s, as well as to the arbitrary and personalized rule that had been characteristic of the Gheorghiu-Dej period. On both accounts his demands were even more extreme than those of his predecessor. Investment rose to unprecedented heights (see Table 6.4), and Ceauşescu's leadership cult intensified. He did increase investments in agriculture after 1970, but he focused on capital investments rather than incentives to raise productivity. His demand that all energies be devoted to production led to a radical reorientation of the educational system toward technical subjects (see Table 6.5), a shift that aroused intense resentment among the nonpolitical elites.

Essentially, Ceauşescu returned to the coercive strategies of the Stalinist period, alienating workers, peasants, and intellectuals, and not taking advantage of the potential for acceptance and legitimacy that had appeared as a result of the new foreign policy. His economic strategies would be so harsh that by 1985 Romania's per capita GNP would be the lowest of any East European Comecon member.[72]

Ceauşescu's rhetorical commitment to participatory democracy continued, but the implementation of that concept in Romania allowed no challenge to his personal power. Instead of using nationalism to bridge the gap between himself and the population, and then building a permanent causeway founded on the development of citizens' capacities, resources, and choices, Ceauşescu tried to substitute

Table 6.4
Romania: Percentage of National Income Used for Consumption and Investment

	Consumption	Investment
1951-1955	75.7	24.3
1956-1960	82.9	17.1
1961-1965	74.5	25.5
1966-1970	70.5	29.5
1971-1975	66.3	33.7
1976-1980	64.7	35.3
1981-1985	72.1	27.9

Source: Anuarul statistic al RSR (Bucharest: Direcţia centrală de statistică, 1987), Table 11, p. 13.

nationalism for political development. This attempt was temporarily successful—when he gained tremendous popularity by denouncing the Warsaw Pact intervention in Czechoslovakia in 1968, for example—and his diplomatic successes and promises of legality and participatory democracy initially generated considerable popular support. By the mid-1970s, however, the unfulfilled promises had worn thin, and after 1979 living standards actually went into a decline. The gap between regime and population once again widened into a chasm.

Although the underlying causes were much deeper, the initial sign of crisis was a shortage of hard currency resulting apparently from structural imbalances in the international petroleum market.[73] Because of their oil resources, the Romanians had long specialized in petroleum-related products and had developed a major refining capacity. As the needs of their domestic industries grew, in the late 1960s they began to import larger and larger quantities of oil. The 1973–1974 rise in international oil prices caused serious problems, but it was not disastrous because the price of Romanian exports—refined products—also went up. The Romanians failed to protect themselves from further increases, however, and in 1978, when the price of crude oil jumped again, the value of refined products did not. The Romanians were caught in a price squeeze. Their supply problems were worsened first by the Iranian revolution (Ceauşescu had worked out a favorable barter arrangement with the Shah) and later by the Iran–Iraq war. By the 1980s the Romanians were buying oil even from the Soviet Union, although they have had to pay in hard currency or equivalents.[74]

By 1981 the previously rather self-sufficient Romanian economy[75] was seriously in debt to Western banks. Although initially stimulated by the unfavorable balance in oil trade,[76] this debt also had roots in unwise investment decisions of the 1960s and 1970s. Indeed, two crucial economic decisions—to invest heavily in petroleum and petrochemical products and to minimize cooperation in

Table 6.5
Romania: Students in Higher Education by Field of Specialization

	1938-1939	1965-1966	1986-1987
Total Students Enrolled	26,489	130,614	157,174
Technical	5,169	52,265	106,155
Mining	*	1,782	4,569
Petroleum	*	1,743	5,563
Electrical	*	8,505	18,092
Metallurgy and Machine Building	*	11,988	41,269
Chemical	*	3,853	7,264
Wood	*	935	848
Light Industry	*	1,094	2,698
Food Processing	*	1,350	1,422
Transport	*	764	3,326
Architecture and Construction	*	10,290	14,242
Agriculture	*	5,685	4,490
Veterinary Medicine	*	3,420	1,722
Forestry	*	856	650
Medical-Pharmaceutical	3,451	9,345	17,597
Economics	3,101	12,866	15,641
Law	7,900	4,534	2,392
Education	5,532	49,185	14,480
Arts	1,336	2,419	909

*No figure given.

Source: Anuarul statistic al RSR (Bucharest: Direcţia centrală de statistică, 1987), Table 58, p. 86.

Comecon—increased the country's dependency on hard currency imports of technology and raw materials, and the cost of these imports together reached unprecedented levels in about 1980. As Marvin Jackson has demonstrated, the "serious deterioration" of Romanian economic indicators did not begin until that year. In 1980 Romania's debt service ratio was better than that of Hungary or Bulgaria, its ratio of convertible currency debts to convertible currency exports was lower than that of Hungary, the German Democratic Republic (GDR), or Yugoslavia, and its debts per capita were a third less than those in any of those three countries.[77] Nevertheless, in 1981 Poland's potential default created among Western bankers a crisis of confidence in all the East European economies.

Romania found it particularly difficult to obtain extensions on its loans—harder than Hungary or Yugoslavia, for example. As Jackson suggests, perhaps the banks lacked confidence in the Romanians because of their excessive secrecy, restriction on contacts with foreigners, and erratic leadership.[78]

Simultaneously, Romanian agriculture, the traditional source of exports that had in the past contributed favorably to the balance of payments, fell short of its production goals owing in part to several years of bad weather, but also to long-term structural problems that reached crisis proportions only after 1979. Despite the RCP's ability to consolidate the tiny private holdings into cooperative farms, the regime had never created an efficient and effective agricultural sector. Instead, the entire economy had been structured to encourage labor to move into industry by depressing the monetary rewards and social facilities in rural life. Moreover, there had been little incentive for the ever shrinking and inefficient agricultural workforce to raise productivity. Investment in agriculture increased significantly after 1970, but the increase occurred too rapidly to be utilized efficiently, and 1979 brought major shortages in planned production for internal and external markets.[79]

Nevertheless, Ceauşescu solved the balance-of-payments difficulties in the same way that he had found investment funds: by reducing imports, exporting consumer goods and agricultural products, and depressing the domestic standard of living still further.[80] Food shortages were severe: bread, sugar, oil, meat, and other staples were rationed, eggs would disappear for weeks at a time, and even the peasant markets with supplies from their private plots were often empty. Gasoline for private cars was strictly rationed, and homes were dark and cold due to restrictions on electricity and heating fuel. In contrast to the interwar governments, the communist regime did not need to worry about instability. The coercive capabilities established by Gheorghiu-Dej and refined by Ceauşescu allowed such stringent controls on imports and consumption that the Romanian president announced the complete repayment of the country's $12 billion debt as of March 31, 1989.[81]

Romania paid off the debt at a tremendous cost in living standards, but the regime did not take steps to meet the fundamental challenge facing the Romanian economy: the need to shift from methods appropriate for extensive growth—adding inputs such as land, labor, and capital—to those that would promote intensive growth, such as the more efficient use of the inputs and production of quality goods competitive on the world market. This shift would have required a number of important changes in the Romanian economy, including close links between effort and reward; a price structure closely aligned to the costs of inputs and outputs; flexibility in decision making so that responses reflect and adjust to demand; and a long learning process on the part of both labor and management to enable managers to take over some decisions and central planners to yield some of their authority. A number of decrees and campaigns did link labor and income more closely in the 1980s, but they stressed penalties (not incentives), tightened labor discipline, and imposed more regulations, tightening rather than reducing centralized control.

Perhaps the most notorious of Ceauşescu's strategies to increase production was his plan for the countryside known as "systematization" (*sistematizare*).[82] Initiated in 1960, the original goal of the program was to distribute industrial development more equally throughout the country and to bring industry, higher standards of living, and cultural facilities to outlying and previously disadvantaged regions. By the 1980s, however, systematization had become a scheme to reorganize the entire Romanian countryside by concentrating the rural population in selected villages into high-rise apartments built on sites from which single-family houses had been razed. These new towns would help to shape an urbanized Romanian citizen who would work nearby in agriculture or in newly established factories. Villages not selected for such treatment would simply be destroyed, and their residents moved to apartments in one of the new towns. The original idea had promise—to distribute the jobs and social amenities of economic development more evenly—but it became distorted into a revolutionary scheme to transform the entire country in accordance with Ceauşescu's ideological priorities.[83]

Other grandiose projects introduced by Ceauşescu also provoked strong opposition but were adopted nonetheless. The Danube—Black Sea Canal, associated in the minds of Romanians with the Stalinist era, political prisoners, and thousands of deaths, was started again in the 1970s. After huge investments of labor and materials, it finally opened in 1984 with great pomp but little economic success. The razing of the southern part of old Bucharest to build gigantic government buildings was another dramatic scheme which Ceauşescu forced through at great cost not only in immediate economic inputs, but also in the permanent loss of historic buildings, churches, and homes. Many of Ceauşescu's plans began with great promise in the late 1960s or early 1970s but were altered in the 1980s into caricatures of their original form.

In responding to the crisis of the 1980s, Ceauşescu did not return to the rhetoric of collective leadership, legality, and participatory democracy characteristic of the late 1960s when he was attempting to consolidate his position at the top of the Romanian Communist party. Instead, he made himself infallible and omniscient, and created insecurity for everyone else from top to bottom in both the economic and political systems. A number of high officials were removed in disgrace; the Party Secretariat and county first secretaries, as well as the Council of Ministers, saw rapid rotation; and personnel change became more unpredictable and arbitrary with time, apparently depending totally on Ceauşescu's personal whims. He gradually abandoned any pretense at institutionalizing the political process and instead increased its personalization. An individual's security and promotion depended on placating Ceauşescu rather than on job performance, not characteristic of a politically developed society.[84]

Ceauşescu's activism in foreign policy continued, and he catered to national pride by his visits abroad and his apparent prestige with foreign leaders that was conveyed at home through the press. His attitudes and Romanian polices remained anti-Soviet, especially in Gorbachev's era of *glasnost* and *perestroika*, but Ceauşescu became more overtly anti-West as well, most notably on issues of disarmament and human rights. In 1981, for example, he staged giant demonstrations against both superpowers for engaging in a nuclear arms race, and in 1986 he held a referendum on nuclear disarmament in which over 99 percent of Romanian voters called for military budget cuts throughout the world. Such demonstrations served both his domestic and foreign policy goals by demonstrating his ability to mobilize the Romanian population to specific actions as well as his independence of both blocs. He was also firmer than ever in rejecting outside efforts to influence his human rights policies. In 1988 he unilaterally rejected most-favored-nation trade status from the United States because it was conditioned on his complying with emigration and human rights provisions imposed by Congress. Then in 1989, although Romania signed the final document emerging from the Vienna Conference on Human Rights, Ceauşescu reserved the right to ignore any provisions he did not wish to accept. Soon thereafter, the UN Commission on Human Rights voted to investigate Romania for violations.[85]

Clearly, Ceauşescu's nationalism became xenophobia in the 1980s as he insisted on Romania's need to be self-sufficient and to find methods of continuing development and growth by utilizing internal resources. The original plans for Romania's broadly based industrialization and foreign policy autonomy initiated in the 1960s under Gheorghiu-Dej had resembled the protectionist policies of the Liberals in the 1920s—"import substitution and a diversification of trade, all to avoid dependence"—and Manoilescu's protectionist nationalism of the 1930s.[86] But Ceauşescu carried both industrialization and nationalism to such extremes that six former members of the RCP leadership, including several of the most important architects and practitioners of Romanian policy in the 1960s, signed a public letter of protest to Ceauşescu in early 1989, condemning his systematization campaign, his violations of human rights, his alienation of other governments, and his food exports that threatened the "biological existence" of the Romanian nation. They acknowledged that they risked their lives and liberty in writing, but they felt compelled to because "the very idea of socialism, for which we have fought, is discredited by your policy."[87]

Ceauşescu had thus aroused the open opposition of major figures within the RCP as well as the intense hostility of the Romanian population. During the fall of 1989, as one East European Communist party after another was forced to compromise with its own people and end its monopoly of power, Ceauşescu continued to resist any change in Romania. After all, he did not depend on Soviet troops to keep him in office but rather on his own security forces. When demonstrations began in Timişoara in December, he had such confidence in the loyalty of his followers that he went ahead with a planned trip to Iran. He then compounded his mistake and demonstrated his overconfidence by holding a mass rally in Palace Square in Bucharest the day after his return—and the day before his overthrow. hat rally some demonstrators on the periphery of the crowd began chanting anti-Ceauşescu slogans. Not only were the slogans heard by a national television audience, but Ceauşescu's reactions—his shock and momentary fear—were visible to the entire nation. Ceauşescu had blinked, he was no longer invincible, and the country exploded. The army went over to the people, and the next day Ceauşescu and his wife were fugitives. The violence precipitated by their flight could only be calmed by their rapid trial and execution.

The situation faced by the new temporary government, the Council of the National Salvation Front, was grim. Initially, its members were able to satisfy the people's desire for revenge by the execution of Nicolae and Elena Ceauşescu. The widespread craving for food was sated temporarily by releasing stores held aside for the privileged elites of the Ceauşescu regime. In the long run, however, the task proved more difficult, and violence recurred in the form of anti- and progovernment demonstrations in Bucharest and elsewhere. The new government was enlarged in early February 1990 and renamed the Provisional Council of National Unity, eventually including over 250 members (with a president, five vice-presidents, and an Executive Bureau of twenty-one), representing over thirty political parties.

The promised elections were postponed until May 20 to give the various political groups time to organize and solicit votes. The Council remained dominated by former communists, opponents of Ceauşescu, it is true, but former members and officials of the RCP.[88] After all, in Romania for over four decades only communists were able to gain political experience, and anyone who wished to advance in a professional career was expected to join the RCP. Anticommunist sentiment in Romania is strong, and there was pronounced hostility toward the provisional government.

Yet, when the voters faced the choice between those with tainted political experience and those with little political experience, they turned by an overwhelming majority to the former. The National Liberal Party and the Peasant Party, both revivals from the prewar period, fared poorly as voters perhaps feared they promised too much change too quickly. Ion Iliescu, leader of the National Salvation Front, gained the approval of the voters by promising to link Romania to Europe, thus reaffirming the country's ties with the West, while building a social democratic society at home.

Conclusions

In Romania, as in the rest of the Balkans, hopes were often raised that real change and progress were imminent. During the interwar years significant economic and social improvement in the lives of most citizens did not materialize. After World War II progress did occur in Romania, but it came at a high cost and did not keep up with popular expectations or lead to accommodation between the regime and the population.

Since independence, but especially in the twentieth century, Romanian elites have found it expedient to justify their dominance and to reduce the gap between them and the rest of the population by emphasizing the one major tie they do have to those excluded from elite status: nationalism. Throughout the Balkans, and certainly in Romania, nationalism has been a deeply held set of beliefs, shaping the world view of most citizens and unifying all economic strata. It has been a constant feature of the political process in the Balkans in the twentieth century. The result has been to embrace and glorify one's own nation and history at the expense of others, heightening ethnic tension within states and hindering effective regional cooperation. Ceauşescu portrayed himself as the last in a series of great Romanian rulers, and his views of Romanian history (as well as many of his policies and actions) antagonized neighboring states, ethnic minorities, and many Romanian intellectuals.

An alternative ideology to nationalism was provided by socialism which, it was hoped, would overcome both horizontal class divisions and the vertical divisions of nationalism. Associated as it was with Stalinism and Russia, and imposed on part of the region by a foreign power after 1944, socialism in the Balkans has actually tended to reinforce the vertical divisions between states and, at least in Romania, to intensify ethnic tension and elite-mass conflict. In twentieth-century Romania both nationalism and socialism have helped elites to preserve their own power at the expense of the general welfare.

If we use the broader definition of political development set forth in the introduction to this chapter—the expansion of citizens' capacities through concrete achievements such as economic growth, vocational and educational opportunities, and rising living standards—we would have to conclude that by the mid-1960s the communist leaders in Romania had created many of the prerequisites for political development: a literate populace, a transport and communications infrastructure, an industrial base, health, cultural, and educational facilities, and a system of agriculture in which the small plots had at least been consolidated and rationalized. The Romanian Communist party had also made some concessions toward the ethnic minorities, although reliance on Romanian nationalism to enhance regime legitimacy even under Gheorghiu-Dej threatened any permanent reconciliation with the other ethnic groups. Finally, Bucharest was on good terms with the West, the Third World, and most of the socialist bloc, and had established its autonomy from the USSR.

During the 1970s, the priorities of President Nicolae Ceauşescu and his close supporters did not enhance the capacities of all citizens but instead required the continued and constant sacrifice of their personal welfare to the demands of the party, which Ceauşescu attempted—with initial success—to identify with the Romanian nation. By the late 1970s, and especially in the 1980s, many of Ceauşescu's economic development strategies—for example, his systematization campaign or his xenophobic foreign policy—had become so extreme as to be irrational. His emphasis on certain economic sectors as well as a variety of grandiose projects required high but inefficient investment, distorted the industrialization process, and allowed considerable industrial capacity to be underutilized. During the 1980s much of the infrastructure built up in earlier decades—roads, buildings, factories—deteriorated. Pollution wreaked havoc with the environment and the health of the population.

Until December 1989, the response of most Romanians was to avoid rather than resist the demands of Ceaușescu and the state, in accordance with their traditions. The regime successfully put down what brief episodes of violence did occur (a miner's strike in the Jiu Valley in 1977, for example, or demonstrations in Brașov in 1987) and dealt forcefully with isolated protests by intellectuals, national minorities, or religious groups. In abandoning any attempt at conciliation, the RCP under Ceaușescu exacerbated ethnic and economic divisions within Romania,[89] alienated foreign governments, and returned to the traditional politics of domination rather than the more developed politics of accommodation.

Yet another danger is nationalism. One of the most positive aspects of the December revolution was the cooperation between Romanians and Hungarians in Timișoara and elsewhere. The riots in Tîrgu Mureș in March 1990 were extremely disturbing, a symptom of the continuing economic scarcity that is exacerbating tensions among the various ethnic groups. The violence also demonstrated the ability of certain right-wing Romanian elements to use nationalism to stir up hostility explicitly toward the minorities but implicitly toward the new government. The irony here is the potential for cooperation between former *Securitate* officials and right-wing nationalists to provoke violence and to prevent the emergence of a moderate democratic system in which the rights of ethnic minorities will be guaranteed. The disorder in Tîrgu Mureș provoked the government of Hungary to react critically, intensified nationalist resentments inside Romania, forced Bucharest to use the army to intervene, and thus weakened the new government, which was criticized by the Hungarians for doing too little to protect them and by some Romanians for doing too much.

Romania is once again at a major turning point in its history and facing a familiar dilemma: how to create a political system sufficiently legitimate and powerful to promote progress. In the interwar years recalcitrant elites and a hostile international environment helped to produce fascism, anarchy, and then military dictatorship. We can only hope that the post–Ceaușescu era will bring Romania an outcome more conducive to positive political and economic change.

Notes

1. Romania in this study usually includes the three historic regions of Moldavia, Wallachia, and Transylvania which are now within the borders of the Romanian Republic. Because Transylvania was part of Austro-Hungary until 1918, socioeconomic data before that year sometimes exclude that province; in that case, we will refer to the "Romanian principalities" or the "Romanian kingdom."

2. Andrei Oțetea, *A Concise History of Romania* (London: Robert Hale, 1985), pp. 67, 69.

3. See, for example, Dinu C. Giurescu, *Illustrated History of the Romanian People* (Bucharest: Ed. Sport-turism, 1981), pp. 30–75.

4. See the discussion in Keith Hitchins, *Orthodoxy and Nationality: Andreiu Șaguna and the Rumanians of Transylvania, 1846–1873* (Cambridge, Mass.: Harvard University Press, 1977).

5. Decebal, Stephen the Great, and Michael the Brave were all embraced by Ceauşescu in his search for glorious predecessors.

6. See, for example, Daniel Chirot, *Social Change in a Peripheral Society* (New York: Academic Press, 1976), esp. chs. 3–5.

7. Chirot, *Peripheral Society*, pp. 94–95, and the sources cited; for the contemporary Romanian view of Vladimirescu as a revolutionary hero, see Oţetea, *A Concise History*, pp. 283–98.

8. Barbara Jelavich, *Russia and the Formation of the Romanian National State, 1821–1878* (Cambridge: Cambridge University Press, 1984), p. 33.

9. Chirot, *Peripheral Society*, p. 96. See also John R. Lampe and Marvin R. Jackson, *Balkan Economic History, 1550–1950: From Imperial Borderlands to Developing Nations* (Bloomington: Indiana University Press, 1982), pp. 90–99.

10. See Chirot, *Peripheral Society*, pp. 98–103.

11. For example, the area under cultivation in wheat rose from 249,102 hectares in 1837 to 1,509,683 hectares in 1890; Henri H. Stahl, *Traditional Romanian Village Communities* (London: Cambridge University Press, 1980), p. 97, cited by William Crowther, *The Political Economy of Romanian Socialism* (New York: Praeger, 1988), p. 23.

12. A nutritional disease resulting from an unbalanced diet of grain.

13. On the events of 1848 in Transylvania, see Hitchins, *Orthodoxy and Nationality*. On the principalities throughout the century, see Jelavich, *Russia and the Formation*, and her *Russia and the Rumanian National Cause—1858–1859* (Hamden, Conn.: Archon Books, 1974).

14. Andrew C. Janos, "Modernization and Decay in Historical Perspective: The Case of Romania," in Kenneth Jowitt, ed., *Social Change in Romania, 1860–1940: A Debate on Development in a European Nation* (Berkeley: Institute of International Studies, University of California, 1978), pp. 87–88.

15. The picture is much more complicated than these data suggest; see Per Rönnas, *Urbanization in Romania* (Stockholm: Economic Research Institute, Stockholm School of Economics, 1984), pp. 172, 232.

16. Joseph Rothschild, *East Central Europe Between the Two World Wars* (Seattle: University of Washington Press, 1974), p. 290; Henry L. Roberts, *Rumania: Political Problems of an Agrarian State* (Hamden, Conn.: Archon Books, 1969), p. 7, and Table VIII, p. 362.

17. Chirot, *Peripheral Society*, p. 134.

18. Roberts, *Rumania*, p. 15. Chirot argues very effectively that in this period Romania developed from a protocolonial to a fully colonial political economy; see *Peripheral Society*, ch. 7.

19. Roberts, *Rumania*, p. 1. On the peasant revolt, see Philip G. Eidelberg, *The Great Rumanian Peasant Revolt of 1907* (Leiden: E. J. Brill, 1974). See also Chirot, *Peripheral Society*, pp. 150–54, and Lampe and Jackson, *Balkan Economic History*, pp. 193–95.

20. Roberts, *Rumania* p. 21.

21. Chirot, *Peripheral Society*, pp. 148–49. Lampe's analysis would seem to support this hypothesis; see Lampe and Jackson, *Balkan Economic History*, pp. 186–90.

22. The most complete study of the reform and it effects remains David Mitrany, *The Land and the Peasant in Romania: The War and the Agrarian Reform (1917–1921)* (London: Oxford University Press, 1930).

23. Romania entered World War I in 1916, fought briefly against Austria-Hungary and Germany, and suffered severe casualties and major territorial losses.

24. Janos "Modernization and Decay," p. 103.

25. Lampe and Jackson, *Balkan Economic History*, p. 352. See also Barbara Jelavich, *History of the Balkans*, Vol. 2 (New York: Cambridge University Press, 1983), pp. 161–63.

26. Janos, "Modernization and Decay," p. 103.

27. See the discussion in Stephen Fischer-Galati, *Twentieth Century Rumania* (New York: Columbia University Press, 1970), p. 9.

28. Michael Shafir, *Romania: Politics, Economics and Society* (Boulder, Colo.: Lynne Rienner, 1985), pp. 5–6.

29. Aleksander Gella, *Development of Class Structure in Eastern Europe* (Albany: State University of New York Press, 1989), p. 53. See also Lampe and Jackson, *Balkan Economic History*, pp. 86ff.

30. Rothschild, *East Central Europe*, p. 296.

31. Ibid., p. 295.

32. See the essays in Jowitt, ed., *Social Change*, especially John Michael Montias, "Notes on the Romanian Debate on Sheltered Industrialization," and Chirot, "Neoliberal and Social Democratic Theories of Development." On the National Peasants, see Roberts, *Rumania*, ch. VII; the quote is from p. 165. For an excellent conceptualization and bibliography, see Paul Michaelson, "Romanian Perspectives on Romanian National Development," *Balkanistica* 7 (1981–1982), 92–120.

33. Janos makes the point about Codreanu; see "Modernization and Decay," p. 111.

34. Janos, "Modernization and Decay." p. 89; on the nonnative commercial class, see p. 91.

35. Lampe and Jackson, *Balkan Economic History*, pp. 265–70, 271.

36. Crowther, *The Political Economy of Rumanian Socialism*, p. 30; Janos, "Modernization and Decay," p. 95; Mitrany, *The Land and the Peasant in Romania*, p. 84, Lampe's findings are somewhat different; see Lampe and Jackson, *Balkan Economic History*, p. 192.

37. Crowther, *The Political Economy of Romanian Socialism*, p. 28; Chirot, *Peripheral Society*, p. 146; Lampe and Jackson, *Balkan Economic History*, p. 428.

38. Janos, "Modernization and Decay." p. 96. In comparing Romania to the other Balkan states, Lampe makes a more positive assessment, but, as he points out, often the enterprise owners and skilled workers were not ethnic Romanians; see pp. 238–77, esp. 241–42, 274–76.

39. Crowther, *The Political Economy of Romanian Socialism*, p. 31.

40. Roberts, *Rumania*, p. 68.

41. Jelavich, *History of the Balkans*, Vol. 2, p. 163.

42. Roberts, *Rumania*, p. 75.

43. Lampe and Jackson, *Balkan Economic History*, pp. 339, 341

44. Crowther, *The Political Economy of Romanian Socialism*, p. 35.

45. Ibid., pp. 37–38. On Manoilescu, see Philippe Schmitter, "Reflections on Mihail Manoilescu and the Political Consequences of Delayed-Dependent Development on the Periphery of Western Europe," in Jowitt, ed., *Social Change*.

46. Michael Kaser, *Health Care in the Soviet Union and Eastern Europe* (Boulder, Colo.: Westview Press, 1976), p. 235.

47. Colin Clark, *The Conditions of Economic Progress* (London: St. Martin's 1940), pp. 41, 83, cited in Janos, "Modernization and Decay," p. 99.

48. Janos, "Modernization and Decay," p. 99.

49. Lampe and Jackson, *Balkan Economic History*, pp. 502–504. On the relationship between education and stability, see Janos, "Modernization and Decay," pp. 95–101.

50. On Romanian fascism, see the following: Eugen Weber, "The Men of the Archangel," in George L. Mosse, ed., *International Fascism* (Beverly Hills, Calif.: Sage, 1979); his "Romania," in Hans Rogger and Eugen Weber, *The European Right* (Berkeley: University of California Press, 1966); and his *Varieties of Fascism* (New York: Van Nostrand Reinhold, 1964). See also Emil Turczynski, "The Background of Romanian Fascism," and Stephen Fischer-Galati, "Fascism in Romania," both in Peter F. Sugar, ed., *Native Fascism in the Successor States, 1918-1945* (Santa Barbara, Calif.: ABC-Clio, 1971); and Nicholas M. Nagy-Talavera, *The Green Shirts and the Others* (Stanford, Calif.: Hoover, 1970).

51. The figures on the grain harvest appeared in *Adevărul*, January 4, 1990. Romanian sources have always been regarded with skepticism; see the sources by Marvin Jackson cited in notes 73 and 79 below. For Jackson's evaluation of the postrevolutionary situation, see his "The Economy in the Wake of the Revolution," in Radio Free Europe, *Report on Eastern Europe* 15 (February 2, 1990), 29-32. *România liberă* has published frequently on false statistics under Ceaușescu; see, for example, the series of reports from the new National Commission of Statistics, March 7-9, 1990.

52. In contrast, the failures of Romanian medical care have been dramatically revealed to the world by the AIDS epidemic among children, and there is no question that the country is last in Europe by a variety of other social indicators. Yet there have been some improvements since the 1930s. Life expectancy, for example, rose from forty-two years in 1932 to sixty-nine in 1986-1988, and infant mortality dropped from 179 per thousand live births to 27 in 1988. The latter figure has been rising in recent years, however, and is "2-3 times higher than in other European countries." See note 46 above for the 1932 data; all other figures are from *România liberă*, March 9, 1990. David Binder summarized the *România liberă* series of March 7-9 in the *New York Times*, March 19, 1990.

53. On this period, see Robert R. King, *History of the Romanian Communist Party* (Stanford, Calif.: Hoover, 1980), and the sources cited. See also Shafir, *Romania*.

54. *Scînteia*, May 8, 1966.

55. Kenneth Jowitt, *Revolutionary Breakthroughs and National Development: The Case of Romania, 1944-1965* (Berkeley: University of California Press, 1971), Part II. The data on industry and commerce are from Chirot, "Social Change in Communist Romania," *Social Forces* 57 (December 1978), 461-62.

56. John Michael Montias, *Economic Development in Communist Rumania* (Cambridge, Mass." MIT Press, 1967), pp. 89, 92. On peasant arrests, see Ghita Ionescu, *Communism in Rumania, 1944-1962* (New York: Oxford University Press, 1964), p. 201.

57. See Crowther, *The Political Economy of Romanian Socialism*, p. 56, citing Montias, *Economic Development in Communist Rumania*, pp. 25, 27.

58. For example, disagreements within the Political Bureau in 1956 would result in the ejection of two of its members (Miron Constantinescu and Iosif Chișinevschi) in 1957.

59. Crowther, *The Political Economy of Romanian Socialism*, p. 58.

60. A number of sources discuss this episode such as Ionescu, *Communism in Romania*, Shafir, *Romania*, King, *History of the Romanian Communist Party*, and Jowitt, *Revolutionary Breakthroughs*.

61. Chirot, "Socialist Romania," p. 472.

62. Much has been written on this dispute; see the survey of sources in Ronald Linden, *Bear and Foxes: The International Relations of the East European States, 1965-1969* (Boulder, Colo.: East European Monographs, 1979), pp. 260-63, note 21.

63. *Scinteia*, April 26, 1964.

64. On Ceauşescu, see my *Nicolae Ceauşescu: A Study in Political Leadership* (Boulder, Colo.: Lynne Rienner, 1989).

65. See Fischer, *Nicolae Ceauşescu*, pp. 227–38, and Daniel N. Nelson, "Development and Participation in Communist Systems: The Case of Romania," in Donald E. Schulz and Jan S. Adams, eds., *Political Participation in Communist Systems* (New York: Pergamon, 1981).

66. Donald E. Schulz, "Political Participation in Communist Systems," in Schulz and Adams, eds., *Political Participation*, p. 3.

67. Schulz, "On the Nature and Function of Participation," in Schulz and Adams, eds., *Political Participation*, p. 30.

68. Kenneth Jowitt, "Inclusion and Mobilization in European Leninist Regimes," In Jan F. Triska and Paul M. Cocks, eds., *Political Development in Eastern Europe* (New York: Praeger, 1977), p. 99.

69. Jowitt, "Inclusion and Mobilization," p. 96.

70. Schulz, "On the Nature and Function of Participation,"p. 30.

71. See Fischer, *Nicolae Ceauşescu*, pp. 178–81. Jowitt also dates the beginning of these changes in 1971; see his "Inclusion and Mobilization," p. 110, and his "Political Innovation in Rumania," *Survey* 20, 4 (1974), 132–51.

72. Crowther, *The Political Economy of Romanian Socialism*, p. 154. On Ceauşescu's progressive alienation of various economic groups, see ch. 6.

73. The causes are, of course, much more complex. See Marvin R. Jackson, "Romania's Debt Crisis: Its Causes and Consequences," in U.S. Congress, Joint Economic Committee, *East European Economies: Slow Growth in the 1980s*, Vol. 3, *Country Studies on Eastern Europe and Yugoslavia* (99th Congress, 1st sess., 1986), pp. 489–542, and Crowther, *The Political Economy of Romanian Socialism*, ch. 7.

74. See, for example, Crowther, *The Political Economy of Romanian Socialism*, p. 177, note 17.

75. The country's debt service ratio at the end of 1979 was the lowest in Eastern Europe; see U.S. Department of Commerce, International Trade Administration, Office of East–West Policy and Planning, "U.S. Romanian Trade Trends, January–June 1981" (October 1981), p. 2.

76. For example, in 1979 Romania would have had a positive balance were it not for large deficits with Iran, Iraq, Libya, and Nigeria. See Radio Free Europe Research, Situation Report/4, March 5, 1981, pp. 20–21.

77. Jackson, "Romania's Debt Crisis," p. 494.

78. Ibid., pp. 491–92. See also Fischer, *Nicolae Ceauşescu*, ch. 9.

79. See, for example, Jackson, "Romania's Economy at the End of the 1970s: Turning the Corner on Intensive Development," in U.S. Congress, Joint Economic Committee, *East European Economic Assessment*, Part I, *Country Studies, 1980* (97th Congress, 1st sess., 1981), pp. 231–97, and his "Perspectives on Romania's Economic Development in the 1980s," in Daniel N. Nelson, ed., *Romania in the 1980s* (Boulder, Colo.: Westview Press, 1981).

80. Again, the picture is much more complicated; see Jackson, "Romania's Debt Crisis," pp. 526–34.

81. *New York Times*, April 15, 1989.

82. For the background to systematization, see Steven L. Sampson, *National Integration Through Socialist Planning* (Boulder, Colo.: East European Monographs, 1984), ch. IV.

83. For early Romanian descriptions of systematization, see *Scinteia*, August 4, 1974, or Ion St. Ion, "Perfecţionarea repartizǎrii pe teritoriu a forţelor de productie," in *Perfecţionarea organizarii si conducerii vieţii economice de stat şi sociale* (Bucharest: Ed. Academei, 1972). On its results, see Dinu C. Giurescu, *The Razing of Romania's Past* (New York: World Monuments Fund, 1989).

84. See Fischer, *Nicolae Ceauşescu*, esp. ch. 8.

85. *Scinteia,* November 21, 1981 and November 22–25, 1986; Boston *Globe*, March 10, 1989.

86. On the Liberals, see Lampe and Jackson, *Balkan Economic History*, p. 593; on Manoilescu, see Chirot, *Communist Romania*, pp. 492–93.

87. The letter was translated in *New York Review*, April 27, 1989, p. 9. See also the analysis by Michael Shafir and related materials in Radio Free Europe Research, Romanian Situation Report/3 (March 29, 1988), pp. 1–14. The six signers were Gheorghe Apostol, Alexandru Birlǎdeanu, Cornel Manescu, Constantin Pirvulescu, Grigore Ion Rǎceanu, and Silviu Brucan.

88. On political developments in the first few weeks following the revolution, see the excellent analyses in Radio Free Europe, *Report on Eastern Europe*, by Michael Shafir, especially "The New Romanian Government," 1:2 (January 12, 1990), 35–38, "Ceauşescu's Overthrow: Popular Uprising or Moscow-guided Conspiracy?" 1:3 (January 19, 1990), 15–19, "The Revolution: An Initial Assessment," 1:4 (January 26, 1990), 34–42; and by Vladimir Socor, "Political Parties Emerging," 1:7 (February 16, 1990), 28–35.

89. On ethnic divisions, see Fischer, *Nicolae Ceauşescu*, pp. 238–49, and on social divisions, see Crowther, *The Political Economy of Romanian Socialism*, pp. 109–17.

Bibliography

In addition to the works cited in the text, the following books may be consulted by readers who wish more information about the various aspects of political and economic development among the Balkan states. Articles dealing with various issues relating to development in the area may be found in the journal *Eastern European Politics and Societies*.

General Works

Carter, F. W. *An Historical Geography of the Balkans*. New York: Academic Press, 1977.

Chirot, Daniel, ed. *The Origins of Backwardness in Eastern Europe: Economics and Politics from the Middle Ages Until the Early Twentieth Century*. Berkeley: University of California Press, 1989.

Gianaris, Nicholas V. *The Economies of the Balkan Countries*. New York: Praeger, 1982.

Hoffman, George W. *Regional Development Strategy in Southeast Europe. A Comparative Analysis of Albania, Bulgaria, Greece, Romania, and Yugoslavia*. New York: Praeger, 1972.

Jelavich, Barbara. *History of the Balkans*. 2 vols. New York: Cambridge University Press, 1983.

Jelavich, Charles, and Barbara Jelavich, eds. *The Balkans in Transition*. Berkeley: University of California Press, 1963.

Lampe, John, and Marvin R. Jackson. *Balkan Economic History, 1550–1950: From Imperial Borderlands to Developing Nations*. Bloomington: Indiana University Press, 1982.

Mouzelis, Nicos P. *Politics in the Semi-Periphery. Early Parliamentarism and Late Industrialization in the Balkans and Latin America*. New York: St. Martin's Press, 1986.

Shoup, Paul, ed., George W. Hoffman, Project Director. *Problems of Balkan Security: Southeastern Europe in the 1990s*. Washington, D.C.: The Wilson Center Press, 1990.

Warriner, Doreen, ed. *Conrasts in Emerging Societies*. Bloomington: Indiana University Press, 1965.

Albania

Pollo, Stefanaq, and Arben Puto. *The History of Albania*. London: Routledge and Kegan Paul, 1981.
Prifti, Peter R. *Socialist Albania Since 1944. Domestic and Foreign Developments*. Cambridge, Mass.: MIT Press, 1978.
Schnytzer, Adi. *Stalinist Economic Strategy in Practice. The Case of Albania*. Oxford: Oxford University Press, 1982.

Bulgaria

Brown, J. F. *Bulgaria Under Communist Rule*. New York: Praeger, 1970.
Butler, Thomas, ed. *Bulgaria, Past and Present*. Columbus, Ohio: American Association for the Advancement of Slavic Studies, 1976.
Crampton, Richard J. *Bulgaria, 1878 to 1918: A History*. Boulder, Colo.: East European Monographs, 1983.
Feiwel, George R. *Growth and Reform in Centrally Planned Economies: The Lessons of the Bulgarian Experience*. New York: Praeger, 1977.
Lampe, John R. *The Bulgarian Economy in the Twentieth Century*. New York: St. Martin's Press, 1986.
McIntyre, Robert J. *Bulgaria Politics, Economics and Society*. London: Pinter Publishers, 1988.

Greece

Clogg, Richard. *Parties and Elections in Greece. The Search for Legitimacy*. Durham, N.C.: Duke University Press, 1988.
Dertilis, George, ed. *Banquiers, usuriers et paysans: Réseaux de crédit et stratégies du capital en Grèce (1780–1930)*. Paris: Editions la Découverte et Fondation des Treilles, 1988.
Freris, A. F. *The Greek Economy in the Twentieth Century*. London: Croom Helm, 1986.
Gianaris, Nicholas V. *Greece and Yugoslavia: An Economic Comparison*. New York: Praeger, 1984.
Halikias, D. J. *Money and Credit in a Developing Economy*. New York: New York University Press, 1978.
Legg, Keith. *Politics in Modern Greece*. Stanford, Calif.: Stanford University Press, 1969.
McNeill, William H. *The Metamorphosis of Greece Since World War II*. Chicago: University of Chicago Press, 1978.
Mouzelis, Nicos P. *Modern Greece Facets of Underdevelopment*. New York: Holmes and Meier, 1978.
Zolotas, Xenophon. *Monetary Equilibrium and Economic Development with Special Reference to the Experience of Greece, 1950–1963*. Princeton, N.J.: Princeton University Press, 1965.

Romania

Gilberg, Trond. *Nationalism and Communism in Romania Since World War II*. Boulder, Colo.: Westview Press, 1990.

Jowitt, Kenneth, ed. *Social Change in Romania, 1860–1940: A Debate on Development in a European Nation*. Berkeley: Institute of International Studies, University of California, 1978.

Montias, John Michael. *Economic Development in Communist Rumania*. Cambridge, Mass.: MIT Press, 1967.

Nelson, Daniel, N. *Romanian Politics in the Ceauşescu Era*. New York: Gordon and Breach, 1988.

Spigler, Iancu. *Economic Reform in Rumanian Industry*. New York: Oxford University Press, 1973.

Tsantis, Andreas C., and Roy Pepper. *Romania: The Industrialization of an Agrarian Economy Under Socialist Planning*. Baltimore: Johns Hopkins University Press, 1979.

Turnock, David. *The Romanian Economy in the Twentieth Century*. New York: St. Martin's Press, 1986.

Verdery, Katherine. *Transylvanian Villagers Three Centuries of Political, Economic, and Ethnic Change*. Berkeley: University of California Press, 1983.

Yugoslavia

Burg, Stephen L. *Conflict and Cohesion in Socialist Yugoslavia*. Princeton, N.J.: Princeton University Press, 1983.

Denitch, Bogdan. *Limits and Possibilities: The Crisis of Yugoslav Socialism and State Socialist Systems*. Minneapolis: University of Minnesota Press, 1990.

Dragnich, Alex. N. *The First Yugoslavia*. Stanford, Calif.: Hoover Institution Press, 1983.

Lydall, Harold F. *Yugoslav Socialism Theory and Practice*. Oxford: Clarendon Press, 1984.

———. *Yugoslavia in Crisis*. New York: Oxford University Press, 1989.

McFarlane, Bruce. *Yugoslavia Politics, Economics, and Society*. New York: Pinter Publishers, 1988.

Moore, John H. *Growth with Self-Management: Yugoslav Industrialization 1952–1975*. Stanford, Calif.: Hoover Institution Press, 1980.

Pawlowitch, Stevan K. *The Improbable Survivor, Yugoslavia and Its Problems 1918–1988*. Columbus: Ohio State Press, 1988.

Prout, Christopher. *Market Socialism in Yugoslavia*. New York: Oxford University Press, 1985.

Ramet, Pedro. *Nationalism and Federalism in Yugoslavia 1963–1983*. Bloomington: Indiana University Press, 1984.

Rusinow, Dennison, ed. *Yugoslavia A Fractured Federalism*. Washington, D.C.: Wilson Center Press, 1988.

Schrenk, Martin, Cyrus Ardalan, and Nawal A. El Tatawy. *Yugoslavia Self-Management, Socialism, and the Challenges of Development*. Baltimore: Johns Hopkins University Press, 1979.

Singleton, Fred, and Bernard Carter. *The Economy of Yugoslavia*. New York: St. Martin's Press, 1982.

Sirc, Ljubo. *The Yugoslav Economy Under Self-Management*. New York: St. Martin's Press, 1979.

Index

Agrarian movement, in Bulgaria, 5
Agrarian National Union (Bulgaria), 22,
 36-37, 48; economic policies of, 36
Agrarians (Bulgaria), 47
Agricultural Bank (Greece), 95-96, 115
AGROKOMERC scandal (Yugoslavia),
 72, 77
Albanians, in Yugoslavia, 79
Aleksandar, king of Yugoslavia
 (1921-1934), 38
AMAG (American Mission for Aid to
 Greece), 104

Balkans: interwar development, 13;
 political culture, 33; post-World War
 II development, 13; socialism in, 162
Balkan Wars, 91
BANU. See Agrarian National Union
Basic Organizations of Associated Labor
 (BOALS), 68, 78
Battenberg, Alexander, 20-21
Beron, Petŭr, 17
Boris III, king of Bulgaria (1918-1943),
 24, 25, 36
Brǎtianu, Ion, 142
Bulgaria: Agrarians' educational policies,
 23; Communists take power, 25;
 Compulsory Labor Service, 36;
 Directorate for Civilian Mobilization

(DEM), 44; economic development in
 1970s, 27; economic development in
 nineteenth century, 19; economic
 development in post-World War II
 era, 25-26; economic policies under
 Communists, 25; economic recovery in
 post-World War II era, 47; educational system in post-World War II
 era, 26-27; education in nineteenth
 century, 18-20; government and
 politics in nineteenth century, 20-22;
 interwar development, 33; interwar
 economy, 34-38; modernization in
 nineteenth century, 18; Ottoman era,
 15-16; role of military in nineteenth
 century, 21-22; role of women in, 27;
 social conditions in nineteenth century,
 20; State Planning Commission, 46
Bulgarian Communist Party (BKP), 36;
 economic policies of, 45-46; post-
 World War II development policies,
 48

Carol I, king of Romania (1866-1914),
 139
Carol II, king of Romania (1930-1940),
 142-43, 144, 145-46
Ceauşescu, Nicolae, 147; development
 policies, 11; domestic policies of, in

1980s, 158–59; fall of, 160–61; na-
tionalism, use of, 155–56, 159;
political strategies of, 153–56;
systematization, policy of, 158–59
Chitalishte (Bulgarian reading room), 17
Codreanu, Corneliu Zelea, 143, 145
Common Market. *See* European
Economic Community
Constantine I, king of Greece
(1913–1922), 91
Constantine II, king of Greece
(1964–1973), 114
Croatia: in World War II, 42, 49; na-
tionalist movement, in 1960s, 68
Croatian Peasant Party (Yugoslavia), 39,
42
Cuza, Alexander I., 139

Development: general definition, 2, 136;
in Balkans, 3–4
Dimitrov, Georgi D., 48
Djilas, Milovan, 60
Drăghici, Alexandru, 154

EDFO (Economic Development Finance
Organization) (Greece), 108
Education: *Chitalishte* (Bulgarian reading
room), 17; educational policies under
Ceauşescu, 155; educational system
in post–World War II Bulgaria,
26–27; education in Bulgaria, nineteenth century, 18–19, 19–20; education in Romania, interwar era, 145;
policies of Agrarians (Bulgaria), 23
EEC. *See* European Economic
Community
ETVA. *See* Hellenic Industrial Development Bank
European Economic Community, 112,
115, 119; and PASOK government,
123–124

Fatherland Front (Bulgaria), 45
Ferdinand, king of Romania
(1914–1927), 140
Ferdinand I, prince, later tsar, of
Bulgaria (1887–1918), 21

George II, king of Greece (1922–1923,
1935–1947), 102
Gheorghiu-Dej, Gheorghe, 147,
153–158; control of RCP, 151–52
Greece: agricultural policies in 1970s,
119–20; agricultural policies in post–
Worl War II era, 106–07; agriculture
in interwar era, 95–96; civil war in,
103–04; colonels' regime
(1967–1974), 112–17; development
after World War I, 8; development in
nineteenth century, 8; development
policies in 1960s, 109–12; development policies in 1970s, 118–120;
economic conditions in 1980s,
124–25; emigration in post–World
War II era, 112–14; factors in
development, 90; and the Great
Depression, 98–100; industrial
development in post–World War II
era, 107–108; industry in post–World
War II era, 97–98; and post–World
War II American aid, 104–105;
public works projects, 98, 105;
recovery of in post–World War II
era, 104–109; settlement of Asia
Minor refugees, 93–95; social conditions in World War II, 100–102;
tourism, 99

Hellenic Industrial Development Bank
(ETVA) (Greece), 109, 115
Hranoiznos (Bulgarian grain monopoly),
41, 42, 44

Idryma Koinonikon Asfaliseon, 100
International Financial Commission
(Greece), 91, 99, 103
International Monetary Fund, 71

Karamanlis, Constantine, 116, 120;
becomes president, 121; government
of, in 1974, 117–18
Kardelj, Edvard, 62–63
KEPE (Center for Planning and
Economic Research) (Greece), 111

Khrushchev, Nikita, 152–53
Kosovo, 79–80
Kostov, Traicho, 46, 47

League of Communists of Yugoslavia (LCY), 58, 60, 74; Sixth Party Congress (1952), 60, 75; Eleventh Party Congress (1978), 68; Thirteenth Party Congress (1986), 70, 74, 79; Fourteenth Party Congress (1990), 75
Liapchev, Andrei, 38
Liberal Party (Romania), 143
Luca, Vasile, 151–152

Maniu, Iuliu, 142–143
Manoilescu, Mihai, 144, 160
Marković, Ante, 74, 75, 79; economic program of, 81–82
Megali idea, 90, 91
Mihailović, Draža, 43
Mikulić, Branko, 71, 76
Milošević, Slobodan, 75, 79
Modernization, defined, 15, 33–34

Nationalism: growth of, in Bulgaria, 16–18
National Peasant Party (Romania), 143, 144
National Salvation Front (Romania), 161
Nation formation, in Balkans, 3
Neuilly, Treaty of (1919), 22, 24
New Democracy Party (Greece), 118, 121

Papadopoulos, George, 115
Papagos, Alexander, 104
Papandreou, Andreas: development policies of, in 1960s, 111–12; and economic policies of PASOK, 122–123; forms PASOK, 121
Papandreou, George, 112, 114; government of, in 1944, 102–103; government of, in 1964, 112, 114–15
Partisan resistance movement (Yugoslavia), 72
Partisans, in Yugoslavia, 6
Pašić, Nikola, 39

PASOK (Panhellenic Socialist Movement) (Greece), 121
Pauker, Ana, 151
Petkov, Nikola, 48
Pijade, Moše, 62
Planinc, Milka, 71
Prizad (Yugoslav grain export monopoly), 41, 42

Radić, Stjepan, 39
Radical Party (Yugoslavia), 39
Ranković, Alexander, 64
Romania: agriculture in 1970s, 158; Ceaușescu regime, relations with people, 162–163; Comecon, relations with, 157; development under Communists, 11; economic problems, in 1970s and 1980s, 156–58; educational policies under Ceaușescu, 155; education in interwar era, 145; elite-mass relations under Ceaușescu, 153–55; Great Depression in, 144–45; industrial development in interwar era, 144; industrial development in pre–World War I era, 143–144; interwar development, 10; land reform in post–World War I era, 140–141; nationalism in, 161–62, 163; nationalism in Communist era, 152–53; peasant revolt of 1907, 138–40; peasants in post–World War II era, 149, 151, 152
Romanian Communist Party (RCP), 147; development policies of, in post–World War II era, 149, 151–52; minorities, relations with, 162; relations with USSR, in 1950s and 1960s, 151–53
Romanians: early history, 137–40

San Stefano, Treaty of (1878), 21
Self-management in Yugoslavia, 7; assessment of, 77–81; defined, 59; economic aspects, 61–62; and national question, 67; political aspects of, 59–60; problems of, in 1980s, 76–77

Soviet-Yugoslav break, in 1948, 58
Stamboliiski, Aleksandŭr, 5, 24, 36, 52;
    program of, 22–24
Stojadinović, Milan, 38

Timişoara, 163; demonstrations in, 160
Tîrgu Mureş: riots in, 163
Tito (Josip Broz), 51, 66; and constitu-
    tion of 1974, 69; role in Yugoslavia,
    72–73
Tsankov, Aleksandŭr, 38
Tsouderos, Emmanuel, 103
Tŭrnovo Constitution, 20–21

United Nations Relief and Rehabilitation
    Administration (UNRRA), 50–51
Ustaša movement, 43, 66

Venizelos, Eleftherios, 91–92

Yugoslav Communist Party (KPJ), 40,
    49, 58; economic policies in post-
    World War II era, 49–52
Yugoslavia: Chetnik resistance move-
    ment, 43; constitution of 1974,

68–69; constitutional changes in
    1989, 75; economic development in
    1970s, 70–71; economic recovery in
    post–World War II era, 50–51;
    economic reforms in 1960s, 63–65;
    economic stabilization program,
    1983, 71; federal-republic relations,
    83; first dispute with USSR, 1948,
    58; first Five Year Plan, 51–52; in-
    terwar development, 33; interwar
    economy, 33–36, 39–42; interwar
    political culture, 39; national question
    in, 65–69; and non-aligned move-
    ment, 62; Partisan resistance move-
    ment, 42–43; political and economic
    problems in 1980s, 76–77; political
    life in 1980s, 71–72; political life in
    post–Tito era, 73–74; political
    system, 8; post–Tito political system,
    69–70; second dispute with USSR,
    1957, 63; Vidovdan Constitution,
    1921, 39

Zhivkov, Todor, 28
ZVENO (Bulgaria), 24

About the Contributors

GERASIMOS AUGUSTINOS is Associate Professor of History at the University of South Carolina. He is the author of *Consciousness and History: Nationalist Critics of Greek Society, 1897–1914.*

JOHN BELL is Professor of History at the University of Maryland, Baltimore County. He is the author of *Peasants in Power: Alexander Stamboliski and the Bulgarian Agrarian Union* and *The Bulgarian Communist Party from Blagoev to Zhivkov.*

MARY ELLEN FISCHER is Professor of Political Science at Skidmore College. She has been a fellow at the Russian Research Center, Harvard University, and is the author of *Nicolae Ceauşescu: A Study in Political Leadership.*

JOHN LAMPE is Professor of History at the University of Maryland, College Park. He has served as secretary of the East European Program at the Woodrow Wilson Center for International Scholars, and is the author of *Balkan Economic History 1550–1950*, with Marvin Jackson, and *An Economic History of Bulgaria.*

ROBIN ALISON REMINGTON is Professor of Political Science at the University of Missouri–Columbia. She has been an exchange scholar at the Institute for International Politics and Economics in Belgrade and has held Fulbright Fellowships to Yugoslavia. Remington is the author of *The Warsaw Pact: Case Studies in Communist Conflict Resolution*, and numerous articles and chapters in books on Yugoslav domestic and foreign policy imperatives.